WHEN FABLES FALL

...AND THEY WILL TURN THEIR EARS AWAY
FROM THE TRUTH, AND BE TURNED ASIDE TO FABLES.
(2 TIMOTHY 4:4)

WHEN FABLES FALL

UNMASKING THE LIES OF
DISTORTED SCIENCE, SECULARISM
AND HUMANISM

ARTHUR FRANCIS GREEN

Sovereign World

Sovereign World Ltd
PO Box 784
Ellel
Lancaster LA1 9DA
England

ISBN: 978-1-85240-593-9

The publishers aim to produce books which will help to extend and build up the
Kingdom of God. We do not necessarily agree with every view expressed by the
authors, or with every interpretation of Scripture expressed. We expect readers to
make their own judgment in the light of their understanding of God's Word and
in an attitude of Christian love and fellowship.

Book cover design by The Book Design Company
Typeset by The Book Design Company
Printed in the United Kingdom

Contents

To the greater glory of God and His Holy Word

and

To my dear wife, Jill,
whose loyal and unwavering support has enabled
this book to be written

ACKNOWLEDGMENTS

I would like to acknowledge with grateful thanks the assistance of my wife and children in the proofreading of the text, not only for errors, but also for readability and consistency.

I would especially like to acknowledge the assistance of my eldest son, Allan Peter Green, whose research for his honors dissertation at Stirling University has greatly informed Chapter 10. I owe him a great debt of gratitude for permission to utilize his research freely.

There are many other people, too numerous to mention, who, over the years taken to write this book, have contributed to the development of the ideas within it. I would also like to thank all the authors, living and dead, of all the books I have read in my search for true meaning. There is an extensive but not exhaustive Bibliography at the end of the book, which may give the reader some idea of the journey.

I especially thank all the unsung Christians who get on with the doing of the Word, and with whom over the years it has been my privilege to serve, in some of the difficult places of the world. They have set me an example of the true, long-suffering servant of the Lord.

FOREWORD
BY DR DON HENDER

Here is a heart cry to return to the Bible – the Word of God – and to the Living God who gave us that Word. Faith in the revelation of the God who is almighty is not a leap in the dark, groping for answers, but a reasoned faith (Isaiah 1:18), based on evidence and the fulfilled revelation of Biblical prophecy – with more fulfillment to come.

Today, more than ever, we need to have and maintain the highest view of a personal, just and loving God. We need also to have the highest view of Biblical truth – the self-revelation of a holy and infinite, but merciful and personal God. This treatise highlights not only the absurdity of evolution and modern humanism, but also their profoundly damaging effects on peoples and societies.

The Word of God is unique, so let us return to Scripture for answers to life's questions and human destiny. How much we need this reconciling grace of God for a desperate world: a redemption obtained for humanity at such a great sacrificial cost.

I heartily recommend this book, which lifts up on high God's Word and His assuring promises.

Don Hender MA BTh DTh PhD DLitt FETS
Bournemouth
United Kingdom
27 July 2011

FOREWORD

BY REVEREND ROBERT CROWE

The best way to understand the truth of the Bible is to study it. As you do, the person of Jesus will step forward since Jesus is truth. When Pilate asked "What is truth?" he was facing the source and personification of all truth – and did not see the truth. The same problem in the modern context is that people today have the source of truth readily available to them in the Bible – and still they do not see the truth.

The church is living in a day of compromise with the social world around us. We have seen decisions made and positions taken by church leaders which are widely different from the orthodox beliefs of our early church fathers, and the source of all truth, Jesus Christ Himself. While the fact of who Jesus is and the demands He places on our lives cause controversy in our ever-changing modern world, He provides stability through inspiration in the heart of the individual believer. The Bible as God's living Word is the source of that stability. A man or woman becomes a living person through Jesus, the real source of life.

When Fables Fall provides an avenue by which individuals can throw off today's bleak mindset and come face to face with the God-breathed living Word. The ability of the Bible to meet the needs of all people, whatever their starting point, is one of the evidences of divine authorship. When a study like this one deals with the deepest truths of the Bible, it reveals the power only the Bible contains to release us from the pressures of life and to expose us to all truth. There are demands such knowledge will place on the life of the individual who seeks God. Those demands will change life and thinking. The honest individual who is seeking the truth and the real Author of life will profit from the study.

As you read and study through *When Fables Fall*, pray that the Author of all truth will reveal Himself to you. Seek Him and He will come.

Rev. Bob Crowe

President and Founder of BreakThrough To People Network

Minister of Education, First Baptist Church, Blairsville, Georgia

USA

July 2011

THE BATTLE OVER FAITH

The fool has said in his heart,
"There is no God."
They are corrupt,
They have done abominable works,
There is none who does good.
The Lord looks down from heaven upon the children of men,
To see if there are any who understand, who seek God.
They have all turned aside,
They have together become corrupt;
There is none who does good,
No, not one.

(Psalm 14:1–3)

I was there in the Sixties, when everything was overturned. It was an exciting time to be alive and to be young. I was present at the changing of the "spirit of the times" and the wholesale adoption of the "new morality" without even realizing it. As time went by I became absorbed by the business of earning a living and raising a family, and I watched the rise of Generation X from a distance, without really understanding what was going on. Antisocial behavior, outright violence, crime, promiscuous behavior, drug abuse, all began to grow, and are still growing in a society where nothing seems to be respected anymore.

The one thing that was scorned more than anything else seemed to be the Christian faith and the person of Jesus Christ. As time went on, many scholars noted that the rise in social ills seemed to be in proportion to the rejection of old-fashioned, orthodox Christianity and its practice. A new morality had eaten away at the foundations of the old, and allowed people to think that their own passions were the basis for morality. The mistake that many people made was that they thought they could reject the Christian creed yet retain the Christian code. They resented bitterly the prophetic warnings that the code could not long survive the creed.

I began writing this book in 1997, in response to the writings of John Shelby Spong, then Episcopalian Bishop of Newark, New Jersey. He was clearly of the liberal theology/new morality school. His extreme views have been a considerable embarrassment to many of his peers. In an article entitled, "A Call for a New Reformation," Bishop Spong wrote that, by the effects of the developments of modern science, and out of the theories of Darwin and Freud, the Christian faith had been brought to the point of death. He offered twelve theses as the basis of his new Reformation, in a parody of Martin Luther's ninety-five theses that began the Reformation of 1517.

He saw no future in it if we carry on as we are. He gave a brief review of the Reformation, the work of such scientists as Copernicus, Galileo and Newton, and followed with a review of Darwin and Freud. He assessed their impact on Christianity and concluded that Christianity had degenerated into either "mindless fundamentalism" or "empty secularism." He made no attempt to define what he meant by these terms, but insisted that a new Reformation was needed – which would examine the very nature of the Christian faith. He dismissed the Reformation of Martin Luther as relatively unimportant, that it was not about the nature of the Christian faith, but about form rather than substance. His twelve theses, on the other hand, challenged every aspect of the orthodox Christian faith.

That was only the beginning of my journey. When I investigated his propositions, I also began to realize that the claims of science, on which the bishop based so much of his logic, were flimsy, to say the least. I found that the great edifice of Darwinian evolution had no real foundations in terms of solid evidence, but was rather a collection of suppositions and rationalizations. I have had some scientific training and so I am familiar with the scientific method. I was appalled at what I found.

When I attempted to engage in dialogue with my fellow Christians in different denominations, I realized that they were also misled, and that the overblown claims of science had infected them. The naturalist philosophy of science had poisoned the well of Christianity to a remarkable degree.

How had this come about? I was further led into a study of the progress in philosophy and its effects on theology. Modern liberal theology goes hand in hand with the twin marches of bad science and rationalism, where human reasoning within the closed system of the natural world is held to be supreme. The authority of Holy Scripture has been undermined – almost fatally.

One of the most striking things has been the rapid growth of aggressive, evangelical atheism. Scientist Dr Richard Dawkins has published several books, one of the best known being *The God Delusion*. He also has been a considerable embarrassment to many of his peers. Amazingly, he had a TV series, where he attempted to show that religion is the source of evil, which makes good people do bad things. He is one of those people who, according to C.S. Lewis, put up "a version of Christianity suitable for a child of six and make that the object of their attack."[1]

Dawkins, like all scientists, has his own area of expertise; in his case it is biology. It is this legitimate authoritative expertise which, like many others, he transfers into other disciplines, without justification. When he moves into philosophy, religion and ideas about the origins of life, he is an amateur, just like the rest of us. He is representative of a growing class of philosopher-scientists; we should not take their pronouncements as unchallengeable, but investigate them. Spong and Dawkins express their views in very extreme ways; the majority of churchmen and scientists would disassociate themselves from them. It took me some time to realize that the disassociation is only concerned with the public embarrassment involved. The basic views of Spong and Dawkins are widely held and quietly taught in schools, churches and universities. As John Ankerberg and John Wheldon note: "Even Pope John Paul II issued a formal statement in 1996, widely reported in the press, affirming that some evolution is compatible with Catholic beliefs. He is the fourth Pope to affirm this."[2]

Recently, in September 2010, Pope Benedict XVI visited the United Kingdom. On the eve of the Pope's visit, one of his aides depicted Britain as prey to an "aggressive new atheism." The Pope himself, on the day of his arrival, talked about resisting "more aggressive forms of secularism." How can an academic like Pope Benedict XVI not recognize that resisting aggressive secularism means rejecting the theological conclusions of evolution? Look what has happened to Dawkins and Spong and thousands like them.

Even more recently, on 5 August 2011, the BBC carried a news item about the Dutch Protestant Church (PKN)[3] – a perfect example of the consequences of this process. At the Exodus Church in Gorinchem, central Holland, a certain Reverend Klaas Hendrikse presides. He told the BBC reporter, "Personally I have no talent for believing in life after death ... No, for me our life, our task, is before death." He has written a book entitled *Believing in a Non-Existent God*. He also told the reporter, "God is not a being at all ... it's a word for experience, or human experience." Reverend Hendrikse described the Bible's account of Jesus' life as a mythological story about a man who may never have existed, even if it is a valuable source of wisdom about how to lead a good life. Rev. Kirsten Slattenaar, Exodus Church's regular priest, also rejected the idea that Jesus was divine as well as human. "I think 'Son of God' is a kind of title," she said. "I don't think he was a god or a half-god. I think he was a man, but he was a special man because he was very good in living from out of love, from out of the spirit of God he found inside himself." Mrs Slattenaar acknowledged that she was changing what the Church has traditionally said, but she insisted that she was not changing the "real meaning of Christianity." A study by the Free University of Amsterdam found that one in six clergy in the PKN and six other smaller denominations were either agnostic or atheist.

In the battle over faith, doubt is a permanent part of any faith, and there must be some authority against which we can check that what we believe is true. It must be true in the cosmic sense and apply everywhere, not just be a local faith, made up of wish fulfillment. It must be Truth with a capital "T." In former times the Bible provided this authority. Between liberal churchmen represented by Bishop Spong, and humanist scientists represented by Dr Dawkins, my faith was reduced to almost nothing, just like the Dutch Protestant Church. Between them, the foundation of my faith, the Bible of Holy Scriptures, had been reduced to worthless myths. How, then, could I consult it with confidence? I eventually found that I agreed with Spong that we needed a new Reformation, but not according to his bleak and barren worldview and not in the direction he would have expected; and I totally disagreed with Dawkins.

The contents of this book draw upon many scholars and nothing in these pages is new. If there is any worth in these pages it is that abler men than I have done the original thinking. I am the beneficiary of their wisdom and knowledge. The book is the record of my journey through the issues and challenges. It was originally written as an exercise to clear my mind (I am responsible for any errors). I hope it will also serve in the same way for a wider audience. It tries to show that trust in the authority of Holy Scripture, and a trusting faith in the Creator and His plan of redemption, is the true unchanging reality, unlike the changeable and fallible scientific theories of mankind. We should remember that all people have a created origin, a purposeful life and an ultimate destiny.

This book is my journey out of darkness and into light, where I have rediscovered my faith and found that I have been misled by fables of the human imagination. My journey has been a long one. On the way, many other things have changed. The rise of Islam and the threat it poses is another issue, but that is something for a different study. This book focuses upon the self-destruction of our civilization from within – the deconstruction of Christianity that was once the beating heart of the West.

Finally, I hope that this study will assist people to be ready, in season and out of season, to defend the faith when called, with confidence that theirs is a faith based on a foundation of solid rock:

> *I charge you therefore before God and the Lord Jesus Christ, who will judge the living and the dead at His appearing and His kingdom: Preach the word! Be ready in season and out of season. Convince, rebuke, exhort, with all longsuffering and teaching. For the time will come when they will not endure sound doctrine, but according to their own desires, because they have itching ears, they will heap up for themselves teachers; and they will turn their ears away from the truth, and be turned aside to fables.*
>
> (2 Timothy 4:1–4)

PART I

CHRISTIANITY
IN CRISIS

But know this, that in the last days perilous times will come:
For men will be lovers of themselves, lovers of money, boasters, proud,
blasphemers, disobedient to parents, unthankful, unholy, unloving,
unforgiving, slanderers, without self-control, brutal, despisers of
good, traitors, headstrong, haughty, lovers of pleasure rather than
lovers of God, having a form of godliness but denying its power.
And from such people turn away!
(2 Timothy 3:1–5)

CHAPTER 1

FAITH UNDER ASSAULT

For any of us to be fully conscious intellectually we should not only be able
to detect the worldviews of others but be aware of our own – why it is
ours and why in light of so many options we think it is true.[4]

James W. Sire

The theme of this book is that Christianity is as truthful and meaningful
as it always was, despite the fact that modern philosophical and
scientific worldviews seem to have vanquished orthodox Christian beliefs,
and apparently reduced the Bible to a collection of myths.

The conclusion of this book is that Christianity is intellectually robust,
rational and coherent, supported by many lines of corroborating evidence.
We should therefore return to it.

The main issue is the authority of the Holy Scriptures and their
trustworthiness in all matters of morality, history and the natural world.
Despite appearances, science is not in conflict with the Bible. It is the
philosophy of science and its presuppositions which provide the conflict.

There is no doubt; Christianity is once more in crisis. Yet, if we call for a new
Reformation, where do we start? What form should it take? In the sixteenth
century Martin Luther was fighting against a dominant worldview arising
out of the false doctrines and practices of the medieval Catholic Church.
By the early twenty-first century we had moved to a dominant worldview
arising from the theories of humanism, scientific naturalism and evolution.
Although the situation in the sixteenth century had false doctrines about the
nature of God, His existence was not questioned, whereas our contemporary
worldview is predominantly atheistic: God is not deemed to exist, and even

if He did, he could not act into the completely closed, predetermined system of natural causes that is the modern concept of the universe. Although the two situations are completely different, curiously the fruits of both are very similar. Now, as then, we see despair all around us, manifested in the lack of hope and the increasing desperation of ordinary people, rising violence, irrational behavior, and the breakdown of personal and family relationships.

The approach of Martin Luther (1483–1546) was to reform the Church by correcting the false doctrines. He started this process in 1517 by posting his ninety-five theses for debate on the door of the church at Wittenberg, inspiring a return to the sole authority of the Holy Scriptures. He could do this in a world that had a general acceptance of the existence and power of Almighty God, who could and did act into a universe based on an undetermined open system.

Since then, the change in worldview has been radical. The prevailing view is humanism, a closed and determined system of thought, where man is the measure of all things, not God. The remark that "man is the measure of all things" is attributed to Protagoras of Abdera (c.490 – c.420 BC), a Greek philosopher and mathematician. The full quotation is as follows: "Man is the measure of all things: of those which are, that they are; of those which are not, that they are not."[5] When considered in its entirety, the complete quotation elevates man not only to being the measure but also the judge of all things. He thus replaces God.

The concept of man being the measure of all things found fertile soil in the Renaissance and the Enlightenment, broadly during the sixteenth to the eighteenth centuries, where a shift in thinking took place that was foundational to the modern world in which we live. Rationalism and empiricism had their modern beginnings in the Renaissance, although their roots go back to the Greek philosophers. Very broadly, rationalism is concerned with logic and philosophy and how we think, whereas empiricism is concerned with how we interact with the natural world. They do overlap in many areas. For example, both schools must be able to deal with mathematics, a source of knowledge which could be claimed by both camps. Gradually rationalism and empiricism have become the basis of the modern worldview. Rationalism is variously defined as:

In philosophy: the doctrine that knowledge is acquired by reason without resort to experience;

In theology: the doctrine that human reason rather than divine revelation establishes religious truth;

In morality: the doctrine that reason is the right basis for regulating conduct.

In Biblical terms, rationalism can be regarded as a movement in eighteenth-century Protestantism which abandoned the idea of Biblical inerrancy and adopted the belief that the Bible can be analyzed as literature and as a historical document. Some rationalists assert that the existence of some form of deity can be proven by reason. Others see rationalism and atheism as synonymous. The bottom line is that in rationalism, human reason becomes dominant, where experience of the natural world and revelation from God are subordinated. Every area of life is radically affected. Most importantly, the authority of the Holy Scriptures is fatally diminished, not because they have been truly discredited, but because rationalism excludes consideration of them. There are of course direct attacks on Scripture, but we will consider these elsewhere.

Empiricism is the view that experience via the senses is the most important, or even the only source of knowledge or sound belief. Empiricism was not an organized philosophical point of view at the beginning of the early modern period; by the nineteenth century it had become the most widely accepted philosophy of modern science. Although there were some extreme forms of empiricism, it was the English statesman and philosopher Francis Bacon (1561–1626) who was one of the major contributors to what is now regarded as the modern scientific method. Bacon maintained that the true seeker after knowledge should be neither an empiricist nor a rationalist. The empiricist, he complained, is like an ant that collects much of value but does not put it into a coherent system. The rationalist, on the other hand, was like a spider, who spun wonderful constructions from within itself but whose thoughts did not connect with external reality. The true philosopher, Bacon wrote, should be like the bee that both collects much of value and puts it into an organized system.[6]

What Bacon proposed was an empirical method of "induction," which is the process of arguing from a collection of measured phenomena to a general conclusion. This became the dominant philosophy of science into which Darwinism appeared in the mid-nineteenth century. It is important to realize that this philosophy of science, at that time, still generally regarded the Bible as legitimate and the true authority on the origins of mankind.

Darwin's theory was published into an atmosphere of increasing rationalism and increasing hostility to organized religion. From the middle of the nineteenth century to the start of the twenty-first century, Darwinism, or evolution, has grown and become taught everywhere as the mechanism of our existence. Although there was a mixed reception at the time, Darwinian evolution now predominates. Religion has been marginalized as having nothing to say about the human condition. The act of special creation by God is ridiculed and not even discussed seriously. Since this modern worldview states bluntly that God doesn't exist, there can have been no act of creation. Therefore we must have evolved, however unlikely that seems. There is no point in talking about God or religion.

Our worldview is now rationalist and based on evolution as the source of life and human existence. Even if we were a modern Martin Luther, how could we have a new Reformation on this basis? What is there left to reform? Before we can answer those questions, we must look at the current evolutionary worldview and ask ourselves a simple question that no one seems to want to ask: What are its foundations? On close scrutiny, the massive claim of science, that evolution is the means by which we have come into existence, is quite without substantial foundations of any kind. As surprising as this statement will be to many, the world has been dazzled by fantastic claims made by evolutionary theory, on the flimsiest of evidence. As we will see later, Darwinism is essentially a rationalist approach to the natural world, neglecting the inductive scientific method. The "theory of evolution" is a wonderful and intricate spider's web of internally self-consistent ideas; it does not depend upon external, hard physical evidence.

As an example of this, the fossil record is supposed to show us evolution at work. How then do we explain the article in the online version of *USA Today*, posted on 25 May 2007: "Ancient coelacanth caught in Indonesia."[7] The article describes how a fisherman, named Justinus Lahama, caught a 4-foot, 110-pound fish near Sulawesi Island close to Bunaken National Marine Park, in Indonesia. By "ancient" the reporter was referring to the evolutionary assumption that this fish (pronounced see-la-canth) had died out 65 million years ago. The reporter also referred to the fish as a "living fossil." There are indeed fossils showing examples of coelacanths in rock strata which are allegedly that old. Unfortunately for the assumption, the fish is alive and well and shows absolutely no variation to the fossilized examples. No evolution has taken place over the assumed 65 million years.

The first example of a living coelacanth was found in 1938 off the African coast, causing a worldwide sensation. Several other specimens have recently been discovered, including one off Sulawesi Island in 1998. The coelacanth was once thought to be an intermediary form, leading up to amphibious forms, which then moved to the land and allegedly carried on evolving gradually, into various land animals and even birds. It was thought that they used their substantial, lobed fins for walking on the seabed before emerging on the land.

As long as the coelacanth was "extinct," such speculation was unchallengeable. But since 1938 and the subsequent study of these fish, it has been established that the fins were not used for walking but for precise swimming maneuvers. Also, the soft parts were conclusively shown to be generically fish, not transitional. So finding live coelacanths dealt a death blow to the idea that they were a "transitional form" from which amphibians (and subsequently land animals and birds) descended.[8] There had obviously been no evolution, and no transitional fossils. The abstract evolutionary theories concerning such fish, and their place in the hypothetical evolutionary "tree," collapsed in the face of real evidence. We will consider fossils fully in Chapter 8.

Professor Stephen Jay Gould and Dr Colin Patterson, both world-renowned leaders and senior figures in evolutionary paleontology, now sadly both recently deceased, agreed in their correspondence that there were no intermediate fossil forms, merely a handful, literally, of doubtful cases. Darwin himself pointed out that his theory would stand or fall on the fossil record. In his day there were relatively few fossils. Today there are millions, held in thousands of institutions worldwide, yet, in the opinion of two of the most respected and world-renowned scientists in this field, we do not have a single definitive transitional form. Where, in this case, is the evidence, and why does it not cause difficulties for Darwinian evolution?

Exploring this further, in a letter to Luther D. Sunderland, dated 10 April 1979, the late Dr Colin Patterson, senior paleontologist at the British Museum of Natural History, wrote:

> I fully agree with your comments on the lack of direct illustration
> of evolutionary transitions in my book. If I knew of any, fossil

or living, I would certainly have included them . . . Yet Gould
and the American Museum people are hard to contradict when
they say there are no transitional fossils . . . I will lay it on the
line – there is not one such fossil for which one could make a
watertight argument.[9]

In another comment Patterson also said, ". . . fossils may tell us many things,
but one thing they can never disclose is whether they were ancestors of
anything else."

Many other admissions from evolutionists themselves could be claimed
in support of these statements by Patterson, which are still valid today more
than thirty years later. In fact, one of the main arguments that evolutionists
Stephen Jay Gould and Niles Eldredge put forward for their "punctuated
equilibrium" theory in 1972 was the "extreme rarity" of transitional fossils
in support of neo-Darwinian gradualism. (Punctuated equilibrium is the
proposal that life is in equilibrium, or stasis, for long periods of time; then a
rapid evolutionary burst occurs, followed by another period of equilibrium,
followed by another burst of evolution, and so on). The phrase "extreme
rarity" disguises the undeniable fact that there are no proper transitional
forms; therefore, the fossil record does not support gradual evolution.

The generally accepted worldview among the majority of scientists is
based on the rationalist approach that we must have evolved, since they
can think of no other explanation of our origins without the God they have
dismissed from their universe. Based on this premise, they are being logical.
However, proper application of the inductive scientific method shows that,
in many areas, a great deal of the available scientific evidence opposes the
theory of evolution. This is fully addressed in Chapter 8, where some of the
basic evidence is assessed, and we attempt to show that, on any reasonable
basis and fair assessment of all the evidence, evolution can be shown to be
logically, mathematically and physically impossible.

Yet to the majority of scientists it is obviously unthinkable that the
only option they have left themselves is demonstrably impossible by their
own methodology. What holds them back is that the only alternative is
creation. Most are in the dangerous situation of allowing wishful thinking
to blind them to the obvious. The fact that the evidence of the fossil record
has serious flaws is not seen as a stumbling block. To be absolutely fair to
scientists as a class, a substantial minority is responding to the situation and

wants a fresh look at the evidence, and a new approach to the problem of the origins of life. It is, after all, bad science to make extravagant claims on flimsy evidence.

Many able scientists have serious doubts about evolutionary theories; for example, a book edited by John Ashton PhD is entitled *In Six Days: Why 50 Scientists Choose to Believe in Creation*.[10] However, the modern evolutionary worldview is everywhere and has infected even senior churchmen – who should know better, being well-educated men. Part of the problem is that many Christians have dismissed the intellect as part of faith. This can be laid at the door of the evangelical movement and the response to early Darwinism. We will address this in detail in Chapter 10.

During the period immediately following the publication of Darwin's *The Origin of Species*, Darwin's theories were soon seen as a direct challenge to Holy Scripture, especially the early parts of Genesis. However, at first, Darwin's theory was opposed on primarily scientific grounds, where most of the criticism came from the laboratory, not the pulpit.

One of the biggest criticisms of Darwin's work was that he had abandoned the inductive approach of the scientific method and adopted rationalism. The inductive method relies on past experience and observation; a set of rules or laws can be formulated to allow practical use of this knowledge. Rationalism can be considered the opposite of induction. Rationalism works by constructing hypothetical arguments in advance of experience and observation. These arguments must be logically consistent and follow the rules of logic, not experience. The answer, however absurd, is not the issue. The coherence of the logic and the argument is the main point. For example, in mathematics, if the equation is correct, the answer must be also correct. Rationalists use logic to construct an answer. The inductive method relies on the physical senses, which can be fooled. Rationalism is not troubled by this issue and can propose universal theories and laws without the problems of sensory experience. However, as Francis Bacon recognized, rationalism cannot be used independently of the inductive method, because science is about understanding the universe, an actual physical system that we are aware of through the senses, that provides experiences and a history of physical events. To study the universe, or the natural order of things, the scientist must be part of it, in order to observe, reason and experiment about it.

Initially, then, one of the major scientific criticisms of Darwin was that he had abandoned induction and embraced rationalism. The English geologist

Adam Sedgwick (1785–1873) was a former tutor of Darwin. In a letter to Darwin in 1859, Sedgwick wrote: "You have deserted – after a start in that tram-road of all solid physical truth – the true method of induction." Elsewhere, Sedgwick wrote:

> But I must in the first place observe that Darwin's theory is not inductive – not based on a series of acknowledged facts pointing to a general conclusion – not a proposition evolved out of the facts, logically, and of course including them. To use an old figure, I look on the theory as a vast pyramid resting on its apex, and that apex a mathematical point.[11]

Sedgwick's problem, shared by many others even to this day, was that Darwin had so emphasized the logic of his theory that the evidence of the physical world was almost secondary. This is much the same as the old paradox, where logicians can show, without fault in the logic, that trees do not exist, whereas, in physical reality, they do. Sedgwick's argument can be summarized that Darwin is abandoning the inductive method and his theory is not true science.

The theological argument centered on the challenge to Scripture, and so the debate became polarized and very heated around scriptural authority. At the time of publication of Darwin's theory, the orthodox practice of the Christian faith was centered on three main things:

1. Natural theology – man reasoning from himself and nature to God
2. Holy Scripture – the sovereign revelation of God to man
3. The person and work of Jesus Christ – the prophesied Messiah

Had the theologians of the day considered Darwin's theories as another form of natural theology, confined to the natural sphere, and as another attempt of man reasoning from himself and nature to the divine, the debate might have allowed the genuine processes of the inductive scientific method to deal with Darwinism. As such, Darwinism could be considered as a perfectly legitimate form of intellectual effort, without challenging the nature of faith or the integrity of Scripture. Unfortunately, the aggressive tactics of supporters of Darwinism, such as Sir Thomas Huxley and Sir Charles Lyell, both establishment figures and members of the Royal Society, meant that the assault was consistently maintained in the area of Scripture, no matter the intentions of others.

As we know, since those days, Darwinism has become ascendant and Scripture relegated to myth. The resulting consequence has been the gradual giving up of natural theology as part of the practice of orthodox faith. Thus the intellectual effort of the use of reason, hand in hand with both Divine Scripture and the person of Christ, has fallen into disuse. Scripture is harmonized with the natural, the natural having become authoritative. Many people who would call themselves both Christian and evangelical, no longer have a trusting faith in the authority of Scripture; their faith is full of doubts about the reliability of Scripture, because "it conflicts with science." As far as orthodox Christianity is concerned, there is a great onslaught from without and a tide of compromise within. Much of modern evangelical belief and practice has become reduced to a faith that the Bible contains "spiritual truth" rather than being factually and historically accurate. The major focus of evangelicalism therefore has retreated into the person and work of Jesus Christ. Many modern evangelical authorities insist that faith is accepting a personal revelation and experience of the Messiah, not insisting on the rigor of Scripture. Yet the Messiah Himself is defined by Scripture, not only spiritually, but also historically and factually. A personal revelation can only be subjective and relative. There is thus no objective truth to be had from this approach.

And so faith has been reduced to a blind faith, without objective intellectual rigor, based on internalized emotions and subjective experience. The foundations have become incredibly weak and are under constant threat. It is no wonder many have lost their faith in the existence of the Creator. Consider the following from *God in the Dark* by Os Guinness:

> The world of Christian faith is not a fairy-tale, make-believe world, question-free and problem-proof, but a world where doubt is never far from faith's shoulder.
>
> Consequently, a healthy understanding of doubt should go hand in hand with a healthy understanding of faith. We ourselves are called in question if we have no answer to doubt. If we constantly doubt what we believe and always believe-yet-doubt, we will be in danger of undermining our personal integrity, if not our stability. But if ours is an examined faith, we should

be unafraid to doubt. If doubt is eventually justified, we were
believing what clearly was not worth believing. But, if doubt
is answered, our faith grows stronger still. It knows God more
certainly, and it can enjoy God more deeply. Faith is not doubt-
free, but there is a general assurance of faith that is truly beyond a
shadow of doubt.[12]

This passage requires doubt to be answered – but how? By allowing the
scientific debate about the natural order of things into the realm of scriptural
revelation, Scripture has been virtually destroyed as the trustworthy basis
for faith. People have always been full of genuine doubt but are now without
an authority to examine their faith in the face of that doubt.

Without Scripture, Christ has no meaning. Throw away Scripture and
we automatically throw away Christ. Today we are seeing the next step in
the process: the gradual destruction of the person and work of Christ.

The tragedy that stands out so clearly is that people are throwing away
the Christian faith for nothing. Without realizing it, they are exchanging
Christ for a secular faith, a belief in nothing! God's wrath was visited upon
Israel for rejecting Him and following other gods, but at least those other
gods had some kind of personality.

Today we reject God and worship nothing, a non-person, the material
universe.

CHAPTER 2

FAITH, KNOWLEDGE AND WISDOM

My son, keep my words,
And treasure my commands within you.
Keep my commands and live,
And my law as the apple of your eye.
Bind them on your fingers;
Write them on the tablet of your heart.
Say to wisdom, "You are my sister,"
And call understanding your nearest kin,
That they may keep you from the immoral woman,
From the seductress who flatters with her words.

(Proverbs 7:1–5)

There is no absolute certainty on this side of the grave. It is spiritual life that is fundamentally important in providing enough confidence, through faith, to provide a framework within which we are to live. It is confidence based upon spiritual faith that enables us to relate to each other and to God. It allows us to make definite statements and hold clear views upon morals and social behavior. It allows us to live with dignity and mutual respect. Spiritual faith gives meaning and purpose to our lives and our physical deaths. Unfortunately, mankind has always disliked this dependence on God for meaning and authority and has tried to find a way out. Throughout history, natural philosophers have always tried to put forward a view of life without God. The modern application of rationalist and evolutionary theories to our society has apparently succeeded, and in doing so has produced misery and hopelessness in the West.

Many philosophers have tried to construct a humanist philosophy – a unity of knowledge – based on mankind rather than God. On the whole, the philosophers failed. Each new proposal created more difficulties than it solved. By the time of the great Renaissance in Europe, this effort had extended to art and literature and was no longer confined to philosophy. For example, Francis Schaeffer in his book *Escape from Reason* describes how Leonardo da Vinci sketched and sketched in the hope of expressing the essence of life in his art. Having done away with God, Leonardo followed the humanist school and tried to create his own unity. He failed, like all the others before him.

Since the time of the Renaissance, great scientific leaps have chased each other down the centuries, extending our knowledge of the universe beyond all previous imagining. Technology has improved from generation to generation. In the West, our technological prowess has removed the apparent need for faith in God. In the first years of the twenty-first century we have become masters of the universe and arbiters of nature. Science is king, so who needs God? Today we have knowledge, not simple-minded faith. For the first time in history, philosophers have something to work with and they have built on modern technological achievement, extending the humanist worldview into the greatest civilization the world has ever known. They have taken the discoveries of science and our growing mastery of the natural world as an excuse for doing away with the need for God. After all, we have explored the evolution and development of life itself; we have looked far out into the cosmos and seen the very ends of the universe.

According to this, we should, as a civilization, be moving towards greater self-understanding and better behavior. As our knowledge increases, so our philosophies should improve and we should become more mature in our relationships – able to create better and better societies without God as their basis. Sadly, this proves not to be the case. As we have increased our knowledge of the universe and its properties, we have used that knowledge to extract more and more from an exhausted planet and to create more and more powerful weapons of war. More people died violent deaths in the twentieth century than in the entire record of previous human history. There have been more totalitarian dictatorships and more wars (large and small) in the last 250 years than ever before. It is no coincidence that this period coincides with the growing atheism of the modern worldview and the amplifying effects of industrialization and technology.

Yet the advances of science, technology and humanist philosophy have, in the last few centuries, created an extraordinary situation. On the one hand we have discovered so much in the various branches of science that we are now dealing with the basic building blocks of the universe. On the other hand, modern scientists no longer claim to have reached the limits of knowledge – as the classical scientists of the nineteenth century used to boast. As our knowledge has increased we have come to the point that not only are we becoming more aware of what we don't know, but we are also less confident about what we do know. Therefore the modern hallmark of a mature approach to anything is one of uncertainty.

Scientific results are always accompanied by an indicator of confidence in the results, based on the limits of experimental accuracy. Modern scientists studying the universe have come to the startling conclusion that, in the inherent nature of things, nothing is certain to happen at all! Events and causation can only be given an index of probability. It may surprise you to know that according to quantum theory there is a very small possibility that the sun will not be on the eastern horizon tomorrow, as the earth turns on its axis for each new day. It might be somewhere else! Common sense laughs at such a notion, but in the scientific sense it is not possible to be absolutely sure of anything at all.

In philosophy, the rather defiant conclusion of the rationalist French philosopher Descartes (1596–1650) – "I think, therefore I am!" – is, in some way, a desperate acknowledgment of this lack of certainty – a soul crying out. Descartes had set out to reject everything that could not be proven without the slightest doubt. He wanted to retain only the undoubted facts and construct his philosophy from there. By the time he had finished there was almost nothing left. He failed, as others had failed before him. He was forced to accept the fact that rationality and reasoning (the mind and consciousness) cannot be explained by this approach; they are, in fact, the indispensable evidence of meaning and existence – a paradox indeed. There is a story about the renowned Scottish philosopher, David Hume (1711–76), who was sitting and thinking about the very same problem in his study one day, when he suddenly became unsure about whether anything at all was real. He had a panic attack and ran out into the billiard room where his friends were playing, just to reassure himself that there was a real world out there! As philosophers reasoned themselves further and further away from God, they gradually lost touch with reality, and could no longer be sure of meaning, objective reality, or purpose to life.

In our postmodern society, where philosophers have failed to find a true basis for objectivity, and we are influenced by the uncertainties of modern science and technology, dogmatic assertions are impossible. Gray is the new black and white. The principles of uncertainty have become embedded in every means of expression. This affects the way we can construct our morality: this, in turn, affects our behavior, and this determines the nature of modern society.

This state of affairs has gradually woven itself into Christian thinking. The ascendance of scientific authority has replaced the authority of Scriptures. A simple faith in God and His Word, giving a dogmatic approach to life, would demonstrate to the world that a person holding such a faith had not yet reached the level of knowledge, experience and maturity of the more advanced and sophisticated world. We often hear the double mantra: "There are no absolutes; your truth is not my truth." This places a great deal of pressure upon the faithful to reject traditional doctrine, based as it is upon the unchanging will of God.

We find that many Christian leaders are actually paralyzed and cannot give a lead for fear of expressing certainty, which will be interpreted as being judgmental and prejudiced, but, more importantly, outdated and irrelevant. This attracts much scorn and ridicule from the world and criticism from Christian colleagues. In an attempt to be sophisticated, up-to-date and "mature," church leaders have watered down and restated doctrine after doctrine, gradually reducing the impact of the Christian faith. It would not be extreme to claim that they have actually lost their faith under the onslaught of scientific naturalism, and the philosophical challenge of humanism. As a consequence, no assured lead is given to help people to express their faith and live their lives with definite meaning and hope for the future. For this reason many have stopped attending church; paradoxically, the more that leave, the less controversial the Church becomes, for fear of turning away the remainder.

This situation has come about from fear of conflict with academic and scientific authority. This is so terribly sad, because such conflict is actually the heart of a witnessing church and should be the norm of the faithful. Without it any church becomes gradually more and more irrelevant. If the Church agrees with the world, or at least avoids conflict with the given opinions of the day, what does the Church have to offer?

Have you noticed that if any Christian leader expresses a firm moral opinion based on Scripture, his own Christian peers undermine him? He is criticized as being authoritarian, or fundamentalist. We seem to have reached the position whereby to be firm, convinced, or definite in what you do or say is a sign of naivety or immaturity and inevitably invites personal attacks. It demonstrates how far we have gone down the path of rejecting scriptural certainties. A clear reliance on Scripture for guidance is no longer exercised. Worldly concerns filter the gospel message. Is it any wonder that people turn away from inconclusive, non-judgmental, uncertain, modern liberal Christianity?

Another huge pressure is the external onslaught from those who point out the many acts of barbarity carried out in the name of Christ throughout history. Most Christian leaders wilt under such attacks. Instead of wilting they should send the very clear message that condemning people to death in the name of Christ is the opposite of His teaching. Ruthless people with worldly ambitions, interpreting the Scriptures for personal gain, are the true architects of such barbarities. There have been many people who called themselves Christians, and who knew that God would eventually judge them for their actions, who committed real atrocities. When you examine this in detail, as bad as they were at the time (and without excuse) they are a mere shadow of the atrocities committed by the atheist ideologies of fascism, socialism and communism, where there is no restraining fear of divine retribution.

The gospel message, properly understood, remains the one true hope of mankind. At the very least it restrains the worst excesses. Scripture must be held in high regard, worthy of study, and viewed as the ruler of our behavior and how we look at the world. When Holy Scripture is misused to justify murder it is brought down to the level of humanity. It becomes just another book of rules for oppressing the poor and powerless, rather than the Book of Truth that gives life and freedom. A perfect example of this was the situation faced by Martin Luther, when he challenged the medieval Church of Rome.

Knowledge and wisdom are not the same thing, yet the explosion of worldly knowledge through the twentieth and twenty-first centuries has dazzled people by its achievements. We can genetically modify plants and animals. We can harness the atom. We can do all sorts of things based on our ever-increasing knowledge of the natural universe and how it works. Knowledge is a seductress who flatters to deceive. Such knowledge masquerades as wisdom in the minds of many, but the ability to do things is not wisdom. On the contrary, we must use wisdom to restrain ourselves from doing something that may have harmful consequences.

What is wisdom? I have come to a definition that serves me very well. Wisdom can be defined as:

> ### The capacity to foresee consequences and the will to modify our behavior accordingly.

To amplify this, wisdom carries with it a sense of what is right, or "what ought to be." Wisdom also carries with it a sense of moral force in action: to think rightly and to do what is right. This means there must be an underpinning set of standards against which we measure our actions; there must be an "ought" in morals – but where do we get it from?

In the natural world there can be no basis for wisdom as we have defined it here. What is, simply is, without moral force. The philosopher David Hume set this out in his major work, *A Treatise of Human Nature*. Hume was an empiricist (one who believes that true knowledge can only be derived from the physical senses and sensory experience) and he explored where we can find morality in nature. He pointed out the illegitimacy of jumping from an "is" to an "ought" when confined to the natural world.[13]

Wisdom can therefore only have a supernatural origin. Wisdom can only draw its moral force from the ethics of God, out of His objective, external, eternal and unchanging character. Wisdom draws its understanding about "what ought to be" from God Himself. Scientific knowledge does not contain wisdom or moral force and has no ethic. Scientific knowledge is simply a collection of facts, plus some theories about how the universe works. Science is concerned with the "how" of things, not the "why." Similarly, science is not concerned with ethics, morality, or "what ought to be." It is only concerned with "what is." Wisdom, however, is a spiritual phenomenon. It is prescriptive and judges the "what is" on the basis of "what ought to be." Wisdom then commands obedience to its conclusions.

We must not be led astray by technological achievements, magnificent though they are. Modern technology has a very powerful effect upon the way people think. It draws them away from God and dazzles them with worldly achievements. "What is" has begun to define "what ought to be."

Under these conditions idolatry is the most dangerous temptation of all. The first commandment of God is that we shall have no other gods before Him. Philosophers have endlessly tried to devise a worldview that does not need God. Seeking a way of life without God, or exalting ourselves above

God, is perhaps the root form of idolatry. Philosophers today have modern science and evolution, and all the technological wonders of the world, to insist that God does not exist. Modern Christians have temptations the likes of which have never been seen before. We need to exercise caution and wisdom.

We must understand what is happening to our world and be firm and certain in our faith. Satan once took Jesus to the top of a mountain and offered Him the world – provided, of course, that Jesus rejected His Father and worshiped Satan instead. Jesus resisted and kept His Father's will. Science and technology are taking each of us to the top of our own individual mountains and offering us the world; not just a material world of physical comforts, but also a moral world of self-centeredness and autonomy. To embrace wisdom, and the divine ethic it embodies, is to foresee and avoid the seduction of our selfish and cruel human natures. We must be able to resist the worldly temptations of science and technology and acknowledge God as the Creator and Sustainer of all things. Only wisdom from above can help us.

CHAPTER 3

A FIGHT TO THE DEATH

If the foundations are destroyed, what can the righteous do?

(Psalm 11:3)

A t the beginning of the twenty-first century, most scholars in the West would agree that the evolutionary theory of origins and humanist philosophies have consigned religion to the level of myth at best, and dangerous delusion at worst, responsible for many of the world's ills. Many concerned and influential people on both sides of the argument accept that the take-up and development of these ideas have brought the Christian faith to the point of death.

The apparent opposition of modern science and the Bible is one of the foundational problems. A deliberately distorted review of the Renaissance, the Reformation and the work of such scientists as Copernicus, Galileo and Newton, is almost always used to show the opposition and persecution these scientists faced from religion. Their work on taking the Western worldview away from Christianity is extolled, because the Church resisted the "true march of science and progress."

The Reformation of Martin Luther could be considered as relatively unimportant compared with today's situation; then, it was not about the nature of the Christian faith, but about form rather than substance; now, however, it is about the very basis of the Christian faith, where the resurrection, the virgin birth, miracles, prayer – are all reduced to myth, fallacy or fabrication. Collectively this constitutes an overwhelming challenge to every aspect of Christianity. It would appear that there is no future for the Christian faith if we carry on as we are. It is a fight to the death between man and God, between human knowledge and divine revelation. The battlefield is the hearts and minds of people everywhere. The outcome has eternal consequences.

I want to take up the challenge of this fight to the death and attempt to examine the problems of Christian faith and spirituality at the start of this, the third millennium since the advent of Christ. As a starting point, we need to look at the meaning of two words: "fundamentalism" and "secularism."

Fundamentalism

Paul Tillich (1886–1965), in the introduction to his work *Systematic Theology*, describes fundamentalism as failing to make contact with the present situation, of speaking from the past and elevating something finite and transitory to something infinite and eternal. In other words, something that was once useful in the past cannot be useful today, or in the future. Tillich goes on to say that, "In this respect fundamentalism has demonic traits. It destroys the humble honesty of the search for truth . . ."

On this view, fundamentalism does not therefore speak into the current situation of the beginning of the twenty-first century. It retreats into past forms and tries to impose these on a radically new situation. In contrast to this view, there is another aspect of the traditional faith known as orthodoxy. Orthodoxy states that the Christian faith has certain truths, expressed in the Bible, which are timeless and applicable to all situations in all times. Upholders of Biblical orthodoxy would say that they are restating the unchanging truth of the gospel message into an increasingly secular world. Many liberal theologians, such as Tillich, have a tendency to discount orthodoxy and place everyone who upholds the inerrancy and inspired nature of the Bible in the fundamentalist category; they tend to ignore the possibility that orthodoxy has anything meaningful to say.

"Fundamentalism" as a Christian movement arose out of British and American Protestantism in the late nineteenth and early twentieth centuries among evangelical Christians, in an effort to restate the fundamentals of the orthodox faith. There were different strands of thought that went into it. One such strand was reaction against liberal theology, and it restated ideas that were fundamental to the Christian faith:

- The inerrancy of the Bible
- The sole authority of Holy Scripture (*Sola Scriptura*)

- The virgin birth of Jesus Christ
- The doctrine of substitutionary atonement
- The bodily resurrection of Jesus
- The imminent personal return of Jesus Christ

Another strand was "dispensationalism," an interpretation of the Bible developed in the 1830s in England. It was a theory that divided all of time into different "dispensations" which were seen as stages of God's revelation. This reinforced a more literal interpretation of the Bible. A third strand came from Princeton theology, which developed the doctrine of inerrancy in response to higher criticism of the Bible. A fourth strand came from a collection of ninety essays in a twelve-volume study called *The Fundamentals*, published between 1910 and 1915.[14] This strand emphasized the literal nature of the Biblical accounts, especially Christ's miraculous ministry, and the creation account in Genesis.

By the late 1920s, inerrancy and literalness of the Bible texts had become central to fundamentalism. Yet another strand was of growing concern among many evangelicals: the moral consequences of modernism and higher criticism. This strand focused its major efforts on opposition to Darwinism.

The term "fundamentalist" quite quickly grew to be a dismissive epithet; it is often used to attack or ridicule those who attempt to defend the "fundamentals of the faith," or orthodoxy in preaching and practice.

Secularism

Secularism is often used in the opposite sense to fundamentalism, and can be explained as the process whereby the great doctrines of the Christian faith are gradually reinterpreted in the light of non-religious, humanist influences. This is not new. Biblical doctrine has always been ameliorated and watered down to please the demands of church members, let alone external critics. This is one of the great tragedies and paradoxes of the Church. There has always been, however, the great normalizing pull of orthodoxy, like a piece of elastic that snaps back into shape when released. The core of the faith has always been there to correct the compromising tendencies of its members and, over time, draw the faithful back to God. However, secularism in the context of the postmodern worldview of the twenty-first century can only be taken to mean that there is no spiritual or religious content left. It is a completely "empty secularism" without any faint tinge of Christian content. This time the process is complete – the historical tendency to secularism has been amplified and extended by the dual march of science and philosophy. At the same time, alleged contradictions and mistakes in the Biblical texts have fatally undermined orthodoxy. The rational and orthodox faith of former times was based on the exercise of reason using scriptural evidence. This has been destroyed. Secularism in the twenty-first century thus becomes the total rejection of Holy Scripture and the complete substitution of scientific knowledge and humanist principles as the authoritative source of guidance.

Consequences

Many people are indeed retreating into the kind of fundamentalism described by Tillich, but many more are surrendering to secularism as their personal response to the meaningless existential world they inhabit. On Tillich's definition, fundamentalism is simply a cry for help, a retreat from threatening changes by sticking to familiar formulas. On the other hand, secularism is actively giving up, in the sense that religion has no further relevance. The traditional Church has no effective answer to this devastating situation. Many denominations imitate secular marketing and recruitment programs in a vain attempt to retain or attract members. The Church is apparently powerless in the face of modern science and philosophy.

By the word "Church" I mean the institutionalized denominational Churches, whose hierarchical structures are political and worldly. I can only speak from my experience of the Western Churches – Roman Catholic and Protestant: I have no personal experience of the Eastern Orthodox or Apostolic Churches, and so these are excluded. This definition is used throughout this book. In contrast to the institutional "Church" there is always the faithful remnant of believers in any age, who form the true church, the body of Christ, scattered among the denominations and Christendom generally. There are also individual local churches which have kept the faith and have a high view of God's Word.

Generally, however, the situation is that modern scientific thinking has superseded the Holy Scriptures, although the Church insists there are some spiritual truths contained in the Bible. Unfortunately, having bent the knee to man's science, the Church actually preaches a form of secularism, or faith without the supernatural. The reason is not far away: since modern science and humanism are the touchstones of modern theology, no miracle and no exception to the scientifically determined path of the universe is allowed. The miraculous ministry of Christ is thus denied. This means that, despite evangelical pretensions, a large proportion of modern Christian teaching actively opposes the basic Christian faith and the witness of Christ Himself!

The practical consequences of this are devastating. What is the point of trying to follow Christ if our natures are fixed at birth (Darwin, evolution and genetics) and our whole lives behaviorally determined from cradle to grave (Freud and Jung)? Are we no more than accidental biological machines? Do our lives have any value at all? Are our choices real or imagined? Is guilt real or merely neurosis? Psychoanalysis reduces everything to neurosis, removing true moral guilt. This allows individuals to deny personal responsibility for their actions. How do we cope with this overwhelming situation? What value does the Bible actually have, and what faith should we place in it? What response can we make?

Labeling a belief in the error-free nature of Holy Scripture as "mindless fundamentalism" effectively disempowers those who would quote the Bible in the debate. The evidence-based faith of former generations is fatally undermined by excluding the Bible as a source of credible evidence. So many modern Christians attempt to avoid the issue by emphasizing direct personal revelation and a personal relationship with Christ, rather than the orthodoxy of Scriptures. However, the consequence is that the use of Scripture as the basis for debate is much reduced. Humanist secular arguments are widely used instead. It is this process, the removal of Scripture from the heart of the practice of Christianity, which is causing the decline of the Church. The increasing secularization is happening in part because church leaders have compromised their faith. There can be no effective discussion of Christianity that does not involve extensive use of Scripture.

The crisis within the Church is the result of giving away the only weapon it possesses: the Sword of Truth from the inspired Word of God, which gives meaning, life and hope, and cannot be dismissed or changed without removing the very reason for the existence of the Church. We see this all around us. Churches are diminishing both in membership and effectiveness. The message is being lost so the faithful are being lost, and the empty churches are being converted into offices, industrial units and apartments.

It cannot be stated too strongly that the root causes are found in the rejection of Scripture. This has intensified since the Enlightenment and the birth of modern rationalism, and reached its zenith in the evangelical response to Darwinism between 1860 and 1900. Naturalist theories, instead of remaining within the realm of the natural, have risen to challenge the supernatural – the divine revelation of Scripture. We will look at this in some detail in Chapter 10.

It is all very well and necessary to discuss the academic philosophical issues and the historical process, but let us not forget that they have real effects on real people. As one looks at the modern world and the progressive decline of moral behavior, one is filled with growing horror. The way people think about themselves governs the way they behave. If everything is meaningless or personal neurosis, then all behavior becomes irrational. Faith becomes irrational; morals become irrational. It is just as valid to kill and maim as it is to love your neighbor.

Modern morality has become concerned only with this natural life, with individual fulfillment based on individual circumstances. Thus all morals become relative, without absolute standards. This way of thinking is producing terrible effects in modern society. There are many current examples of people deliberately killing others. This is not because they do not understand traditional Christian morality; it is deliberate action against it. In the case of "cult" killings it is the expression of their own "higher morality." Abortion is a different, but related example. Abortion sets aside the moral imperative of the sanctity of human life as subordinate to other considerations, and the rights of the woman. Without Scripture people have no basis for absolutes. They have no God.

The modern Church could not be in a more helpless situation. Faith in God's Word has been fatally undermined and fallible human science exalted as truth. Not only is this a tragedy of the greatest proportions, but also idolatry of the worst kind. We all know that the basis of orthodox Christian faith is rooted in history, and cannot simply be dismissed as mythological or unscientific. It is, however, overwhelmingly miraculous and depends upon the self-revelation of God to man from outside the realm of our natural existence – something totally excluded from the modern worldview. This erosion of the "core" of Christianity has consequences for church discipline. The part of the Church Age in which we are now living is the most divisive in history. Churches are splitting away from the mainstream faith with the greatest of passion, so they can follow their own subjective view of the faith, as the once great anchor of orthodoxy fades away.

A good example of this is the "Emerging Church" movement. Emerging churches are an informal network of Christian communities who believe that God's way for today is based on relationships and emerging ideas, rather than dogmatic truths and traditional statements of faith. They pursue dialogue over doctrine and are filled with people who have left the traditional Church. Typically they might have couches, conversations and coffee in place of preaching. They would normally compromise rather than confront, and seem to prefer questions instead of answers. While those leading the movement say that the gospel can't be clearly known, they make one definite statement: "The Bible doesn't mean what traditional people think it means."[15] That being the case, the Emerging Church is just another attack on the truth and certainty of God's Word – this time from within, based on compromise.

John McArthur, who was interviewed about the Emerging Church in 2007, said:

> This is not an intellectual movement. This is not a movement that has discovered evidence that overturns inspiration, evidence that overturns inerrancy or authority. This is a movement born of people who do not want to accept the clarity of Scripture.[16]

The obvious conclusions about the Emerging Church are these:

1. For any movement to claim that the Bible is not clear is to claim that God's wisdom and integrity are faulty and fallible.
2. God may have spoken, but for practical purposes no one can be really sure what He said. Saying that Scripture is not clear is just another way to undermine Biblical authority.
3. If God's Word is not clear, then no-one is responsible to follow it.

More seriously, these explicit attitudes in the Emerging Church are already implicitly at work in the traditional denominations and growing in strength. The only possible conclusion is that things are going to get much worse.

This is a challenge requiring a response that speaks into the situation of the twenty-first century, without losing the truths of the Biblical message. It requires a response that can look honestly at the advances of science and technology yet legitimately call upon the Bible for guidance and help. The situation of the Church may be helpless but it is not hopeless. It may well be a fight to the death, but we have the one true Living God who will triumph in the end. Let us not be faint and give up hope. If God is for us, who can be against us?

CHAPTER 4

UNCHANGING TRUTH

Jesus Christ is the same yesterday, today, and forever. Do not be carried about with various and strange doctrines. For it is good that the heart be established by grace, not with foods which have not profited those who have been occupied with them.

(Hebrews 13:8–9)

New Testament Greek has a word: *kerygma*. It expresses the concept of "unchanging truth," which is the gospel message at the core of Christianity. This gospel message is applicable to all ages and cultures.

Christian apologetics have long been the method of defending the faith and of interpreting the faith into new situations. The term "apologetic" means "answering" and was held in great esteem by the early church. Latterly it has fallen into disrepute due to the poor way in which this approach has been used to "defend" the faith against the encroaches of scientific naturalism and humanism. It has come to mean "apologize" for the faith, firstly due to a shift in word meaning, but more importantly it is perceived as "apologizing" for contradicting science. There is a common acceptance that the advances of modern science and evolutionary theories, together with discoveries in medicine and psychiatry, are somehow opposed to the Bible and every new discovery undermines some part of the Bible. The traditional apologetic approach has been used piecemeal, in an attempt to bridge the differences and maintain the relevance of the Bible in an increasingly naturalistic and deterministic culture. Sadly, this method of using apologetics has obviously failed to stem the tide. Anyone attempting an "apologetic" approach to another scientific advance is treated with derision. The attitude has become one of fatalism, of the inevitability of the triumph of science and rationalism over the outdated worldview of the Christian faith.

Daniel Dennett, in his book *Darwin's Dangerous Idea*,[17] compares Darwin's theory to a "universal acid" that can eat through anything – nothing can hold it. Darwinism "eats through virtually every traditional concept." By this he means mankind's beliefs about God, meaning, purpose, morality – absolutely everything that gives us value and destiny. Dennett is an atheist and has no brief for Christianity or any religion. He criticizes creationists severely, but he states that they are:

> . . . right about one thing; Darwin's dangerous idea cuts much deeper into the fabric of our most fundamental beliefs than many of [Darwinism's] sophisticated apologists have yet admitted, even to themselves. Even today, many people still have not come to terms with its mind-boggling implications.[18]

A "kerygmatic" approach is very simple. It consists of preaching the message of the gospel of Jesus Christ into the situation in which we live. This is the message of the salvation of mankind through the sacrifice of Jesus. This is not a new idea, of course, but to do it, the preacher needs complete faith in the inspired nature of the Biblical texts. He needs to understand them and fully accept that they contain no error and are the direct revelation of Almighty God. Since it is clear that the modern Church in general has no confidence in the inspired and inerrant nature of the Holy Scriptures, the gospel cannot be meaningfully preached into the lives of modern people. Many Christian clergy, and many who would call themselves Christian, exhibit no evidence of their own salvation. They have been infected with the postmodern worldview. No one can preach the Christian doctrine of salvation without a clear and firm belief in his own real salvation, according to the Scriptures. This is the personal tragedy of many clergymen, preaching a futile message.

We all need a trustworthy authority, a standard against which we can measure everything we see, hear, think and do, to discover our purpose and our destiny. Many things must be studied and considered in the search for meaning. Unfortunately, in our modern society, everything must be easy to digest, prepackaged and, above all, quick: the "sound bite." We have no time to sit and contemplate the great mysteries. This no doubt explains why many take the secular approach, allowing sound bites to take the place of personal reasoning, accepting the findings of science and the comforts of technology without question, and allowing the Christian exercise of reason and intellect to fall into disuse.

The things of God do not fall easily into human categories. Every seeker is unique, every culture unique, every fulfillment unique. Yet these variations all depend upon an objective, unchanging bedrock of common truth. Otherwise there is nothing that one individual can say to another, one nation to another, one age to another, that carries any basic, consistent meaning, independent of the ideologies of the day.

Christianity is a way of life based on a clear, unchanging message. It is not some kind of religious experience divorced from propositional truth.

CHAPTER 5

THE REFORMATION OF 1517

*Unless I am convinced by proofs from Scriptures or by plain and
clear reasons and arguments, I can and will not retract, for it is neither
safe nor wise to do anything against conscience. Here I stand.
I can do no other. God help me. Amen.*

Martin Luther, in his response to the Diet of Worms on 18 April 1521

In our renewed search for a trustworthy authority it is necessary to look
afresh at the Holy Scriptures themselves. The value and trustworthiness
of the Scriptures were also key issues in the Reformation of the sixteenth
century. The great body of taught dogma of the Roman Church, known as
the Magisterium, was, and remains, often in conflict with the Scriptures.
The use of the Scriptures as an absolute authority was neglected. The cry
"*Sola Scriptura!*" (only Scripture has authority) of the Protesting Church
was a clarion call back to the sole authority of Holy Scriptures and the
gospel truth (*kerygma*) they contain.

In a strange way we are also in the same position at the beginning of the
twenty-first century. The outworking of natural philosophy has undermined
the use of the Scriptures. The critics of the Biblical texts have suggested that
the Bible contains errors in the areas of history and nature, thus questioning
the moral and spiritual content. Scientific knowledge has replaced historical
Biblical knowledge, and has become the basis of the worldview of the West
– science and technology are what our civilization believes in above all other
things. Yet the common assumptions behind the rejection of the Scriptures
are often plainly and obviously wrong. Historical records and secular science
in themselves have no conflict with the Bible or what the Bible teaches.

The seriousness and importance of the Reformation of the early sixteenth century is not fully appreciated in the modern world. A view seems to be growing that the Reformation was fought over minor differences and matters of emphasis of church order. Nothing could be further from the truth. There were real and deep differences over the basic tenets of the Christian faith and its fundamental ethos. The principle of *Sola Scriptura* was a real divergence from the Church of Rome. The Roman Church had, over the centuries, accumulated such a large amount of dogma and doctrine that the simple gospel was obscured. The Reformers wanted to reverse this process and go back to the Word of God, rather than the man-made dogmas of the Church at that time.

The great Roman Catholic theologian Thomas Aquinas (1225–74) had introduced humanism into the Church by his conclusions that the fall of man had corrupted everything except the intellect. This allowed the Church to imagine that human thoughts were the equal of the Holy Scriptures. By the time of the Reformation, the body of teaching within the Roman Church (the Magisterium) had been elevated to equal, some would say more than equal, status with Holy Scripture. Access to the Bible was restricted to the clergy, and it was only available in Latin. Anyone attempting to translate the Bible for ordinary people was severely punished and sometimes executed: a well-used method was by burning at the stake. Anyone other than a priest found with a Bible was condemned and punished severely. The Roman Church had become a powerful organization, preventing the teaching of the true gospel while, at the same time, elevating its own doctrines.

The problem did not end there. There were great abuses of ecclesiastical power. One glaring example was the selling of "indulgences" as passports to heaven, or to minimize the time to be spent in purgatory, as though forgiveness and salvation could be bought with money or deeds. The simple truth was that Rome needed the money. The Bible tells us categorically that buying forgiveness is not possible, that salvation and forgiveness cannot be earned "lest anyone should boast" (Ephesians 2:8–9). Consider the abject misery and hopeless condition of those exposed to the Roman dogma; consider their expectations that they and all their loved ones would go to hell because they could not afford Rome's fees. This was not the fruit of the gospel but that of a cruel tyrant.

The Reformation was born out of the accumulated revulsion against all the excesses of the papacy at that time. The Reformation was a demand for a fundamental rethink of the way that the Christian gospel was taught and applied to daily life. It was not a trivial affair. Theology was the crucial issue. The call of the Reformation to return to the teaching of salvation through grace was a major challenge to the temporal as well as spiritual authority of the papacy. Salvation through works was the great lever used by Rome to control the faithful through false guilt, reward and punishment. The doctrine of salvation through grace alone removes this power from any Church, Roman or otherwise.

Since both sides of the argument within the Reformation of 1517 had a common starting point of the Catholic (universal) Church, it is easy to assume from the distance of the twenty-first century that the Reformers were battling over differences of doctrine and practice. The present crisis within Christianity, brewing irresistibly since the Enlightenment and erupting in the twentieth century, is assumed to be of a different, more serious, nature than that which caused the first Reformation. It is scientific humanism which is directly opposed to the Christian faith – an external threat, not an internal battle. Also, what frequently confuses the issue is that modern society is vastly different from that of the early sixteenth century; modern scientific and technological achievements are so powerful that they appear to be the answer to all problems, including the religious questions. However, since the Reformation of 1517 was an attempt to rediscover the true Christian faith for a new era, then today, at the turn of the twenty-first century, we have the same problem.

In spite of the differences between the sixteenth and twenty-first centuries, there is an underlying similarity in the two cases. In the sixteenth century, although the protagonists were indeed starting from a common heritage, the Church of Rome had a worldview and structure based on its position as a great secular power. Salvation was earned through the "works" of men and women, controlled by the Church, which, since the time of Thomas Aquinas, was deeply infected with humanism. The Reformers wanted a worldview based upon salvation as the free gift of God through His sovereign grace, as the only true source of freedom. We see here the basic conflict between earth and heaven, between the interests of man and the will of God, between nature and grace. There was and is nothing new in this conflict. It is the basis of the original act of rebellion of Adam and Eve. It will be the basis of the last sin ever committed. It is also the basis of the present conflict between secular humanism and the Judeo-Christian tradition. We can therefore learn from the previous reform of the Church and apply those lessons to today.

It is worth emphasizing the importance of the Reformation of 1517. If we argue otherwise, we must explain away not only the theological differences, but also the hundreds of thousands of Christians who died because of it. We must also explain the effects of the Reformation on Northern Europe. Since the Reformation, the general culture of Northern Europe has had unprecedented success by any standard in history. This was brought about by a significant change in the way people thought about themselves and their relationship to God. The effect of the reformed Christian faith and the new Protestant dogma on the general society and culture of Northern Europe (and by extension North America and Australasia) over the last 500 years is staggering. Such an effect is not brought about by trivial changes – nor is it brought about by false beliefs that have no relation to reality. Communism, for example, lasted barely seventy years from the Russian Revolution. It bankrupted and ruined all those countries and societies where it was imposed. The human cost of the enforced application of a humanist ideology has been appalling. In the USSR alone, from 1917 to the death of Stalin in 1953, it has been estimated that 60 million people died. Stalin himself ordered the deaths of an estimated 22 million of his own countrymen! The total sum of human suffering from global communism in the twentieth century defies calculation.

Today, in the West, secular humanists have almost succeeded in realigning the worldview of human beings away from the knowledge and love of God and His Son, the Redeemer of mankind. Some would say they have completely succeeded. The spiritual condition of the Church today is very similar to that of the Church before the Reformation. Then, the doctrine of salvation through grace was suppressed by the religious government of the day in favor of a secular agenda that gave them power and control over their fellow human beings. Nowadays the very same condition has come about, but we are no longer in a theocracy. The sociologists and the politicians exercise control. Their ideological aim is to remake the world into a socially engineered paradise. They want to be in charge of their own destiny. The common denominator of all such people is a belief in rationalism, secular humanism and the evolutionary origin and progress of mankind, without the need for God. They are the blind victims of their own pride. They cannot see the lessons of history.

If we go back to the last century, the great English scientist and humanist philosopher Sir Julian Huxley (1887–1975), with fellow-travelers and colleagues, deliberately set out to replace the basis of faith in God with a faith in science and human progress. They knew what they were doing and were explicit in their aims. They saw in the writings of Darwin a scientific basis for their alternative "religion." Evolution was their alternative to creation. They believed that if they set out to sell their "religion" to the general public they could challenge the Judeo-Christian belief in a Creator God and substitute a humanist system. The process can be said to have formally started with the publication in 1879 of Herbert Spencer's book, *The Data of Ethics*. Spencer was a very influential English philosopher. After Darwin published *The Origin of Species* he was the first to begin the application of the theory to society, and can lay fair claim to being the father of Social Darwinism. It was Spencer who actually coined the term "survival of the fittest." Spencer argued that as biological structures and functions evolved, ethics should likewise evolve, and we should be framing a "conception of the evolution of conduct."[19] Huxley himself said:

> Many people assert that this abandonment of the god hypothesis
> means the abandonment of all religion and all moral sanctions.
> This is simply not true. But it does mean, once our relief at
> jettisoning an outdated piece of ideological furniture is over, that
> we must construct something to take its place.[20]

More than a century later we can attest to the success of their efforts in doing away with God. What they may or may not have realized, however, was that by replacing Christianity with a man-made faith, they were also eliminating the possibility of salvation. Without God there can be no grace, no Son, no redemption, no forgiveness and no freedom. Everyone is under the law again. This time it is not the personal Law of God, but the impersonal and predetermined natural law of the physical universe: a closed system where divine intervention is impossible and freedom non-existent. What they also did not realize was that they were creating an intellectual atmosphere where the concept of the survival of the fittest or "natural selection" spawned the doctrine of class struggle, leading to Karl Marx and atheistic communism. More sinister was the development of evolutionary theory into eugenics and the concept of a master race. The results we all know.

As the great ideological wars of the twentieth century slowly recede into history, the spiritual legacy of the shifts in worldview brought about by the efforts of these philosopher-scientists remains. Effectively, this legacy has undone the immense benefits gained from the Reformation of the sixteenth century. By continuing to place their faith in the new religion known as evolution, underpinned by secular humanism, human beings are once again in bondage. Freedom has been lost under this atheistic worldview. Political and business leaders now calculate their fortunes not upon human beings but upon "consumer units." We are all graded according to our credit rating, and targeted for our buying power and our voting power. We are worked to death from stress and lack of real satisfaction in life. We are prepackaged from cradle to grave, regarded as nothing more than evolved biological machines, to be dealt with on the basis of current value to society. Secular humanism has ensured that grace is beyond the means of mere consumer units.

So, just as the first Reformation was based upon the principle of rejecting man-made dogma and returning to the unadulterated Word of God, a second Reformation should have exactly the same principle. We must leave our human delusions of adequacy based upon science and technology and return to a study of God's Word. We must believe God and not the world. We must accept that we cannot achieve our own salvation through science. We cannot buy it with money or by a donation to the political party of our choice, and we cannot delude ourselves for very long that we can do without it.

Do not forget: God is not in crisis. We are.

We are the creatures, not the Creator.

PART II

SCIENCE AND RELIGION

*Then the L*ORD *answered Job out of the whirlwind, and said:*
"Who is this who darkens counsel
By words without knowledge?
Now prepare yourself like a man;
I will question you, and you shall answer Me.
Where were you when I laid the foundations of the earth?
Tell Me, if you have understanding.
Who determined its measurements?
Surely you know!
Or who stretched the line upon it?
To what were its foundations fastened?
Or who laid its cornerstone,
When the morning stars sang together,
And all the sons of God shouted for joy?"
(Job 38:1–7)

CHAPTER 6

ASTRONOMY, MATHEMATICS AND THE BIBLE

In scientific progress a critical part of the process is asking the right question.
Every question contains implicit pre-suppositions, hidden from the casual
observer. If these pre-suppositions are wrong or confused or conflicting,
then the question itself is wrong, in the sense that to try to answer it has no
meaning. One has then to enquire as to the appropriateness of the question.[21]

David Bohm (1917–92), physicist and theorist

The modern myth of our times is that science and the Bible are
opposed and contradict each other. The argument goes something
like this: after Copernicus and Galileo showed that the earth was not
the center of the universe, this destroyed the notion of a personal God;
we are just infinitesimal beings on the outer edge of a nondescript spiral
galaxy, of no special importance. Newton, with his laws of mechanics,
destroyed the concepts of divine intervention and the validity of miracles,
and therefore destroyed the intellectual integrity of the faith. Reference
is always made to the "big bang" theory, and to Darwin and his theory
of natural selection, to show that God wasn't necessary at all. Modern
genetics and genome research seem to reinforce this. The work of all these
scientists and many others is used to show the opposition of an allegedly
mythological Bible to the rational and superior knowledge derived from
scientific progress.

This is a travesty of the truth. Most of these scientists advanced the sum
of human knowledge because of, not in spite of, their Christian faith. They
believed that God had created a reasonable, regular and ordered universe,
which was open to observation and reason. It is well documented that
Copernicus, Galileo and Newton died firmly in the traditional belief of a
personal Creator God. The true barrier to progress was not the Bible or the

gospel message, but the institutionalized Church, thoroughly infected with humanism and Greek philosophy.

So why does modern science maintain the opposite to the known facts? This is an interesting question, since scientists are educated people and should therefore be able to research the facts for themselves. The answer can only be that the scientists see no need for research because the facts are already self-evident. There is no need to go to court; it's an open-and-shut case. This prejudice is unconscious and preformed. The worldview exhibited by most modern scientists has very deep roots, far back in the teachings of the ancient philosophers and academic institutions.

One of the greatest barriers to a modern, scientific understanding of the universe was not the Bible but Greek philosophy. The Greek worldview, especially the teachings of Plato (c.428–347 BC) and Aristotle (384–322 BC), held sway over the known world until the Renaissance – and still linger today. Aristotelianism held natural philosophy in thrall for nearly 1,500 years, until the work of Renaissance and Reformation scientists gradually moved scientific thinking away from its Aristotelian tradition. Many people still think that the barrier to progress was the Bible, but this is not so. Nor is the Bible an obstacle to scientific progress today, despite much propaganda to that effect. The Bible, and the philosophy or worldview derived from it, was the starting point of the revolution in science, and is responsible for much of the material progress the Reformation countries have achieved and exported to other parts of the world.

The common-sense view of things is that the earth does not move because we don't feel any movement. Therefore it follows that everything else moves around us. This is known as a geocentric worldview, and was common to nearly all ancient peoples, not just those of the Judeo-Christian tradition. This is what gave Aristotle his system for the universe, with his concentric spheres moving in circular motion, centered on the earth. The idea of a circle or sphere was not based on any theory or experimental evidence. Greek philosophical thought considered the circle or sphere to be one of the perfect shapes, so circular motion for the great celestial spheres was very natural to their worldview. In other words they brought this preconceived philosophy of perfect circular motion to astronomy and the structure of the universe. It was this Greek preconception that, more than a thousand years later, Copernicus, Kepler, Galileo and Newton challenged – not the Bible, nor anything inferred by the Bible. Granted, the Church was infected with Greek philosophy, but the Bible itself stands unadulterated and uncontaminated.

Aristotle's system had its problems. It could not explain certain observed movements of the planets, with their apparently erratic movements through the sky. Although circles upon circles, called epicycles, were tried in order to explain this strange situation, the problem persisted, especially in the movement of the planet Mars.

Ptolemy (c. AD 90–168), born Claudius Ptolemaeus, a Greco-Egyptian mathematician, tried to deal with it by moving the earth slightly away from the center of planetary rotation. This worked better and became known as the Ptolemaic system, although he still used circular orbits. It lasted for nearly 1,400 years before Nicolaus Copernicus (1473–1543) proposed another system. The Ptolemaic system allowed the prediction of where to find a planet at a particular time, but did not provide an explanation of how things actually worked. The mechanics of the universe were still a mystery. Greek and Aristotelian principles were still very influential, insisting upon a circular or spherical approach.

Copernicus was a man with a mission: to provide a truly universal system, which not only described what was observed, but also provided a real physical explanation of how it all worked. Sadly, he also employed circular orbits, following centuries of established practice. However, after many years of research, Copernicus was led to the amazing conclusion that the earth was not fixed in place, but also moved just like the other planets. This explained the otherwise strange wanderings of the other planets in the sky much better than before. Copernicus concluded that the earth and all the other planets were in orbit around the sun. His system was heliocentric (after the Greek word *helios*, meaning "sun"). The Copernican system was a tremendous advance on the Aristotelian and Ptolemaic systems, but did not conform to common sense, and was not readily accepted because people didn't feel the movement of the earth.

Unfortunately Copernicus had fallen into the old Aristotelian trap: he used circular orbits. He had brought his Aristotelian presuppositions to his work. This resulted in very complicated, lengthy mathematical calculations and did not provide much more accuracy than Ptolemy, 1,400 years before. Also, one of his major concerns was that the Church might reject his theory. His fears were well founded when we consider what later happened to Galileo. Copernicus was a Catholic priest and well aware that the Church was infected with Aristotelian philosophy. In those days one had to be a priest to teach at universities, which were mostly Aristotelian institutions. Copernicus was a very astute politician (unlike Galileo). He was very careful to put forward his views as extensions of Greek philosophy. He learned Greek especially to read untranslated manuscripts and managed to find four Greek philosophers who had put forward views that the earth was not fixed, but moved in an orbit. He contrived to appear reluctant to publish his works and allowed his friends, a bishop and a cardinal no less, to persuade him to publish. Finally, he dedicated his work to the Pope himself. In preparation for the anticipated antagonism, Copernicus wrote:

> If there are idle talkers who take it upon themselves to pronounce judgment, although wholly ignorant of mathematics, and if by shamelessly distorting the sense of some passage of Holy Writ to suit their purpose, they dare to reprehend and attack my work, they worry me so little that I shall even scorn their judgments as foolhardy.[22]

As a Christian priest Copernicus was not worried by the pronouncements of Holy Writ, but he was by those closed-minded people who would distort Scripture in an attempt to discredit him, by claiming divine authority for their criticisms where none existed. As a Christian thinker and scientist, Copernicus found that the universe did not conform to "common sense" or man's prejudices, but to the design of the infinite Creator God. Nevertheless, in 1616 his system was denounced as dangerous to faith.

Copernicus's main achievement was the heliocentric system, even though his accuracy could not improve upon the mathematics of Ptolemy. Accuracy of observation had to wait for Tycho Brahe (1546–1601). Without the use of telescopes Brahe made observations so accurate that they stood unsurpassed, until the systematic use of the telescope improved upon his work. He believed that the earth was fixed, so he proposed a compromise between the Ptolemaic and Copernican systems, with a stationary earth. It never really worked. Brahe's major contribution was the accuracy of his celestial observations, which were inherited by Johannes Kepler, a mathematician.

Kepler (1571–1630) had a very hard life and was frequently ill. Eight of his children from two marriages died in infancy. He was frequently not paid by his employers and lived in a period of war and religious and political upheaval. Because of his Christian commitment, he never enjoyed a secure job and eventually lost his house and home. Fleeing from his troubles, he met Tycho Brahe, something he ascribed to the hand of God. Kepler was another man with a mission, very like Copernicus, and with similar aims. He wanted to provide astronomy with real systematic explanations. For that he needed Tycho Brahe's data. Brahe's observations of the orbit of Mars had an accuracy of 1 minute of arc, whereas the calculations of Ptolemy produced an error of 8 minutes of arc. Not a great deal, you might say, since it takes 60 minutes of arc to equal 1 degree, but sufficient to show that the theory did not agree with observation. It was enough to set Kepler on fire with determination to explain the discrepancy.

For years, without computers, or any other aid, Kepler labored at the task, finally producing the ellipse and not the circle as the planetary orbit. The rigorous mathematical proofs would have to wait for Sir Isaac Newton, but Kepler's achievement was the new system of ellipses for planetary movements. This was the moment in history where the perfect circles of Greek philosophy were discredited by mathematical reasoning based upon observation, not preconceived ideas. He was encouraged by correspondence with Galileo at a late stage in his work and by a deeply held conviction that he was, in a small way, revealing the attributes of a much greater mind than the human. "O God, I am thinking Thy thoughts after Thee," he wrote.[23] He had a deeply religious approach to all his life's work. Once again, a Christian thinker and scientist confounded "common sense" by systematic study of God's creation.

Kepler's work had serious consequences. If the earth moved around the sun with the other planets, it must obey the same laws. What held for one planet was true for the others. It was now possible to imagine a universe where the laws were the same everywhere. This was a new dawn for scientific endeavor. By getting rid, at last, of the Greek philosophical influences, here was a system giving good agreement between observation and theory. Kepler acknowledged the importance of the disagreement between the observed and predicted positions of the planet Mars when he wrote:

> Divine Providence granted us such a diligent observer in Tycho Brahe that his observations convicted the Ptolemaic calculation of an error of 8 minutes. It is only right that we should accept God's gift with a grateful mind. Because these 8 minutes could not be ignored, they alone have led to a total reformation in astronomy.[24]

Kepler, in other words, thought that God had arranged this particular scientific breakthrough.

Our Western culture represents science and scientists as advancing the cause of the intellect and reason against the unscientific superstitions of the Bible. In our postmodern condition this conflict is everywhere apparent, which no doubt helps to explain the apostate condition of many churchmen, but leaves us with no ready understanding of how we came to this pass. All the great scientists usually quoted in support of this theme of conflict were very open in their acknowledgment of God, in all they saw and discovered. This applied to Galileo Galilei (1564–1642) as much as anyone. The "book of nature" and the "book of Scripture" were to Galileo simply the two aspects of the one God. He wrote in January 1633 (before the Church pronounced its infamous verdict upon him) " . . . the world is the work and the scriptures the word of the same God."[25] Galileo affirmed to his dying day that the Bible was without mistake or error in all it said. Towards the end of his life Galileo was almost blind, yet he kept on working at astronomy. He was so infirm that he had to be carried to the local chapel daily.

The schism of the Church and science started with the Galileo affair[26] and the sentence of life imprisonment, imposed on him by the Roman Church on 22 June 1633. It was the alleged contradiction of Scripture that was the cause célèbre of the trial. Yet Galileo was a Christian fundamentalist in his views about the Bible. He held the Scriptures in the highest regard, as a lifetime of correspondence shows. How, then, did this monstrous situation come about? Careless historians and theologians have always used the judgment against Galileo as typical of a blindly intolerant religious attitude. They hold Galileo as the original hero of rationalism and humanitarianism, being unjustly condemned by religious mysticism and bigotry. The Bible is portrayed as the source of the conflict. From the time of Galileo, the Church and the Bible have been held as the villains, as prejudiced, reactionary and incompatible with scientific understanding of the natural world.

The character of Galileo is part of the problem. He was an extremely intelligent man, quick-witted and observant. He was arrogant and suffered fools very little, if at all. He had a great sense of the theatrical and was a showman *par excellence*. Such a man gathers many admirers but also many enemies. He had the great ability to present his arguments in ways that were overpowering. He devised thought experiments that were astounding in clarity of mind and simply unanswerable. He was brought up in Florence during the great flowering of the Renaissance. When he went to Pisa as a medical student his loud character and un-Aristotelian thinking were a source of constant trial to his teachers and he left without a medical degree. When he later returned to Pisa as a mathematics professor, he antagonized the academic fraternity with his famous experiments with falling balls. Tradition has it that he used the Leaning Tower of Pisa, probably the highest profile venue available. It would certainly fit with his character, but it is at best an apocryphal story – this was originally a thought experiment. Galileo disagreed with Aristotle's proposition that the speed of falling objects was proportional to their weight, where heavier objects fall faster than lighter ones. Galileo argued that this could not be the case and proved it by simultaneously releasing balls of varying weights, allegedly from the top of the famous tower, which all hit the ground at the same time.

Galileo disagreed with Aristotle on other matters. He favored the Copernican heliocentric system for the solar system. His activities and teaching did not endear him to his colleagues in the university – he was challenging their beloved Aristotle. As with many other universities of the day, Pisa was an Aristotelian institution. Galileo became so extremely unpopular that his academic peers would sit at the back of his lectures and barrack him, wrecking his lectures. It is not surprising that once his three-year appointment was complete he took another position at Padua.

At this point in history, after one-and-a-half millennia, Aristotle was still in command of the worldview. Most university staff were Aristotelians, who handed on their rote-learning as had always been done. Original thinking was not encouraged and Galileo was therefore not a very welcome colleague, since he threatened their sense of security and position. His academic peers were enraged into active opposition against him and eventually formed *La Liga* (The League), a secret society with the aim of bringing about his downfall. As we might say in the context of the argument, they were "Aristotelian fundamentalists." La Liga met in the house of the Archbishop of Florence, a very significant factor in what follows. It was the academic community who poisoned the Church firstly against Copernicus and then against Galileo, not the Church deciding on first principles to persecute him on matters of interpretation of Scripture.

In 1609 two significant events happened: Kepler published his work on planetary orbits, and the telescope was invented. Galileo made his own telescope and put it to great use. At the time he was the professor of mathematics at the University of Padua. One of the first things that he did was to demonstrate the military applications of the telescope to the Doge of Venice. He was rewarded by a lifetime appointment at the University of Padua and his salary was doubled. Then he started to look at the night skies – and the rest, as they say, is history. In 1610 he published his findings. The moon had mountains and valleys in contradiction to Aristotle (again!) who had called the moon a perfect light. Galileo also found sunspots, proving Aristotle's other "perfect" light to be blemished. We must not belittle or dismiss Aristotle's real achievements. The fact that his system had lasted so long is a testament to his work and philosophy. However, the world was moving on and the limitations of his worldview were beginning to show. Aristotle, Plato and Ptolemy were seriously challenged and Copernicus was shown to be correct. Kepler was overjoyed to learn of the new discoveries. Further afield, however, Galileo's success in overturning the established Aristotelian worldview was creating many enemies in academic circles. La Liga was very active in opposition.

Galileo, for all his qualities, was extremely naive. Politically he was a babe-in-arms. His observations from 1609 to 1610 that changed the world were made in Padua, where he had a job for life with a good salary. Padua was within the rule of the Doge of Venice, where he was quite safe from La Liga. He could have spent the rest of his life there in reasonable security. What he did next dumbfounds common sense. He resigned his position at Padua to become the chief mathematician and philosopher to the Duke of Tuscany. There he was not so secure. His enemies could reach him.

His opponents were initially university academics based in Florence. By themselves they were not strong enough to bring Galileo down. They needed an ally and the Church was it. By 1611 the campaign against Galileo on purely scientific grounds had failed. The arena was then enlarged into theology. Sermons were preached to persuade public opinion against Galileo, calling all mathematicians "agents of the devil." Note that is was against all mathematicians, not just Galileo, since the Aristotelians were fearful of the whole thrust of Renaissance thought, which was by now threatening to overturn their comfortable intellectual beliefs and their way of life. For his part, Galileo was able to respond, because his papers were all published in Italian, readable by non-academics, rather than the usual Latin, the language of learning at that time. He, too, could influence public opinion. Of course, the use of Italian also caused problems with his peers, who would rather have kept their work obscure and in Latin. In modern parlance he was not a team player. In 1615 Rome became involved, through a complaint from the Aristotelian academics within La Liga in Florence, that Galileo and his supporters were undermining the Holy Scriptures.

It was this alleged challenge to Scripture that now became the focus of the debate, just as, in a later century, Darwinism was to provide. The Church of Rome was at that time a great world power. The Reformation was challenging its pre-eminent position. The single, united structure of the Roman Catholic Church was being broken up. The Council of Trent had been formed to counteract the damage caused by the Protesting Church, or Protestant Church as it came to be known. Inevitably, the matter was referred to the Council of Trent. Had Rome not been in such difficulties with the Reformation, had Rome not lost so much ground in previous battles, events might have had a different outcome, and the judgment on Galileo might have been much more moderate. His views might have been allowed to be studied by others – a normal procedure in similar cases – and time allowed for extended debate, for years if necessary. The Roman Church had precedents enough for such a solution to be quite acceptable under normal circumstances. Unfortunately, times were not normal.

The great tragedy in the whole affair was the lack of attention given to Galileo's respect for the error-free nature of Scriptures – the same Scriptures he was accused of undermining! The same lack of attention was given to the motives and the vested interests of La Liga. Galileo had a clear view of the importance of Scripture when he wrote that the Bible was written at the inspiration of the Holy Spirit and with "the primary purpose of the salvation of souls and the service of God."[27] His Christian faith was not some expedient cloak worn carelessly. His entire life and correspondence demonstrate that he had a deep relationship with the one God of both Scripture and nature. In 1612 Galileo sent a letter to a colleague, Marcus Welser, where he wrote:

> . . . in whatever way we spend our lives we ought to receive them
> as the highest gift from the hands of God who might have done
> nothing at all for us. First and foremost we should receive them not
> only with thanks but in infinite gratitude for His goodness . . .[28]

Galileo was a true man of God.

Now we arrive at Sir Isaac Newton (1642–1727), possibly the greatest scientist of all time, who was born in the year that Galileo died. As he turned his attention to astronomy and the movements of the planets, Newton was already a prodigy, having invented, among other things, his own type of telescope, the binomial theorem and calculus. The work of Copernicus, Brahe, Kepler and Galileo now came together in Newton's mathematical genius. Newton's universal law of gravitation, together with Newton's laws of motion, produced a system of mechanics that described the movements of the universe. Newtonian mechanics was to be the cornerstone of science until the advent of the general theory of relativity and quantum mechanics in the twentieth century. It finally overturned Aristotle and released the shackles of Greek philosophy from the scientific study of the universe. In his comments on his discovery, Newton wrote:

> This most beautiful system of the sun, planets and comets, could only proceed from the council and dominion of an intelligent and powerful Being . . . and on account of his dominion he is wont to be called the Lord God.[29]

The modern worldview about the adversarial nature of science and religion is both inaccurate and misleading. The Church of Rome may have imposed its will on one of the many challenges it was facing throughout the period of the Reformation, but it was a victory for which we have been paying ever since. The antagonism between science and Scripture is artificial, completely wrong-headed and damaging to the whole of human endeavor. It was Francis Bacon (1561–1626), in many ways the father of modern science, who said in his *Novum Organum Scientiarum*:

> Man by the Fall fell at the same time from his state of innocence and his dominion over nature. Both of these losses, however, can even in this life be in some part repaired; the former by religion and faith, the latter by the arts and sciences.[30]

CHAPTER 7

FROM DETERMINISM TO UNCERTAINTY

I believe that we are at an important turning point in the history of science.
We have come to the end of the road paved by Galileo and Newton, which
presented us with an image of a time-reversible, deterministic universe.
We now see the erosion of determinism and the emergence of a new
formulation of the laws of physics.[31]

Viscount Ilya Prigogine
Nobel Laureate in Chemistry

The consequences of Newtonian mechanics were to have a very serious effect on the worldview of the West. The idea that each action was the result of an action before it, and one before that, and so on, gave rise to the concept of determinism. This is the idea that events within a given system are bound by cause and effect in such a way that any situation, state, or condition is determined by previous causes. This included not only mechanical operations, but developed so that everything, including human reason, behavior, decision-making and actions, was eventually brought under the idea of cause and effect. Determinists believe the universe is fully governed by causal laws resulting in only one possible state at any point in time, with an unbroken chain of causes back to the origin of the universe.

Determinism arising from humanist philosophy in a world without God had already established itself in the minds of intellectuals everywhere, and Newton's work rapidly became the bedrock of scientific thinking about the universe. Newton's work was on the large scale, where we imagine billiard balls caroming around and colliding with each other. We can imagine planets orbiting the sun, or objects falling under gravity, where everything can be calculated mathematically and every condition either known or predicted. However, there was the little problem of the orbit of Mercury, which didn't quite conform to the predictions of Newtonian mechanics. Like Mars before it, Mercury had to wait for another breakthrough before its behavior would come within the understanding of scientific thought.

Newton contributed to many branches of science. In one of his more famous experiments, he separated light into the colors of the spectrum by means of a prism, an experiment many schoolchildren now perform as part of their science lessons. In Newton's time there were two views of the nature of light. Newton defended the view that light consisted of a stream of fast-moving particles of very small mass. This view easily accounts for the reflection of light from a plane surface, like bouncing balls off a flat surface. He accounted for refraction by arguing that when light particles were very near any optically dense medium, such as glass, they were attracted to it and this attraction increased the component of the velocity of light directly towards the surface of the glass. So Newton's view results in the conclusion that light travels faster in a medium such as glass than it does in free space. The scientist Christian Huygens, on the other hand, supported the view that light consisted of waves. The most important evidence supporting Huygens was the fact that two light beams can cross without colliding. He could also explain reflection and refraction. His explanation of refraction agreed with Newton about the change of direction, but disagreed about the change in velocity, which he said was slower.

Over the next century, work done on optics by many scientists proved that the particle theory was not tenable. Thomas Young of England proved the principle of interference of waves. In France, the physicists Foucault, Fresnel, Arago, Malus, Cornu and Fizeau performed experiments that confirmed the wave theory to be correct. Huygens's view completely displaced Newton's when Foucault demonstrated the velocity of light in a dense medium to be less than its velocity in free space.

As we move into the nineteenth century, we find two tremendous men of science: Faraday and Clerk-Maxwell. Sir Michael Faraday (1791–1867) worked with electricity and magnetism, discovering the relationship between the two, and formulating the basic laws of electromagnetic theory. James Clerk-Maxwell (1831–79) was the scientist who gave mathematical form to the discoveries of Faraday.

In 1864 Clerk-Maxwell announced his results in putting the laws of electricity onto a firm mathematical foundation. He had succeeded in his efforts and there was another very important by-product. His results could be put into the mathematical form of the wave equation for electromagnetic waves. He showed conclusively that the velocity of these waves is the velocity of light. In one giant step forward he integrated the sciences of electricity and optics into the same theory. Clerk-Maxwell's proposals were confirmed in 1888 when Hertz showed that oscillating current in an electric circuit could radiate energy to another similar circuit. This was the birth of modern telecommunications. Hertz used rather crude spark gaps to show the transfer of energy was taking place, but he nevertheless showed that the radiation generated by electric circuits obeyed the same laws as optics (as far as they were then known). This was a tremendous experimental confirmation of the mathematical work of Clerk-Maxwell. But that was not the end of the story. Hertz noticed that the sparks induced into the receiving circuit were more easily produced when the spark terminals were illuminated by the light of the sparks from the transmitting circuit. Further work by Hallwachs, a student of Hertz, showed that a negatively charged plate of zinc loses its charge when illuminated by ultraviolet light. So the experimental confirmation of Clerk-Maxwell's work led immediately to the discovery of the photoelectric effect. This in turn led to a dramatic and fundamental revision of the wave theory of light. We shall see how important this was to be.

One of the features of Newtonian mechanics is that no consideration is given to time. According to Newton's mathematics, everything happens instantaneously. No time was possible between action and response. However, the work of Faraday and Clerk-Maxwell included the factor of time. Time was now needed for the transmission of an electromagnetic event from one place to another. Clerk-Maxwell had shown that electromagnetic radiation traveled at the speed of light. Not only that, but the concept of "fields of force" put forward by Faraday contradicted the Newtonian view that force emanated from a point. Newtonian mechanics was unable to account for these discoveries. The limitations of the Newtonian worldview were becoming apparent, as later scientists advanced the range of human knowledge.

Another step forward was needed. It was not long in coming. Albert Einstein (1879–1955) produced his monumental theory of relativity in 1915. This was mind-boggling in its massive departure from a "common-sense" view of the universe. Einstein proposed that time slowed down when traveling at speeds close to that of light, mass increased and size decreased. What was going on? Was all this necessary just because Faraday and Clerk-Maxwell had been experimenting with electricity and magnetism? Did the theory of relativity really describe what was actually, physically, going on in the universe, or was it just an interesting concept? Einstein viewed the equations of Clerk-Maxwell as the most important development since Newtonian mechanics for two reasons. Firstly, because they were a huge advance in understanding; and, secondly, because they were a pattern for a new type of law, a new approach to the universe.

Although Newton's theories had been tested experimentally many times, they could not adequately explain the variations in the orbit of Mercury. This was reminiscent of the old problem with the orbit of Mars, solved by Kepler. Einstein now proposed a solution based on the relativistic effects on time and motion when close to a massive gravity field. He proposed that space itself had been warped by the sun's gravitational field. It was this space–time warp that caused the variations in the orbital velocity of Mercury that Newtonian or classical mechanics could not explain. Observations proved his theories were accurate in their predictions. Mercury's behavior was explained! Einstein's theories were real! The scientific worldview had just been turned upside down. The old concept of space and time and mass and energy being independent of one another had to be modified into a new worldview of a space–time continuum, where everything was interrelated according to new mathematical equations. The awful accuracy of these equations was to be demonstrated in the development of atomic power, where a tiny amount of matter could produce enough energy to power or destroy a whole city. The twentieth century was to be a century like no other before it.

Another world-shattering twentieth-century development also challenged the Newtonian worldview. Max Planck (1858–1947) proposed his quantum theory in 1901. He was dealing with the problem of calculating the amount of energy in electromagnetic radiation emitted from bodies at high temperatures, like the sun. Classical physics had produced what had become known as the "ultraviolet catastrophe," where the mathematics had produced results which matched experimental evidence quite well at low frequencies, but at high or "ultraviolet" frequencies the mathematics produced results where the amount of energy seemed to be heading off towards infinity! This "ultraviolet catastrophe" was clearly impossible and caused a real crisis in physics. The problem could not be solved using the classical physics of the Newtonian worldview. To solve the problem Planck proposed that energy did not radiate continuously but in discrete packets or "quanta" of radiation. These could be treated as "particles" of light of a fixed energy, rather than as electromagnetic waves. Planck's quantum theory, treating radiation as discrete particles after the ideas of Newton, gave an accurate mathematical answer to the problem. The ultraviolet catastrophe had been averted, but at the cost of the achievements of classical science. This apparent reversal of a century of progress was very difficult for scientists of the day to accept. After all, many scientists had contributed to the international century of effort to establish the wave theory of light. This apparent reversal was a serious blow. Recanting a lifetime's work is no easy matter for anyone, let alone a scientist of some reputation.

Let us now return to the photoelectric effect. As was related earlier, the photoelectric effect was discovered as a result of the study of electromagnetic waves and still needed a solution. It was Einstein himself who proposed the solution to this problem using Planck's quantum theory. Einstein assumed that each light "particle" hit an electron, transferring its quantum of energy to the electron, which was then knocked out of the metal surface. Einstein's solution worked well and gave an accurate description of the process. The quantum theory had been quickly demonstrated to have practical applications in the real world, the physical universe.

What a time to be working in the field of physics! But the dramatic explosion of ideas did not stop there. In 1924 the French scientist Louis Victor Pierre Raymond, Duc de Broglie (1892–1987), gave a simple mathematical treatment that indicated that matter as well as energy could be treated as either particles or waves. He had no reason for doing this except that of symmetry in nature. He reasoned that if electromagnetic radiation could be treated as either waves or particles, perhaps matter could be treated in the same way. In 1926 Erwin Schrödinger (1887–1961) announced his system of wave mechanics, which described the wave nature of matter. Wave–particle duality was established as a working concept for both matter and energy.

However, it became clear through the work of other scientists such as Werner Heisenberg (1901–76) that there was a problem with what we could know at the atomic level of the universe. In 1927 Heisenberg announced his "uncertainty principle." He demonstrated that we could know either the position or the energy of a particle, but not both. Therefore, we could not accurately know its present state. Based on this uncertainty it was not therefore possible to predict with any accuracy its future state, say after a collision with another particle, because we could never have sufficient prior knowledge of the collision conditions. The billiard ball concept of atoms caroming around was no longer viable – there was no absolute answer for an individual particle.

Also, when considering radioactive decay, it was not possible to predict when any individual particle would be emitted. Similarly, if a beam of electrons was focused on a target, just as in a TV tube, it was not possible to predict or calculate the trajectory of an individual particle. This was appalling for the determinist school of thought. It meant that the fundamental level of the universe was unpredictable! How could this be? Cause and effect in the macro-universe could clearly be observed, in an orderly and predictable way, yet according to Heisenberg it was based upon completely unpredictable subatomic behavior in the micro-universe.

The answer lay in statistical probabilities. It may not have been possible to predict the behavior of a single particle, but the statistical sum of the behavior of a large number of particles can be observed and predicted with reasonable accuracy, using statistical mathematics. Probability now becomes the way to deal with subatomic behavior. Since we have incomplete information about the starting conditions, there are many possible solutions to the problem for an individual particle, but the statistical sum of a large number of particles can be estimated with a great deal of accuracy. However, there is always a margin of error, no matter how small. Whereas classical physics had given absolute answers for movements of individual objects in the Newtonian universe, this was no longer possible in the quantum universe.

Look at the problem from the reverse point of view: at some time after a collision has occurred, a particle has moved to a different location. There were many possible paths for the particle, which it may or may not have taken. Which one did it take? The mathematics of probability will indicate the most likely path, based on the energy of the system and all the particles present, but cannot give complete certainty for an individual particle. We have to consider the possibility that the particle may have taken a low-probability path. There is also another consideration: since the particle can also be treated as a wave, perhaps the wave was diffracted, or spread, and took more than one path simultaneously! There is mounting evidence to show that, from an energy point of view, matter waves may move along all the probable paths! But this would mean that matter could be in two places at once! This is a paradoxical idea, but it is known as a quantum superposition. Conversely, two particles may coexist in the same place, forming a single entity known as a Bose–Einstein condensate. Condensates up to 16 million merged beryllium atoms have been formed in the laboratory. The entity is large enough to see with the naked eye and has been photographed.[32]

Quantum theory, which Einstein hated so much even though he used it, has shaped the development of twentieth-century science and technology. Quantum mechanics are used to explain the behavior of transistors and microchips, which provide us with our telecommunications and personal computers. Although the concepts of quantum physics appear strange, they have had a powerful practical effect on our civilization in a very short period of time. Yet it is the basic uncertainty contained within the theory that caused Einstein to make his often quoted remark, "God does not play dice with the universe!"

What does all this mean? It means that science has moved on, away from a deterministic worldview. Unfortunately, after innovation in any field, it always takes a certain amount of time before other fields catch up. Philosophy and theology, always subject to the worldview of their time, have not yet caught up and are still caught in the web of determinism.

The philosophy of science, despite some individual pioneering efforts, seems for all practical concerns to be stalled at Newton. Eventually it will continue into the twenty-first century. After all, something like 80% of all the scientists who ever lived are alive today. Many advances in human knowledge have been made since the time of Newton, and their cumulative effect has been to replace Newtonian mechanics with the general theory of relativity, quantum mechanics and wave mechanics. The deterministic macro-universe of Newton has been replaced by the indeterminate micro-universe of modern science.

Without stretching belief very far, it is now possible to see that God could intervene in the universe without breaking his own natural laws. The natural order of things means that most events take the high-probability path. There are some events that take the low-probability path, and these are sometimes called "miracles." They appear so unlikely that they challenge common sense. However, as many scientists have found in their studies of God's creation, common sense is usually the first thing to go, because it is very subjective. Objective knowledge always challenges the subjective ideas of a culture.

We must be careful not to take these ideas too far. God is not subject to finite human reasoning. Yet it is clear that the march of science and progress, having moved through a closed, deterministic universe, is moving into an open, non-deterministic universe.

We can see from this brief survey of the scientific landscape of the last few centuries that there never was a conflict between science and the Bible. Unfortunately, the resistance to change of the Aristotelian worldview and academic animosity towards Galileo's discoveries produced a prejudice within the scientific community from which we have never really recovered. The subsequent influence of the deterministic school of thought has poisoned the philosophy of science to a tremendous degree. Most scientists genuinely believe that they are the epitome of rational behavior, logically discarding the prejudiced dogma of a religion more suited to an earlier, more primitive age. They little see that they, in turn, are subject to their own institutionalized prejudices, soaked up with their scientific studies during attendance at their universities and colleges. This worldview can be called scientific naturalism, where the universe, or matter, is all there is. There is nothing else and so we have a closed system of deterministic cause and effect. Matter is king and so most scientists are materialists with a problem of how to think about the origins of the universe and of life.

The following extract from an internet article on the life of de Broglie shows how powerful the concept of determinism can be in the minds of scientists:

> The central question in de Broglie's life was whether the
> statistical nature of atomic physics reflects an ignorance of the
> underlying theory or whether statistics is all that can be known.
> For most of his life he believed the latter although as a young
> researcher he had at first believed that the statistics hide our
> ignorance. Perhaps surprisingly, he returned to this view late in
> his life stating that:
>   "The statistical theories hide a completely determined
> and ascertainable reality behind variables which elude our
> experimental techniques."[33]

De Broglie, like many other extremely able scientists, was profoundly shocked and disturbed by the increasingly open, non-deterministic nature of scientific advance and was forced into what can only be described as a "faith" position, in order to make sense of his life and the universe.

CHAPTER 8

EVOLUTION AND BIBLICAL CREATION

The greatest derangement of the human mind is to believe
because one wishes it to be so.

Louis Pasteur (1822–95), chemist and biologist
Founded the science of microbiology

An honest man, armed with all the knowledge available to us now, could
only state that in some sense, the origin of life appears at the moment to be
almost a miracle, so many are the conditions which would have had to have
been satisfied to get it going.[34]

Francis Crick (1916–2004), Nobel Laureate in Biochemistry
Co-discoverer of the DNA double helix

Today, at the start of the twenty-first century, the broad concept of
evolution (in all its forms and variations) holds sway over our civilization.
Yet there is so little scientific evidence to substantiate evolutionary theory.
Any casual internet researcher, looking at the vast array of literature covering
hundreds of specialisms, could not fail to be impressed by the breadth and
depth of the work done. Yet the more the actual empirical evidence for
evolutionary theory is sought throughout the literature, the more it recedes.
There are many places where some idea or concept is put forward as proof,
but little actual evidence. When evidence is quoted, it is frequently based on
circular reasoning. Yet it is this theory, from about 1860 onwards, that has
challenged Scripture and changed the worldview of the West. Evolution
is such an important idea, is so widely held and promoted, and has such
profound consequences, that despite the fact that this is not a scientific
textbook, we need to look at it in some depth.

In 1966 the geneticist H.J. Muller produced a manifesto signed by 177
American biologists claiming that the organic evolution of all living things,

mankind included, from primitive life forms, and ultimately from non-living materials, is a fact of science as well established as the fact that the earth is round.[35]

Evolutionists everywhere claim that the theory of evolution is the pinnacle of science – many vilify non-evolutionists as unscientific in their approach. Richard Dawkins goes out of his way to denounce people who reject evolution in the following terms: "It is absolutely safe to say that, if you meet somebody who claims not to believe in evolution, that person is ignorant, stupid or insane (or wicked, but I'd rather not go into that."[36]

When creationism is mentioned in front of evolutionists, stand back and watch the sparks fly. They spare no effort to discredit those who challenge evolution. Their attitude is appallingly closed-minded; their language very ill-advised and extreme, as the Dawkins quote above shows. He is not alone in his position. A common theme is that non-evolutionists are scientifically illiterate and should never be allowed to express their views at all. Creation science is labeled as non-science, and absolutely no interaction is permitted on pain of loss of job or research funding. In actual fact there are very many pieces of evidence in the natural world which can be better explained by a creationist model, so there is a scientific basis upon which to base sensible debate. In fact, the creationist position could be argued as more scientific than evolution. Certainly it is more rational. One cannot observe the atomic precision of living cells, and the interdependence of all living processes, without challenging the established evolutionary view that it is all irrational and random.

When evolution is assumed as a first principle, everything must be made to fit. Difficult pieces of evidence are ignored or placed into a future realm when science will have progressed further; and so science tomorrow will explain away difficulties today. Evolutionists then have the cheek to claim that other views are unscientific. Not only that, but other views are ruthlessly suppressed. There are very many highly qualified scientists who cannot fully accept evolution as a valid theory, and a significant proportion of scientists profoundly disagree with evolution. Some want a revision of the theory; others are more radical. Authors and contributors to books such as *Cosmos, Bios, Theos*, written by sixty scientists including twenty-four Nobel laureates, have a variety of views, some surprising. They reflect on science, religion and the origins of the universe, the complexity and intimately related order of life on earth, and *Homo sapiens*.

How do we explain these contradictions? If nature alone were able to explain the origin of life and its complexity, why do so many Nobel Prize-winners express doubts? If evolution were so obvious a fact, why do thousands of scientists reject it? Thousands of qualified scientists from many disciplines and many countries simply would not reject well-established principles. So why do many say no to evolution? The reason is not hard to find: there is a substantial body of evidence that shows very clearly that the theory of evolution is plainly wrong on the matters of which it claims to speak; in other words, evolutionary theories do not correspond with reality. On page 14 of the preface to their book *Darwin's Leap of Faith: Exposing the False Religion of Evolution*, John Ankerberg and John Wheldon write:

> Evolutionists are, unfortunately, often rather condescending
> to Christians for allegedly taking an irrational "leap of faith"
> in believing in God, miracles and the supernatural. Not only
> are their charges false . . . we will seek to show evolutionists
> themselves take an incredible "leap of faith" that far exceeds in
> credulity anything Christians have ever believed.[37]

And in Chapter 11 they quote Howard Byington Holroyd: "In the minds of critics, evolution can rationally be classified as one of the 'worst superstitions of all time.'"[38]

Before we can look at the consequences of evolution, we need to examine a little of the evidence. The two statements above, quoted from Ankerberg and Wheldon's book, are strongly worded. Are they justified? The following sections attempt to look at the evidence.

A Few Small Difficulties

One of the major scientific criticisms of Darwin when his work was first published was the "fixity of the species." No new species were being formed, so this was seen as a major flaw in his theory. This basic situation remains unchanged today. In the *New Scientist* magazine of 14 June 2003, there was a seven-page article entitled "Evolution: Five Big Questions."[39] The questions were:

1. How did life begin?
2. How do mutations lead to evolution?

3. How are new species formed?
4. Is evolution predictable?
5. What's God got to do with it?

Five experts in their respective fields were asked to answer these questions. The inadequacy of the answers betrayed the extent of the lack of real evidence to support the concept of evolution.

In Question 1, the first expert ignored the show-stopping problem of the biological complexity required in a simple cell, let alone the coherent information contained in the DNA/RNA mechanism – all of which had to be present in the first place, before the cell could be viable. His opinion of the origin of life in a chemical ocean is a nice feat of imagination, but hardly scientific. We know that amino acids disassociate in water and rapidly break up. His thesis is very weak. In simple English the real answer is: "Don't know."

Responding to Question 2, the second expert noted that rare beneficial mutations led to evolution by natural selection, but qualified this by stating: "However, many gene sequences show hardly any change over millions of years . . ." This is not what we would expect as a conclusive statement from an expert in this field. In simple English the real answer is: "Don't know."

In answering Question 3 about the formation of new species, the third expert was not happy with then current thinking, based on a founder population model, where a "genetic bottleneck" is created by a pregnant female being swept off to a remote island, where her subsequent offspring mate with each other. The expert commented: "[This] just didn't hold up. Despite evolutionary biologists' best efforts, nobody has even got close to creating a new species from a founder population . . ." In simple English the real answer is: "Don't know."

Question 4 asks, "Is evolution a predictable science?" like, say, physics or chemistry, where physical and chemical laws predictably produce the same results under the same conditions, time after time. Our fourth expert notes that there are so many random mutations and selective forces that if the "tape of life" could be rewound and replayed, it would not repeat – it must produce a different outcome. The conclusion can only be that evolution is not a testable theory: each incident in an evolutionary chain must be classified as unique, unrepeatable and untestable and therefore completely outside the definition of modern science! One can only say that a great deal of non-rational faith must be placed in evolutionary theory for so many scientists to continue to support it on such uncertain grounds. Certainly, our fourth expert does not help to clarify matters. In simple English the real answer is: "No."

Which brings us to the fifth and final question: "What's God got to do with it?" Our fifth expert begins with the statement, "A growing number of biologists think that we must offer some insight into the question of why religion exists and at what point in human evolution it began." So our final expert begins by begging the question. Implicit in this opening statement are two false premises: there is no God and evolution is an historical reality. Therefore, the original question is not what it at first seems; the sole purpose in asking it is to get rid of the possibility of God and His special creation and leave evolution as the only credible alternative. In simple English the real answer is: "Nothing."

It is useful to list the questions and answers together at this point, to clarify the overall position at the end of the exercise carried out by *New Scientist*:

Question	Answer
1. How did life begin?	Don't know
2. How do mutations lead to evolution?	Don't know
3. How are new species formed?	Don't know
4. Is evolution predictable?	No
5. What's God got to do with it?	Nothing

This is hardly a robust "scientific" position. Why is there so much fudging and lack of clear evidence? Where is the rigor found in other scientific disciplines? In the years since this article appeared, the situation remains substantially unchanged, despite reams of scientific papers on this subject.

Science or Speculation?

The confusion begins with the fact that there is an observed adaptation of a species to cope with changes in the environment. This is what Darwin observed so well on the Galapagos Islands, during the voyage of HMS *Beagle*. At the end of the adaptation, however, there is no new species, no new type of organism, but a variation of the same *adapted* organism living in a different environment. This is what we should term "observed adaptation."

Unfortunately, this is then extrapolated, on no firm evidence whatever, into what we should term "speculative evolution," where newer, more complex organisms are supposed to develop spontaneously and randomly from older, less complex organisms.

It must be said that there is nothing wrong with speculation. It is the source of all original thinking and progress, but there must be a reality check at some point. Any speculation must be related back to the real universe, with its physical evidence and processes. This is what Francis Bacon pointed out so clearly, centuries before.

The speculative theory of evolution runs counter to all observed physical processes in the known universe. The second law of thermodynamics states that all things are running down, that disorganization always increases. Therefore, by themselves and without outside intervention, more complex and more organized organisms cannot arise from the less complex and less organized. This can be understood better by thinking about the quantity of DNA information needed, say, to produce a single-celled creature, the amoeba. Evolution proposes that mankind eventually arose from the amoeba, but consider the vastly increased amount of DNA information needed for a human being. Where did it come from? After all, it is new DNA information, not a variation of the existing amoebic DNA. How did it get there? Evolutionists say that it came from random mutation followed by natural selection. As we have just seen, they don't really know this to be true, but they believe it must be true. However, random mutations in the DNA cannot produce new information. Laboratory results show that randomly mutated DNA always deteriorates from the original material. Random mutations tend to produce lethal or sterile mutations by disorganizing the existing structures and relationships within the creature. This is what we would expect anyway, according to the second law of thermodynamics. New DNA is never produced, unless the outside agent, or the experimenter, intervenes and puts it there. In other words, long periods of time and blind chance are not sufficient to produce the living world as we see it. There must be another explanation, one that includes the demonstrable fact that the complexity of life already exists, *before* this so-called evolution begins to work on it.

Ask yourself a simple question. How did the amoeba itself originally acquire its DNA? Or, where did it come from? After all, there are no ancestors to the single-celled organism. It is the original ancestor in evolutionary theory, from which all else descends. How do we get from inanimate matter to a live creature, with all its complex functions simultaneously in place? A cell is irreducibly complex. The absence of even one of the cell functions would prevent it from existing. Even at the single-celled level there is such a complex interaction of all the different parts of the cell that the disruption of even one of them causes the cell to die. Evolutionists seem to ignore the fact that they work with pre-existing complexity in the simplest of creatures. Charles Darwin may be perhaps forgiven, since the science of his day knew so little about cellular structure and functions. Modern scientists have no such excuse.

All the different parts of the organism must be there and working together from the beginning, otherwise there would be no organism. A jar of chemicals will not produce a living cell, no matter how much it is mixed, heated, shaken, stirred, or struck with bolts of lightning.

Chance: the Agent of Evolution

There is a widely accepted idea that everything began as a result of random chance, from the big bang to the occurrence and development of life itself. There are serious problems with this idea. The concept of randomness applied to physical processes is one of the basic tenets of evolutionary theory, where chance determines outcomes. Chance becomes the agent of causality. Nobel Prize-winning biologist Jacques Monod wrote: "Chance *alone* is at the source of every innovation, of all creation in the biosphere. Pure chance, absolutely free but blind, at the very root of the stupendous edifice of evolution . . ."[40]

We have irrationally given the concept of chance causative power. Chance is only a way of accounting for the probability of something happening. Chance cannot make something happen as though it were a real power or agent of action. If I toss a coin nine times and it comes down "heads" every time, what are the odds of it coming down "heads" on the tenth throw? Answer: the same odds as the first throw. We know that the odds of the coin coming down "heads" or "tails" for any given throw are 50/50. A long string of "heads" is unlikely in the nature of things. Statistically it becomes more likely that the next throw will produce the opposite outcome. Chance, however, is not the agent or cause of the outcome of any of the results. The odds are still 50/50 for any given throw. Randomness is an idea, not a force of nature.

The late Professor Sir Fred Hoyle (1915–2001) was a noted astronomer and cosmologist. Professor Hoyle, together with Thomas Gold (1920–2004) and Sir Hermann Bondi (1919–2005), developed the "steady state" theory. This was an alternative to the big bang theory, which was running into grave difficulties over star and planetary formation (and still is!). They proposed that the observed expansion of the universe could be accounted for by the continuous random appearance of hydrogen molecules in interstellar space. The word "appearance" is used here because the word "creation" is not possible in this context. The continuous random (chance) appearance of matter would thus try to explain some of the observed properties of the universe.

"Creation" implies purpose and intention, which is why the word "appearance" was used to describe the formation of hydrogen molecules in space. Creation implies an agent. This is not just semantics or splitting hairs. There is a real difference. The term "random creation" is a contradiction in terms. One of the adjustments to the theory of evolution, in order to explain the lack of intermediate types in the fossil record, is the theory of "abrupt appearances," proposed by Professors Eldredge and Gould. They could have said "abrupt creation." Evolutionary scientists themselves recognize this issue and use language appropriately.

Creation demands an *agent*. The phrasing of Jacques Monod that "chance alone is at the source of every innovation, of all creation in the biosphere," gives the agency to the dead, inert matter of the universe. How can inanimate matter, without will or power to act, or the ability to do anything at all, create and destroy itself? A rock today is a rock tomorrow, and will be to the end of time. Even if we grant the existence of the universe in the first place, how can we explain complex multicellular life? Every living thing depends upon the fantastically accurate transmission of the DNA record, atom by atom within the cell, a self-copying, self-correcting code of unbelievable complexity. Chance and random processes cannot give rise to coherent information that has a purpose.

We are all subject to subtle influences on our thought processes, which affect the language we use. The evolutionary influence on our society has caused a massive shift in thinking. This comes out in the way we express ourselves. Despite the logical flaws, power is given to the dead matter of the universe to create itself and exist. This is a philosophical assumption, not a scientific discovery, and cannot be justified.

When serious thought is given to it, all of these theories come down to efforts to deny the Creator and give the creative power to something we can understand and hence control. Science gives us apparent control over our universe and so we notionally give the power of being and creating to the universe of matter; this is usually referred to as materialism. This sleight of mind places mankind in control and removes the need for a transcendent God – the real Agent. We are back with the Greek philosopher Protagoras: "Man is the measure of all things . . ."

Geology

Before I begin, I want to be very clear that I am not trying to discredit the science of geology. The science of geology is a legitimate body of knowledge with many practical uses. However, once we step outside of the operational science and into paleontology, the application of geology to the consideration of origins needs very careful handling.

One of the most quoted lines of evidence for evolution is the fossil record in the strata of the geologic column. Having established the principle that certain rocks were older, being lower, and others younger, being higher, the geologic ages were thus fixed in the geologic column. It was given its present form in about 1840 when nearly all that was known of the geology of the earth was part of northwestern Europe. This is not unreasonable – many working theories are formed in a similar manner in many branches of science. The theories are then modified in the light of further evidence and new knowledge.

In geology, however, the problem soon arose that there were very many sites in the world where the so-called younger rocks were below the older rocks, and the accepted geologic column did not fit.[41] Astoundingly, the early geologists made what they found fit the theoretical model, even where the evidence was in serious conflict. Huge discrepancies with the early geologic column of 1840 have been explained away by amazing theories, such as "overthrusting" and "crustal subduction," among others. These theories require the sideways movements of single slabs of rock hundreds of miles across and weighing billions of tons, without causing any disturbances to the surrounding rock strata. Sometimes, thin layers of undisturbed rock only millimeters thick lie between these great plates of rock that are supposed to have "slid" over each other. How can this be? Surely a billion tons of rock sliding for many kilometers over other rocks would have torn a passage obvious to the naked eye?[42]

The uniformitarian approach, which had come into prominence by about 1830, was the presupposition brought to the evidence. This concept was based on the work of James Hutton (1726–97) the founder of modern geology, and Sir Charles Lyell (1797–1875) the promoter of the concept of "gradualism," later known as "uniformitarianism." According to this principle, the rock layers can only have been formed by the processes observed in the present day, acting over long periods of time – measured in millions of years. There has been no global catastrophe involved. Finding rocks out of sequence with the accepted column therefore means other processes must be involved, which "slide" the rock plates around to fit the initial presuppositions. As ingenious as this is, there are still massive problems. Many strata are missing and others are in the wrong order, in different ways and in different places around the globe. The physical evidence suggests that a global uniformitarian approach cannot be applied.

There is another area of geology that needs attention. When geologists first began to study the relationships of differing rock strata, they found fossils. It seemed to be a correlation that the simpler the fossilized animal, the lower the rock strata. Therefore the ages of the rocks were determined because of the range of fossils associated with them. Geologists assumed the evolutionary theory that the simpler the fossil animal, the older it must be. In this way the strata of the geologic column became dated by the fossils, and fossils became dated by the strata. Also, occurrences of fossils that did not fit the accepted model were largely ignored. Even today, out-of-sequence fossils are found in out-of-sequence rocks in many parts of the world. Fossils found out of their normal place in the accepted sequence are called displacements, or anomalies, and, according to the accepted theories, are "reworked" back into the place they would have been had not some "unknown" process moved them out of their "normal" place.[43] The circular reasoning involved with this approach destroys any intellectual integrity it may once have possessed. Once again, evolutionary theory and uniformitarianism are the presuppositions brought to the table, and the evidence is "fudged" to fit.

There is a very dramatic example of what happens when the obvious is ignored and the evidence is made to fit the theory. Let us look again at those out-of-sequence rock strata. There are many places where the "older" strata are laid evenly on top of "younger" ones, without evidence of any sideways movements, with many of the intervening strata missing. Whole epochs of time seem to be missing or out of sequence in the geological records in many parts of the world. Even with these absences, if we add together the thickest currently known depositions of each so-called geologic age and make a real column, it would be more than 100 miles high. It is, of course, impossible to have a significant portion of this in one place. The Grand Canyon of Arizona is only one mile high.[44]

After examining the available evidence with an open mind, the conclusion must be that the uniformitarian evolutionary method of dating rocks and constructing the geological epochs utilizing the fossil record has serious defects. There must be another explanation that better fits the plain observations of the natural world. This is our first warning about the credibility of the evidence behind evolution.

Fossils

If we turn to the fossils themselves, it is generally claimed that the fossil record contains some of the strongest evidence for evolution. In his 1956 introduction to *The Origin of Species*, W.R. Thompson wrote: "The only available evidence is provided by the fossils." This sentiment is echoed many times over by individual scientists and by prestigious institutions worldwide. One example will suffice: The American National Association of Science Teachers states that: "The fossil record, which includes abundant transitional forms in diverse taxonomic groups, establishes extensive and comprehensive evidence for organic evolution."[45] Nothing could be clearer than that. The fossil record with its abundant transitional forms is clear evidence for evolution. This kind of statement is very common and it can be considered as typical of the given wisdom on the subject.

In the very early days after the publication of Darwin's *Origin of Species*, Sir Thomas Huxley realized the importance of the fossil record. Among the then known fossils there were empty gaps where there should have been transitional fossils to bridge the species. In his lectures Huxley stated that if it could be shown that the gaps in the fossil record had always existed, the fact would be fatal to the doctrine of evolution.[46] The fact is that the fossil record should produce countless examples of transitional forms. Paleontologists should trip over them everywhere. As we discussed in Chapter 1, there are none to be found at all. Darwin himself wrote: "But, as by this theory, innumerable transitional forms must have existed, why do we not find them imbedded in countless numbers in the crust of the earth?"[47] Darwin identified the gaps in the fossil chain as fatal to his theory. Those gaps still remain. The noted paleontologist and Harvard professor Stephen Jay Gould pointed out that "The fossil record with its abrupt transitions offers no support for gradual change . . . All paleontologists know that the fossil record contains precious little in the way of intermediate forms; transitions between major groups are characteristically abrupt."[48] What he means is that there are no transitions between groups. The phrase "characteristically abrupt" is evolution-speak for the lack of transitions.

In Darwin's day there were relatively few fossils that had been collected and categorized. He hoped that the "gaps" would be filled in as time went by. Today we have an estimated 250 million catalogued fossils, of some 25,000 species. Dr Raup of the University of Chicago summarized the situation, stating that about 120 years after Darwin there were fewer examples of evolutionary transition than in Darwin's time.[49] Well, Darwin said he had none. So where does that leave us?

The naked truth is that the fossil record is composed entirely of gaps between the species. This conclusion continues to be reinforced as time goes by. If the fossil record is the mainspring of evolution, then all I can say is, "The Emperor has no clothes!"

Evidence for a Young Earth

One of the requirements for evolution and uniformitarian processes to be true is vast amounts of time. Evolution needs billions and billions of years of time, sometimes known as "deep time." If there is any evidence to show that such amounts of time are not available then evolution is in deep trouble. There are lines of evidence that show that the earth is much younger than the billions of years needed for evolution. They are fascinating and challenging:

1. Salinity of the oceans

Many processes bring salt into the sea and some take salt out. There is a net inflow of salts and minerals into the oceans annually. Since we can measure the amount of salt and minerals in the oceans, and we can estimate the net inflow, we should be able to estimate the age of the oceans, and hence the age of the earth. This method was first proposed by Sir Edmond Halley (1656–1742)[50] who discovered the comet since known by his name. More recently, John Joly (1857–1933), the pioneer of radiation therapy, estimated the age of the oceans to be a maximum of 80–90 million years,[51] a figure far too low for evolutionists to accept.

More recently still, in 1990, geologist Dr Steve Austin and physicist Dr Russell Humphreys analyzed figures from geoscientific sources for the quantity of sodium in the ocean and the input and output rates. We need to remember that the slower the input and the faster the output, the greater the age of the oceans, and hence the earth, will be. Granting the most generous assumptions to evolutionary requirements, that is, taking the lowest input data and the highest output data, these two scientists calculated that the oceans must be less than 62 million years old.[52] This is not the actual age, but a maximum age; the oceans could have any age, including the Biblical age of about 6,000 years. If the assumptions are examined so that they are less generous to evolutionary "long ages" presuppositions, the age would certainly be significantly less than the 62 million years quoted. In any case this modern research is consistent with the earlier results of Halley and Joly, in producing an estimated age far too low for evolutionary requirements.

2. Magnetic field intensity

The earth's magnetic field protects us from very dangerous and lethal charged particles from the sun. If it were not there, we could not long survive. In the 1970s the physicist Dr Thomas Barnes noted that measurements of the intensity of the earth's magnetic field, since 1835, show that it is decaying by about 5% every 100 years.[53] Archaeological research shows that it was about 40% stronger in 1000 AD compared with today.[54] Barnes theorized that the earth's magnetic field was caused by a decaying electric current in the earth's nickel-iron core. He calculated that the earth could not have been more than 10,000 years old, since beyond that point in time the magnetic field would have been strong enough to melt the earth! The model that evolutionists prefer is of a self-sustaining dynamo, in accordance with the need for long ages, but there are many problems with the evolutionary model that have not been resolved.

Barnes's model is clearly out of sympathy with evolutionary timescales: however, a major criticism of his model is that the earth's magnetic field has reversed many times. The nuclear physicist Russell Humphreys thought that Barnes's idea was the right way to go and he also accepted that the field had reversed many times. He modified Barnes's theory to account for the liquid nature of the earth's core. Convection currents within the core could account for the rapid reversals. The moving conductive metallic liquid would carry magnetic flux lines with it, and this would generate new currents, producing new flux in the opposite direction.[55] (This model also explains why the sun reverses its magnetic field every eleven years. The sun is a massive sphere of hot, electrically conducting plasma gas; and the overall energy of the sun's magnetic field is decreasing.)

Dr Humphreys predicted that, if his model were true, magnetic reversals should be found in rocks that had cooled quickly, in days or weeks. For example, in a thin lava flow, the outside would cool and solidify first, preserving the magnetic field direction in its crystalline structure; the inside would cool later and record the field in another direction, if such rapid reversals had taken place. Three years after this prediction, researchers Robert Coe and Michael Prévot found the evidence in a thin layer of solidified lava.[56] So the Barnes–Humphreys model accords with the physical evidence so far discovered.

The decaying magnetic field of the earth is powerful evidence that the earth is young. The mathematics of the model indicates less than 10,000 years. The evolutionary model cannot account for the measured data, and in any case would reject such a ludicrously low age.

3. Continental erosion rates

It was James Hutton, the father of modern geology, who suggested in 1785 that the earth was immensely old. He famously said that there was "no vestige of a beginning, no prospect of an end,"[57] thus clearing the way for Darwin's theory of evolution. Hutton's views are generally accepted today without question. The continents are held to be about 2–3 billion years old by modern scientific reckoning. There are many geological processes and lines of evidence that do not agree with this evolutionary assumption. One of these is the process of erosion. Water is the main agent of erosion, dissolving and loosening soil and rock and transporting them via the river networks to the ocean. This process goes on all the time. Millions of tonnes are taken in this way each year and deposited in the oceans. By sampling the mouth of a river, we can measure the volume of water and the amount of sediment in it. Some solids roll along the bed of the river, so it is difficult to be precise. Of course, there are also rare catastrophic events, almost impossible to measure, that can dump huge amounts of sediments into the oceans.

Allowing for the inaccuracies, many of the world's rivers have been researched by sedimentologists, who have estimated how fast the land is eroding. The average height reduction for all the continents of the world is about 60 mm (2.4 inches) per 1,000 years.[58] Looking at this on a human scale it doesn't seem very much, but if we do the arithmetic and multiply this by the 2–3 billion years of modern evolutionary theory, we find that we would have eroded about 150 kilometers (93 miles) of continental height, using an average figure of 2.5 billion years for the age of the earth. This defies reality. If erosion had been going on for 2.5 billion years there would be no continents left! A number of geologists have calculated that, at the measured rates, the North American continent should have been leveled in about 10 million years.

These rates not only challenge the concept of billions of years for the age of the continents, but they also challenge the widely held idea that mountains are ancient. Mountains, with steep slopes and deep valleys, are eroded fastest. Erosion rates of 1,000 mm per year are common in mountainous regions around the globe, the Himalayas being a good example.[59] Why do the mountains and continents still exist? There are many factors to be considered, for example, new land being thrust up by geological activity, but the real issue is the problem of the assumed age of the continents and the measured erosion rates. The simple solution is that the vast geological time periods, first suggested by James Hutton, do not apply. This would harmonize with the observed measurements of the natural world. This would mean that the earth and the continents are much younger than evolutionary theory can allow. Since evolution needs the time, this line of evidence is not normally admitted.

4. Population statistics

When we look into a Petri dish and see bacteria dividing and "doubling" every few seconds, we are amazed that, within a few hours or days, the colony of bacteria has grown into billions and begins to die through overpopulation. There isn't enough food, or the waste products accumulate sufficiently to poison the bacteria, or a combination of both takes place. There are literally billions of bacteria in a very short space of time by this action of "doubling." When looking at population growth, any statistician will tell you that it is the population "doubling time" that is the critical issue.

Just for a moment, consider the Chinese inventor of the game of chess. He was offered a reward by his emperor. He didn't ask for gold, but instead asked for one grain of rice doubled for each square on the chessboard. Here we have the "doubling" effect again. The number of grains would have been 1, 2, 4, 8, 16, 32, 64, and so on. The tenth square would have 512 grains, the twentieth 524,000, the thirtieth 537,000,000. The last (sixty-fourth) square would give a number so great – 2^{63}, or very approximately 10^{19}, or ten million trillion – that the emperor could not afford to pay it. Such is the power of compounding or "doubling."[60]

If you are not familiar with scientific notation of numbers, all you have to do is remember that the number itself is called the "base" and the quantity above the number is called the "index." Let us take the example of 10^{19}. The base is "10" and the index is "19." This means we multiply 10 by itself 19 times, giving 10,000,000,000,000,000,000. In English this is ten million trillion. It takes a lot less space to write 10^{19}. Remember, though, that every time we increase the index by 1, we are adding another zero to the base number, and so in reality we are multiplying by 10, so 10^{20} would be one hundred million trillion!

Population growth is defined as the number of live births in excess of the number of deaths per year. Average current world population growth is about 1.7% per year.[61] This means that for every thousand people, 17 are added every year. This means that in about forty years the population will double. I remember the worry back in the 1960s, when the world population was about 3 billion, about how we would feed 6 billion in the year 2000! Today we have the 6 billion and are heading off towards 12 billion by about 2040.

If we allow for wars, famines and pandemic diseases, we still see substantial growth rates. Some areas of the Third World have growth rates in excess of 3%. The population of the earth carried on doubling about every forty years throughout the twentieth century, with its mass wars and genocides, not forgetting major influenza pandemics and other serious diseases and epidemics.

Evolutionists claim that we are descended from apes about a million years ago. Let us be very conservative and assume a growth rate of 0.01%; this would give a population doubling time of about 7,000 years. Dividing 1,000,000 by 7,000 gives us about 143. Do you remember the chessboard with "only" 64 squares? The chessboard doubling effect gave us 10^{19} rice grains in 63 doublings. Those supposed 143 population doublings would give about 10^{43} people alive today.[62] The quantity 10^{43} is a 1 with 43 zeros after it. This number applies only to humans and excludes all the other creatures and their populations. How would we calculate the population problem of all the other vertebrates who lived and died within this period of about 1 million years? This excludes all the evolutionary false starts, dead ends and alternative branches. All these things would multiply the problem by some unknowable factor of gigantic proportions. Furthermore, the assumption of a 0.01% population growth rate is very lenient to evolution. The real figure will be in excess of 1.0%. A growth rate of 1.0% would give a population doubling time of 69 years; after 1 million years this would give 14,493 doublings to the nearest whole number; starting from a population of 2 would mean approximately $3 \times 10^{2,171}$ people! Remember, that's a number with 2,171 zeroes!

Keeping our feet on the ground, to try and put just 10^{43} people in context, let us divide up the entire surface area of the earth into units of just one square meter and allocate one person per unit. The total surface area of the earth is about 150,000,000,000,000 or 1.5×10^{14} square meters. Let us consider the situation in simple terms and ignore the figure 1.5 and just look at the number 10^{14}. If every one of those square meter units were made into *another earth* with exactly the same surface area, we would get an available area of $10^{14} \times 10^{14}$ square meters, or, in other words, we could accommodate 10^{28} people.[63] This is nowhere near the size of the number 10^{43}. We still need to accommodate a further $10^{43} - 10^{28} = 10^{15}$ people.

To summarize, we have here 10^{14} earths, each with 10^{14} square meters. Looking at it another way, we have 100,000,000,000,000 earths, or 100 million million earths, or 100 trillion earths, depending upon how we want to express it, each with 100 trillion people. We are still short by 10^{15} or 1,000,000,000,000,000 or one thousand trillion people! This excludes all other vertebrates with all their countless generations that ever walked the face of the earth. Where are all the bones of their passing? We can't imagine such things. Evolutionists with their million years of human evolution really need to look again at the implications of their theories.

What you must realize is that, however much you play with the population growth rate and the starting population, the most significant term is the time factor and the doubling rate. You can adjust the numbers all you like, but once you go beyond a few thousand years, let alone tens of thousands or millions of years, the population grows exponentially, doubling itself every few years, to reach unsustainable numbers.

Evolutionists recognize the issue and argue that wars, natural disasters, plagues and famines kept mankind on the brink of extinction for most of this time. Does this mean that all other vertebrates were also on the brink of extinction? This stretches belief to the limit. The one simple thing that any unbiased observer would do is to examine the basic assumptions. Don't forget that every vertebrate animal would also achieve uncountable trillions in a million years. Time is the culprit here, not the mathematics or the well-understood dynamics of population growth. Time, however, is non-negotiable in an evolutionary context. Evolution is the prisoner of its presuppositions about time.

5. Living fossils

In Chapter 1 we mentioned the coelacanth. There are many other living fossils. By this we mean that there are organisms alive today whose ancestors are fossilized in rock strata and there is no difference between the two: evolution never happened to these organisms. The evidence is quite striking: the fossilized forms are identical to the living examples. Space precludes giving this fascinating subject the full attention it deserves, but there is a significant conclusion to be drawn from the existence of these creatures that should have died out millions of years ago and been replaced by their "evolved" descendants. The list is impressive:

- Neopolina molluscs – 500 million years
- Lingula lamp shell – 450 million years
- Coelacanth fish – 340 million years
- Cockroaches – 250 million years
- Tuatara lizard – 200 million years
- Horseshoe crabs – 200 million years
- Crocodiles – 140 million years
- Gingko trees – 125 million years

The list is not exhaustive, but the above examples suffice to demonstrate the principle. The conclusion can only be that, in these cases at least, either the time frame is all wrong and there hasn't been enough time for evolution, or the time frame is correct and evolution hasn't happened. Either way, these specimens are a huge issue for evolutionists. Based on our examination of all the other features of evolution, we would be justified in concluding that not only has the time not been available, but evolution hasn't happened either.

Mathematical Probability

There have been several scientists and mathematicians who have calculated the probability of life developing from non-life, or the appearance of the smallest living organism. When we looked at the subject of population growth, we looked at how to express large numbers in powers of 10 – see the section starting on page 91. There is a great need to be able to do this when talking about probabilities in evolution.

Before we begin, a French expert on probability, Emile Borel, has established that a probability of one chance in 10^{50} is the absolute limit for anything to happen by random chance. Beyond this number the thing would never occur – not ever. Keep this in mind when we discuss some of the numbers that will shortly appear: 10^{50} represents one chance in 100 trillion, trillion, trillion, trillion!

One mathematician, Professor David Rodabaugh, demonstrated that the probability that a simple living organism could be produced by mutations is "less than one chance in $10^{2,999,942}$" anywhere in the universe.[64] In another article, Professor Rodabaugh gives evolution every possible benefit of the doubt and assumes that evolution is 99.99% certain. There is still only one chance in 10^{132} of evolution happening. Therefore: "Even with the beginning assumption that evolution is a virtual certainty, a conditional probability analysis of the fossil record results in the conclusion that evolution is a demonstrable absurdity."[65]

Even one chance in 10^{132} is no chance, according to Borel. Sir Fred Hoyle calculated that there was one chance in $10^{40,000}$ that a single bacterium could be spontaneously generated. Hoyle said:

> The likelihood of the formation of life from inanimate matter
> is one to a number with forty-thousand noughts after it. It is
> enough to bury Darwin and the whole theory of evolution. There
> is no primeval soup, neither on this planet nor on any other, and
> if the beginnings of life were not random they must therefore
> have been the product of purposeful intelligence.[66]

Fraud in Evolution

There are many cases of scientists, who "know" evolution to be true, deliberately reworking their results to vindicate evolutionary assumptions. Why they do this is not clear. In some cases there is the desire to achieve recognition, although when the fraud is discovered they achieve notoriety rather than acceptance and recognition. In their book *Betrayers of the Truth: Fraud and Deceit in the Halls of Science*, William Broad and Nicholas Wade write:

> A continuous spectrum can be drawn from the major and minor acts of fabrication to self-deception, a phenomenon of considerable importance in all branches of science . . . In the spectrum that runs from hard sciences to soft sciences, from physics to sociology, the centre is probably occupied by biology, a discipline in which fraud is by no means rare.[67]

In Volume 2 of *The Origin of Species Revisited*, Wendell R. Bird comments:

> Many examples of scientific dishonesty with data and observation also exist. These include many instances of evolutionists' suppression or discounting of unfavorable data, according to Lipson: "In fact, evolution became in a sense a scientific religion; almost all scientists have accepted it and many are prepared to 'bend' their observations to fit with it."
>
> Eisley and Romar mention casual discarding of anomalous fossils; Weidenreich describes how "paleontological facts are disregarded and replaced with purely speculative constructions" on the evolution of man; and Keith recounts arbitrary rejection of human remains mixed with alleged pre-human remains.[68]

Yet, even though many of these frauds have been clearly shown for what they are, some iconic frauds are still found in biology textbooks and are still taught in schools and universities! Below are two examples:

1. The peppered moth

Textbooks around the world have used the story of England's peppered moth, *Biston betularia*, as proof of evolution. This moth has a grainy, peppered coloring and comes in two varieties, light and dark. The story goes that before the Industrial Revolution in England, the dark form rested on light-colored tree trunks and were easily spotted by birds and eaten – hence the predominance of the lighter form. When pollution from the Industrial Revolution coated the tree trunks, the dark variety was now better camouflaged, so the birds ate the light ones and the darker form became predominant. Later, as the pollution was cleaned up, the position reversed itself again.

This story was welcomed by evolutionists and quickly became one of their favorite examples of evolution in action. Much of the experimental work was carried out by H.B. Kettlewell, who said that if Darwin had seen this, "He would have witnessed the consummation and confirmation of his life's work."[69]

Even as it stands, this is not proof of evolution, but a demonstration of an organism adapting to a changing environment, or "observed adaptation." What we have at the beginning and end of the sequence is *the same moth*, exhibiting the same properties as before, with no change in the DNA nor any other changes, not even minor ones except the trivial color changes. No evolution has taken place. However, the "science" was made to fit a story sympathetic to evolutionary theory. The experiments were fraudulent. Consider, where do moths rest during the daytime, the time during which birds forage and hunt? Certainly they do not rest exposed on tree trunks! Later work has shown that they hide in the forest canopy, possibly under leaves, but it is still a matter of speculation. They are very good at hiding.

Kettlewell and others attracted moths into traps by night, the only time they actually fly. The moths that were filmed being eaten by birds were bred in the laboratory by Kettlewell; the still photographs of moths on tree trunks were made possible by dead moths glued onto the trees![70] Kettlewell later admitted the fraud.

Jerry Coyne, an evolutionary biologist at the University of Chicago, agreed that the "peppered moth" story had to be thrown out.[71] It is still around in some textbooks, however, and is still taught in some schools. Why is this fraud still taught to children? It does no service to the intellectual integrity of the scientific community.

2. Haeckel's theories of fetal development

This is probably the most damaging and enduring fraud of all. One of the most pervasive evolutionary ideas is that as the human embryo develops, it goes through the main evolutionary stages. This theory is often referred to as "recapitulation," where human life begins as a single cell and progresses through fish, reptile, and mammal stages before ending up at the highest evolutionary achievement thus far, the human being. This is often expressed as "ontogeny recapitulates phylogeny," which means that the fetal development of the individual repeats the evolutionary development of the race.[72]

Many people have absorbed in some form or another that this is, in fact, what happens to the fetus during pregnancy. Evolutionary biologists have known for a very long time now that this is not the case. Despite this, the theory is still around in many biology textbooks and is still taught, despite (at least some of) the teaching profession knowing better. How did this come about? German biologist Ernst Haeckel (1834–1919) was a Darwinist who started with the assumption that evolution is true. He then doctored his drawings of fetuses from different species to establish the "embryonic recapitulation law," sometimes known as the "biogenetic law," discussed above.

In 1866 he published a set of twenty-four sketches of fish, salamander, turtle, chicken, pig, cow, rabbit and human fetuses, in three stages of their development, to show how similar they were: for example, that mammals had embryonic gill slits. (These are nothing of the kind; they are the beginning of important structures in the head and neck.) Darwin himself considered the embryonic recapitulation argument to be of primary importance to his theory of evolution. In his *Descent of Man* he gave the entire first chapter to this line of evidence.

When photography came along, there was no need for sketches – the fetuses could be photographed exactly as they were. Sadly, no one did this systematically. Even so, Haeckel's work was declared fraudulent in 1874 by Professor Wilhelm His; as early as 1900 Haeckel's theories were refuted and his drawings have long been known to be frauds.[73] There is absolutely no excuse for these drawings and the theory they support being taught to generation after generation of biology students. However, it was not until Michael Richardson, a lecturer and embryologist at St George's Hospital Medical School, London, performed a thorough *photographic* investigation using an international team, that the full extent of Haeckel's fraud was exposed.[74] In 1997 he published his results in the journal *Anatomy and Embryology*.[75] In an interview for *The Times* of London, Richardson is quoted as saying:

> This is one of the worst cases of scientific fraud. It's shocking to find that somebody one thought was a great scientist was deliberately misleading . . . What he did was to take a human embryo and copy it, pretending that the salamander and the pig and all the others looked the same at the same stage of development. They don't . . . These are fakes.[76]

Perhaps the most damning statement comes from the mouth of Haeckel himself:

> To cut short this unsavoury dispute, I begin at my numerous drawings of embryos (perhaps six or eight percent) are in a sense falsified – all those, namely, for which the present material of observation is so incomplete or insufficient as to compel us, when we come to prepare a continuous chain of the evolutionary stages, to fill up the gaps by hypotheses, and to reconstruct the missing links by comparative syntheses . . . After this compromising confession of "forgery" I should be obliged to consider myself condemned and annihilated if I had not the consolation of seeing side by side with me in the prisoner's dock hundreds of fellow-culprits, among them many of the most trusted observers and most esteemed biologists. The great majority of all the diagrams in the best biological textbooks, treatises and journals would incur in the same degree the charge of "forgery," for all of them are inexact, and are more or less doctored, schematised and constructed.[77]

Despite all this, Haeckel's drawings are still found in many textbooks and his "law" of embryonic recapitulation is still taught. The establishment of these "scientific" discoveries as fraud has not brought evolution into disrepute, or caused any questioning of its basic assumptions, or of the motives of the scientists involved. More alarming is the statement that such forgery is widespread and the great majority of diagrams in the best biological texts of all kinds would incur in the same degree the charge of "forgery." Even more alarming is his statement that "hundreds of fellow-culprits, among them many of the most trusted observers and most esteemed biologists" were doing the same! Can we ask: is this practice still prevalent?

Apart from quiet retractions, these episodes are simply never mentioned. Sometimes the false, or hoax, material is left in textbooks for years afterwards, without any consistent effort to set the record straight. What does this say about the integrity of modern science and modern scientists? Why do we still trust them?

Summary and Further Thoughts

In our brief review of the "science" of evolution, we have looked at the geologic column, the fossil record, the age of the earth, population statistics, living "fossils" and mathematical probabilities. In each case there are some serious and fatal flaws in the evolutionary assumptions, and much contradictory evidence that does not fit into an evolutionary worldview with its "deep" time. There are many other areas where such discrepancies can be found. Even from our brief review, it is clear that, based on freely available evidence, evolution is not what it claims to be, that is, a complete theory of life and its origins.

This chapter could not look at all the aspects and developments of evolutionary theory. The theory of evolution has been developed from its simple Darwinian beginnings to the "modern evolutionary synthesis" – a blending of ideas from several biological specialties, accepted by nearly all working biologists. Sir Julian Huxley coined the term in 1942 in his book, *Evolution: The Modern Synthesis*. Since then, the synthesis has largely remained the operational framework in evolutionary biology. This modern synthesis, sometimes known as neo-Darwinism, allegedly solves the difficulties and confusions between biologists in the early years of the twentieth century. Discoveries of the early geneticists were difficult to reconcile with gradual evolution and the mechanism of natural selection. The synthesis was an attempt to reconcile the two. It drew together ideas from several branches of biology that had become separated, particularly genetics, cytology, biological systematics (the study of the diversification of life on planet earth, both past and present, and the relationships among living things through time), botany, morphology, ecology and paleontology.

Since then there have been enormous strides in DNA research and genetics. The modern evolutionary synthesis does not include the relatively new field of "molecular evolution" because it wasn't around in 1942. One might be forgiven for asking why a latter-day Huxley has not brought this new field into the synthesis by now. It is simply not feasible. The gradual uncovering of the increasingly complex interdependency and atomic precision of biological functions, tends to point towards design rather than randomness; and molecular evolution has no scientific credibility. Michael J. Behe, in his book *Darwin's Black Box*, writes:

> There is no publication in the scientific literature – in the prestigious journals, specialty journals, or books – that describes how molecular evolution of any real, complex, biochemical system either did occur or even might have occurred. There are assertions that such evolution occurred, but absolutely none are supported by pertinent experiments or calculations.[78]

The Swedish biologist Søren Løvetrup discussed neo-Darwinism in *Darwinism: The Refutation of a Myth*. He wrote: "To all intents and purposes, the theory has been falsified so why has it not been abandoned? I think that the answer to this question is that current evolutionists follow Darwin's example. They refuse to accept falsifying evidence."[79] So yet again we find hard evidence retreating from us.

In 2008 I was in a "blog" conversation with an evolutionist and we were discussing this question of supporting evidence. I was pointed to an article in *New Scientist* by Bob Holmes, dated 9 June 2008.[80] In the article, a series of experiments[81] by evolutionary biologist Richard Lenski, of Michigan State University in East Lansing, USA, took a single *Escherichia coli* (*E. coli*) bacterium and used its descendants to found twelve laboratory populations. One of them developed the ability to metabolize citrate, a second nutrient in their culture medium that *E. coli* normally cannot use. Claims were made in the article that this was "evolution in action" and definitive proof of its validity. In the article, Professor Jerry Coyne, from the University of Chicago, stated:

> Lenski's experiment is also yet another poke in the eye for anti-evolutionists. The thing I like most is it says you can get these complex traits evolving by a combination of unlikely events . . . That's just what Creationists say can't happen.[82]

Despite the blatantly unjust sideswipe at "anti-evolutionists" and creationists, this article from *New Scientist* is just another example of natural selection at work, or "microevolution." Everyone accepts that this is part of the natural world. Lenski started with *E. coli*, and he ends with a recognizable variant of *E. coli*. Variation within a kind has occurred. This can in no way be extrapolated to the generation of a new kind, or "macroevolution." The article is guilty of making outrageous claims on a flimsy evidential base. Yet again evolution is assumed to be the paradigm and everything is filtered through it. Evolution really does blind scientists to considering other explanations. The theory of evolution has become institutionalized in very much the same way that Aristotelian philosophy was institutionalized in Galileo's day.

I am more convinced than ever that evolutionists need to examine their own evidence, and recognize wishful thinking and circular reasoning. Scientists should devote themselves to more study outside the "evolutionary box" in which their intellects have been trapped these last hundred years or so. The man who pointed me to the article genuinely believed it was an example of evolution in action. What he couldn't see was that Lenski started with a pre-existing living organism and this is also where he ended. Where do living things come from in the first place? That is the real question.

The "Darwin-is-king" school of philosophy is laying its foundations in the wrong place. It is a complete paradox that, on the one hand, there is a constant search in all the disciplines of science for the key underlying principle of all things, and to find the design and unity of all knowledge; yet, on the other, when modern science proposes its answer to the origin of life, it says that there is no design, no unity, only randomness and blind chance. In itself, this logical flaw destroys the philosophy of modern science and the basis for any possible unity of knowledge.

The evolutionary worldview is not only a great hindrance to scientific progress, but it could be fairly claimed that is also in the process of destroying science and the scientific method.

We might also say, with considerable reason, that it is destroying our civilization. We discuss this in the next chapter.

CHAPTER 9

SCIENCE, FAITH AND CONSEQUENCES

The crisis inherent in the political and economic situation of Britain is a moral one...History shows that societies rise and fall, flourish and decay, by what they believe in and by what their way of life stands for.

The Times, London, 11 February 1963

Charles Darwin's theory of evolution exists without metaphysical foundations. This means that the theory of evolution does not explain what life is, how life came about, how life exists, how life interacts with other life, how life reproduces, and how this caused life to evolve and adapt. It is, however, used as a metaphysical tool to deconstruct the Bible and the Christian worldview. As we have shown with considerable justification, if someone truly believes evolution then they do so on no substantive evidence. All they have is the belief that this is the way it happened. They bring this presupposition to all they see and interpret about the universe and our world. It is a faith position, only maintained by rejecting lines of evidence that do not fit their worldview, and by considerable judicial "fudging" of the remaining evidence.

Despite the real scientific difficulties, and the not inconsiderable fraudulent claims, our society now believes in evolution and an evolutionary worldview. Long eons of time, blind chance, and the twin mechanisms of random mutation and natural selection have produced all that we see. Based on these suppositions, the Bible is wrong about the world and God is not necessary – a more blatant metaphysical position is hard to imagine.

Why does all this scientific controversy matter? It matters because evolution affects everything. The American attorney Wendell R. Bird, in his book *The Origin of Species Revisited: The Theories of Evolution and Abrupt Appearance*, wrote: "That single volume has had a massive influence not only on the sciences, which increasingly are built on evolutionary assumptions, but on the humanities, theology and government."[83]

Robert Downs, a former president of the American Library Association, also viewed Darwin's work as world-shaking:

> Viewed in retrospect, Darwin's impress on nearly all major fields of learning was, and continues to be, profound. The doctrine of organic evolution has been accepted by biologists, geologists, chemists, and physicists, by anthropologists, psychologists, educators, philosophers, and sociologists, and even by historians, political scientists and philologists. Charles Ellwood declared: "When one reflects upon the immense influence which Darwin's work has had on practically all lines of human thought, and especially upon the biological, psychological, and social sciences, one is forced to conclude that . . . Darwin must be given the seat of highest honor as the most fructifying thinker which the nineteenth century produced, not only in England, but in the whole world. And the social significance of Darwin's teachings is even yet only beginning to be apprehended."[84]

Evolution and scientific naturalism have changed the way people think about themselves and their lives. Every aspect of family, society, government and international relations has been radically affected. Belief in a closed system or universe, where no outside intervention is possible, means there is no God and we are not made in His image. If no outside intervention is permitted and we live in a closed system of cause and effect, evolving by random chance, then how do we come to be here? What meaning is there to our lives and hopes? We simply become accidental biological machines with no real reason for existing, and, since everything is only the accumulation of random causes and effects, there can be no freedom and no moral content to the universe. The consequences of such a belief system are truly devastating.

War and Peace

The terrible events of the twentieth century, the mass wars and genocides, the political and ideological revolutions, cannot be understood without knowledge of the impact of Darwin's theory of evolution. We could not understand Marx and the development of communism, because Karl Marx (1818–83) ascribed to Darwin the inspiration for his "class struggles." Adolf Hitler (1889–1945) with his national socialism would not have been possible without the philosophical foundations of Darwinism. Both of these men explicitly credited Darwin as their inspiration.

The influence of this theory has become the dominant worldview of the age. It is this view of the world and nature that is responsible for the strength of the atheistic humanist philosophy that now governs our civilization. Any theory or religion can be misused and manipulated for evil purposes by unscrupulous people, but evolutionary ethics have a basis that does not need manipulation for such purposes. As mentioned above, the two cruelest ideologies of the twentieth century were Marxism and fascism. Here is the thinking of Adolf Hitler:

> If Nature doesn't desire the mating of weaker with stronger
> individuals, even less does she desire the blending of a higher
> with a lower race, since if she did, her whole work of higher
> breeding, over perhaps hundreds of thousands of years, might be
> ruined with one blow.[85]

Also: "Should I not also have the right to eliminate millions of an inferior race that multiplies like vermin?"[86] Was Hitler misguided? Did he misunderstand and misrepresent the theory he loved? Evolutionary anthropologist and anatomist Sir Arthur Keith (1866–1955), Fellow of the Royal College of Surgeons of England, explained: "Hitler is an uncompromising evolutionist, and we must seek for an evolutionary explanation if we are to understand his actions."[87] And: "The German Führer, as I have consistently maintained, is an evolutionist; he has consciously sought to make the practice of Germany conform to the theory of evolution."[88]

Sir Arthur Keith was one of the most renowned evolutionists of modern times. He was strongly opposed to Christianity. His book *Evolution and Ethics* shows clearly that Keith believed that Christian ethics and evolutionary ethics are not compatible. He came to the conclusion that the two worldviews are at war with each other – completely irreconcilable. He also clearly saw the impact of Darwinism on world peace:

It was often said in 1914 that Darwin's doctrine of evolution
had bred war in Europe, particularly in Germany. An expression
of this belief is still to be met with. In 1935, a committee of
psychologists, representing 30 nations, issued a manifesto
in which it was stated that "war is the necessary outcome of
Darwin's theory . . ." The law of evolution, as formulated by
Darwin, provides an explanation of wars between nations, the
only reasonable explanation known to me.[89]

Joseph Stalin (1879–1953) was another ardent evolutionist, the inheritor of
Marx, Lenin and Trotsky, who surpassed even Hitler, murdering at least ten
times as many "inferiors" as Hitler (estimates vary depending on the source,
but it was certainly tens of millions). Was Stalin morally wrong? Was Hitler?
If you subscribe to the evolutionary worldview they were perfectly correct.
Further, to the consistent, uncompromising evolutionist, Hitler and Stalin
ought to be considered role models.

Let us consider the statement by those psychologists representing thirty
countries, that war is the necessary outcome of Darwinism. This was said in
1935. Since then it can be reasonably claimed that Darwinism has become
the prevalent worldview on every continent. Our societies are becoming
more and more bound up with the ethics and morals of an evolutionary
worldview. Is it not strange that the professed aim of every government, the
United Nations and a host of supranational bodies, is "world peace"? With
their evolutionary mindset, on what intellectual and ethical basis do they
propose that "world peace" can be achieved?

As we remarked at the end of the last chapter, logical flaws within
evolution destroy the philosophy of modern science and the basis for any
possible unity of knowledge. The incompatibility of evolutionary ethics with
world peace is just such another logical flaw that will one day bring down
our civilization in a burst of alleged "natural selection." These considerations
are not academic or unrealistic musings – they are the practical moral
consequences of evolution.

Family and Society

On a personal level, behavior is influenced by the way we think; the way
we think is influenced by what we believe. If we believe we are meaningless
and without purpose, we will think that nothing matters. We will begin to

serve ourselves in all parts of our lives. We will worship our own thoughts, idols and icons as the fancy pleases, to suit our own passing tastes. Morality becomes relative and situational, rather than absolute. Restraint is no longer a virtue, since all we have is this life; one passing moment of eternity during which we draw breath and live our short, pointless lives. Eat, drink, and be merry, for tomorrow we die. This selfish and self-centered view of life is at the root of the breakdown of family and society. Eric Fromm, an existential psychoanalyst, in the 1960s said: "Alienation as we find it in modern society is almost total; it pervades the relationship of man to his work, to the things he consumes, to the state, to his fellow man, and to himself."[90]

Since the initial United Kingdom Abortion Act of 1967, subsequent amendments have been applied which make it extremely easy to have an abortion. Whereas abortions were once only allowed for overwhelming medical reasons, now they are available on demand. Perfectly healthy children are aborted for financial, social and lifestyle reasons. It works out that, statistically, one of the most dangerous places to be in the UK is in the womb. In any given year, if live births, stillbirths and abortions are added together as a measure of the total number of pregnancies, then since about 1980 abortions account for approximately 20%, *or one fifth*, of all pregnancies. In the first ten years of the twenty-first century (2000–09) the average number of live births annually was 647,680; the number of stillbirths averaged 3,460; the number of abortions averaged 186,797 or 22.29% of the total pregnancies. What other cause – disease, calamity, or outright warfare – on any conceivable basis, could account for the deaths of *more than one fifth of all children*? Pause, and think about this.

Think also about the "demographic time bomb" and the ageing of the population. By killing so many of its children, this generation has killed its own future. It's not difficult to see the connection, but this link is never publicly debated. People don't want to face the consequences of their selfish actions.

The total number of legal abortions in England and Wales from 1968 to 2010 is 7,003,416 (Source: UK Office for National Statistics). The sense of personal identity and self-esteem is eroded in our children who are survivors of the abortion lottery. This can express itself in sometimes bizarre ways. Many children grow up alienated, disoriented, antisocial and rebellious. In turn they bring this damage to their own relationships and their own children. Even if extremes of behavior are avoided, the lives of those who think of themselves as cosmic accidents, or meaningless bits of biology, are bleak: they have no origin, no purpose and no destiny. Many young people commit acts of seemingly random violence and hedonistic irresponsibility. I believe this is a cry of desperation, stating, "Look! Take notice! I am here! I want to mean something! I am not nothing!" Unfortunately, all modern society can offer is a meaningless life. Bleak despair is all around. The suicide rate among young men is high. In the United Kingdom, since 1997, the highest rates have been in men aged fifteen to twenty-four, peaking in 1998 at 24.0 per 100,000 and then steadily decreasing. In 2008, the rate for this age group increased to 18.6 per 100,000 from 17.6 per 100,000 in 2007 (Source: UK Office for National Statistics).

Throughout history, people and societies have come through extreme events, such as war, disease and natural disasters, without producing alienated individuals and dysfunctional families on a large scale. During the last war, children were shipped off to distant places to avoid the bombing of cities, to live with perfect strangers. During the Black Death in medieval Europe many families were decimated and the children farmed out to distant relatives, sometimes several times. Society did not fundamentally break down or produce antisocial individuals on the scale we see today. The disease runs much deeper. It is to do with loss of roles for men and women; roles which children observe and emulate, and take as their own as they grow to maturity in their turn. There is a loss of purpose and a loss of the sense of the sanctity of life behind the suicides and the abortions.

In the Biblical worldview, men and women each have a role and a purpose: they are valued for who they are, and not as mere consumer units. They have an eternal destiny with a loving God, who is the source of their existence and the fulfillment of their lives. Children see this and in their turn are valued and given a real role in life, a sense of purpose and a destiny.

In the secular evolutionary worldview, humanity is distanced from God. Male and female roles are blended into one. Somehow, all male characteristics have been demonized; male instincts of protective strength have been labeled as aggression and therefore bad. Since God represents Himself as male, this worldview sets up tremendous barriers to Christian spiritual life. The human soul was designed to have a spiritual relationship with God. When the genuine relationship is blocked off, spirituality is sought elsewhere. There has been a huge growth in alternative spiritualities since the 1960s. In most bookshops there is a section on "Mind, Body, Spirit" dealing with everything from astrology to Zoroastrianism. It is no surprise to see the resurgence of goddess spirituality and the sacred feminine.

Even the role of mother is diminished, and classed as secondary to a career, or some other "meaningful" activity outside the home. Many children are put to one side at an early age, with a child minder or in a crèche facility. Against their better instincts and deepest feelings, mothers are strongly encouraged to find their value not as a mother, but as something else. The children's need for role models and moral structure is not being met, and as they mature they find the only consistent message is, "You have no purpose or meaningful role, except what you make for yourself. You only have this life so don't blow it. Eat, drink, and be merry, for tomorrow you die." The only wonder is how so many parents do so remarkably well in such an environment, providing clear role models in spite of the contrary pressures, and providing moral guidance in a moral vacuum.

Conclusion

Since the great shift in Western culture and worldview during the 1960s, the behavioral changes can be seen in the succeeding generations. The impact on individuals, families, social order and morality has been significant and rapid. When the Bible describes the falling away of the people of Israel into idolatry and immorality, I used to think this was a gradual and long-term decline, over many generations. Having watched the behavioral changes in my own country, I now recognize that this is not the case. Such changes can happen rapidly over very few generations, even one or two, to match the changing worldview of society. One follows the other like night follows day. Most people now consider that the Biblical story of the perfect and finished creation from which human beings fell into sin is pre-Darwinian mythology. They believe that since Darwin, we have the real story of origins. We don't need a God to explain how we came to be here.

It is, of course, much more comfortable to believe that there has been no creation, since we can also believe that there is no God, no beginning, no end, no moral responsibility and no judgment in an eternal universe. The consequences are perpetual conflict and frequently open war between nations, individual alienation and stress, and the breakdown of family and relationships.

Chapter 10

The Response of Evangelicalism

Science without religion is lame; religion without science is blind.

Albert Einstein (1879–1955)

Introduction

The great schism between science and religion may have begun with the Catholic Church and the judgment on Galileo, but it was reinforced following the publication of Darwin's book *The Origin of Species* in 1859. The theories about the origin and development of life contained within this book were deliberately used by such people as Sir Thomas Huxley and Sir Charles Lyell (both Fellows of the Royal Society and extremely influential establishment figures) to challenge the Christian worldview of science prevailing at the time. As these gentlemen knew, the real issue was the authority of the Holy Scriptures.

Before we go any further we need to understand the nature of evangelicalism. It is quite difficult to define, or, equally, to state what makes an evangelical. It is not a Church but rather a broad movement, with members drawn across many of the great denominations and the free churches. Lord Shaftesbury said in later life, "I am still not sure what makes an Evangelical."[91] Professor D.W. Bebbington, in his book *Evangelicalism in Modern Britain*,[92] gives a definition of what makes an evangelical: he or she is someone who, in the doctrinal sense, holds to four major points:

1. **Biblicism:** A particular regard for the inspired and authoritative nature of Holy Scripture as revealed by God

2. **Crucicentrism:** The cross as the key event of history and the atoning sacrifice of Jesus Christ in the life of a believer

3. **Conversionism:** The salvation of the individual – in order to be a genuine Christian one has to be converted and "saved"

4. **Activism:** The necessity of activism in the community as the outworking of faith

Evangelicalism was a great influence on public life from about 1750 to about 1900. William Wilberforce, the anti-slavery campaigner, was an evangelical. The Methodist temperance movement and Lord Shaftesbury's reforms are examples of the activism and influence of the evangelical movement.

While many evangelicals were antagonistic to Darwin's theory, many others supported it. Furthermore, many evangelicals were educated in both science and religion. Many of the early naturalists were Christian clergy. There was no clear-cut position, no party line. This was due to the dispersed and informal nature of the evangelical movement. There was no institutional position, only the four [unstated] principles. It is also worth quoting from the research of Allan Green: "Firstly, Evangelicals were not solely theological beings and, secondly, scientists as well as Christians have rejected Darwinism and a significant number of those rejections had little or nothing to do with revelation or religious experience."[93]

The evangelicals of the Victorian period were always interested in scientific advancement and were always willing to hear new theories about the natural world. Some evangelicals were sympathetic to Darwinism and presented scientific papers accordingly. Others objected to it on scientific grounds; yet others objected to it on scriptural grounds and sometimes a mixture of both. The majority of criticisms were scientific in nature and were usually presented first, before scriptural considerations were investigated. Evangelicals usually made their theological points *after* stating their scientific objections. Ironically from today's perspective, Darwin was initially criticized from the laboratory, not the pulpit.

Let us remind ourselves that there were normally three legs to the platform of the Christian faith:

1. Natural theology – man reasoning from himself and nature to God
2. Holy Scripture – the sovereign revelation of God to man
3. The person and work of Jesus Christ – the prophesied Messiah

From the time of the Enlightenment we see the rise of empiricism and rationalist philosophy. We shall look at these in Part III. For now we merely need to note that these methods of thinking were used to attack orthodox Christian beliefs. It was not completely one-sided, because Christian theology also moved on and incorporated elements of Enlightenment progress into the Christian worldview. This was especially true of inductive empiricism in the natural sciences – what has since become known as "the scientific method." Natural theology became a method of thinking about the world around us. It combined the revelation of Holy Scripture with the natural philosophy of science. Isaac Newton had demonstrated that the universe was a well-ordered machine, as befits the God of Scripture, who desires order, peace and structure. Newton's Christian beliefs demonstrated the happy coexistence of faith and science. William Paley developed Newton's ideas of a structured universe from the eighteenth into the nineteenth centuries and attempted to show that the universe was designed for the habitation of mankind. This implied a benevolent God and was entirely in harmony with Scripture and the revelation of God to man.

By the mid-nineteenth century the orthodox worldview of Christianity included natural theology. The intellectual effort of the use of evidence-based reason, hand in hand with a trusting and submitting faith in the revelation of Scripture and the person and work of Christ, was the norm of orthodox belief and practice. None of these three aspects of orthodox faith was contradictory or exclusive to the others. The workings of nature, or the natural condition of man, were seen as only one aspect of the universe and God's creation. It was into this orthodoxy that Darwin's theory and German higher criticism burst like a slow-burning explosion, with far-reaching effects.

The Course of the Debate

During the period immediately following the publication of *The Origin of Species*, Darwin's theories received a very mixed reaction. At that time, Mendel's research and experiments had not been published, and the science of modern genetics had not been born. What we understand today about Darwinism, or neo-Darwinism, is radically different from the Darwinism of 1859. Then, it was simply defined as a means whereby successive generations could improve their chances of survivability through adaptation.

In parallel with the publication of Darwin's theory, the effects of the "higher critics" in Germany were being felt. In Britain, *Essays and Reviews* was published in 1860. This collection of essays advocated a more liberal reading of the Bible; contributions from several authors, notably from Bishop J.W. Colenso (1814–83), asserted that there were alleged "contradictions" within the Bible. Bishop Colenso also published his own work, *The Pentateuch and the Book of Joshua Critically Examined*, in 1862. This was initiated out of his knowledge of some of the sciences:

> My own knowledge of some branches of science, of Geology in particular, had been much increased since I left England; and I now knew for certain, on geological grounds, a fact, of which I had only had misgivings before, *viz.*, that a Universal Deluge, such as the Bible manifestly speaks of, could not possibly have taken place in the way described in the Book of Genesis, not to mention other difficulties which the story contains. I refer especially to the circumstance, well known to all geologists . . . that volcanic hills exist of immense extent in Auvergne and Languedoc, which must have been formed ages before the Noachian Deluge, and which are covered with light and loose substances, pumice-stone &c., that must have been swept away by a Flood, but do not exhibit the slightest sign of having ever been so disturbed.[94]

His comments on the volcanic hills of Auvergne and Languedoc were based on the uniformitarian assumptions of the immense time required for geological formations to develop. We have already challenged these in the last chapter. Bishop Colenso was also led to the conviction – painful, he said, both to himself and his reader – that:

> The Pentateuch, as a whole, cannot personally have been written by Moses, or by anyone acquainted personally with the facts which it professes to describe, and, further, that the (so-called) Mosaic narrative, by whomsoever written, and though imparting to us, as I fully believe it does, revelations of the Divine Will and Character, cannot be regarded as historically true.[95]

The origin of his opinions on the Pentateuch (the five books of Moses) came from the theories of Jacob Wellhausen. Wellhausen's "documentary hypothesis" was based on the style of the writing and the different names of God that were used within the Pentateuch. He proposed that there were four different authors operating later than Moses, plus some kind of editor to pull it all together. This was a rationalist approach for which he had no evidence; and there were many tortuous and unreasonable assumptions. His motives were evolutionary and materialistic; he aimed at re-evaluating Scripture to invalidate the supernatural and miraculous content. His method was to show that there was an evolutionary development of Judaism from animistic beginnings to a more abstract concept of a unified God. This reduces the miracles of the Pentateuch to mere natural events, magnified into the miraculous by later writers and the editor, who wished to promote their own religious views.

One of Wellhausen's false assumptions was that writing had not been developed at the time of Moses, so Moses could not have been the author; this, of course, is in direct contradiction to the explicit and unequivocal claims of the Bible itself. Archaeology has since falsified the documentary hypothesis. To deal with our example of writing, it had been around since well before the time of Moses, and Moses was an educated prince of Egypt; he could read and write as well as anyone. There is no credible alternative to the Mosaic authorship of the Pentateuch.

At the time, there was little documentary or archaeological evidence to support the documentary hypothesis and so it was a rationalist proposition, difficult to refute because of the lack of tangible evidence one way or the other. It made great inroads into the theological schools and gradually became the dominant view of the authorship of the Pentateuch. Today we have plenty of archaeological and documentary evidence that completely invalidates and falsifies the documentary hypothesis. Yet it is still taught in theological schools and seminaries. Just like the theory of evolution, it has been falsified, yet it lingers on. Scholars and theologians really do need a house-cleaning of discredited ideas and false presuppositions.

It was a very testing time for Christian orthodoxy, with attacks coming from many directions. In summary, German higher criticism was a movement that challenged the doctrine of scriptural infallibility, and proposed errors and contradictions in the Bible. "Neology" was the name given to the rationalist theology of Germany, or the increasing rationalization of the Christian religion. Darwinism was a scientific proposal that seemed directly to contradict the book of Genesis, and which lent force to the Biblical critics. The almost synchronous arrival of German higher criticism and neology, together with Darwinism, presented a very serious challenge to the traditionally accepted view of the natural world as God's creation.

The Victoria Institute was founded in London in 1865 to meet these challenges and to provide a "platform to demonstrate how scientific advances were not anathema to existing theology."[96] The Institute was not solely concerned with Darwinism, but published a great many scientific papers on a wide variety of topics. The contributors were both Christian and qualified scientists, and represented a cross section of the views of eminent scientists and theologians of the day. The *Transactions of the Victoria Institute* in London, from 1866 onwards, show a gradual shift in the emphasis of the debate.[97] The first editor of the *Transactions* was a Mr J. Reddie. In his introduction to the Institute, he stated that the aim of the Institute was to "investigate fully and impartially the most important questions of philosophy and science, but especially those great truths revealed in Holy Scripture, with a view to defending those truths against the opposition of science, falsely so called."[98]

Initially, Darwin's theory was opposed on both scientific and scriptural grounds. Many evangelicals were qualified and respected scientists. Mr Reddie put forward a view that Scripture and science should be complementary and mutually supportive. However, he did assume that Scripture was authoritative and therefore any scientific theory or law would only be correct if it conformed to Scripture. He finished his article on page 6 of the initial issue of the *Transactions*, by giving his opinion that if science and religion are opposed to one another, then it will result in "nothing less than the truth or falsehood of revealed religion, the maintenance or abandonment of Christianity." In the event he has been prophetic to a remarkable degree. His comments would seem to sum up the views of a considerable proportion of evangelicals at that time, that an attack on the inerrancy of the Bible was an attack on the revealed nature of the Christian religion.

Although the supremacy of Scripture was claimed, science, or natural philosophy as it was known then, was fully embraced. It is important to remember that many of the scientific arguments put forward by evangelicals against Darwin's theory are still valid today. As we noted in Chapter 1, Adam Sedgwick (1785–1873), one of the founders of modern geology and Darwin's teacher in geology, criticized Darwin on the grounds that his theory did not conform to empiricism, the inductive scientific method. Therefore it could not be subject to testing and was therefore outside of the realm of science proper. It was an untestable proposition and no more.

Be that as it may, Darwin's theory gained ground rapidly and in the process has done great damage not only to orthodox Christian faith but also to natural theology. There were three main lines of development:

1. **Natural theology** was unprepared to deal with the issues raised by Darwinism:

   - Orthodox natural theology presupposes a benevolent world, created by a God whose goodness and compassion are seen all around us.
   - Darwinism is "red in tooth and claw" – and that is the way it has always been.[99]

2. **Conflict between science and religion** was emphasized continually until it became the accepted wisdom.

3. **The growth of premillennialism** hardened the evangelical view of the inerrancy of Scripture, making it even more difficult to accommodate Darwinism.

Each of these three contributed to the polarization of the debate. The theological argument eventually and unavoidably centered on the challenge to Scripture, therefore Darwinism was increasingly considered a threat by some because it affected the credibility of the divine revelation; and so the debate became polarized and very heated around scriptural authority. The critical issue is that if God is wrong about the story of man's origins, then what else did He get wrong?

1. Natural theology

Within natural theology, the evangelical readily accepts natural selection as an observed part of the created order. If it was only the arena of natural theology in which Darwinism was contested, the conflict might have been minimal, largely because science and theology use similar methods.

Theology was once known as the "queen of sciences." The natural meeting-ground for science and religion is natural theology.

Natural theology assumes a benevolent God and an ordered universe, where the presence of evil is the result of the fall of man; it assumes that the world is naturally degenerating and cannot be rescued by anything less than divine intervention. Natural theology uses the inductive empirical method: observe the phenomena and then come up with a theory to explain them.

Darwinism assumes a universe of random, chance occurrences and ever-increasing complexity of development in the natural world. No divine intervention is necessary. Darwinism is based on rationalism and the hypothetical method: develop the theory and then seek evidence to support it.

Because of these differences, it was very difficult for evangelicals to come to grips with Darwinism using the normal approaches of natural philosophy. Despite the fact that many scientists agreed with the criticisms of Sedgwick, and despite all the other scientific objections to Darwinism based on the inductive approach, it was not easy to challenge something that was based on the hypothetical method. Additionally it was not in the interests of the supporters of Darwinism to focus on the deficits of the theory, but rather to pursue the Enlightenment rationalist aims of attacking organized religion by whatever means possible. Here was an apparent scientific basis for objecting to religion, and the Christian religion in particular.

Had the evangelicals of the day maintained Darwin's theories as another form of natural theology, confined to the natural sphere, and as another attempt of man reasoning from himself and nature to the divine, the debate might have allowed the genuine processes of inductive scientific method to deal with Darwinism. As such, Darwinism could be considered as a perfectly legitimate form of intellectual effort, without challenging the nature of faith or the integrity of Scripture. However, it is not easy to see how this could have been achieved. Sadly, and inevitably, the debate moved into the realm of scriptural authority. Since then, science and Darwinism have become ascendant and Scripture relegated to myth. The perception of science in opposition to religion was reinforced and compounded by people such as Huxley and Lyell. The famous debate between Sir Thomas Huxley, president of the Royal Society, and Bishop Samuel Wilberforce is frequently mentioned, in order to claim a decisive victory for the scientific camp. The true outcome of that debate is not so clear-cut as the supporters of Darwinism claim; both parties thought they had won the argument.

However, through this ongoing conflict of irreconcilable opponents, science was deliberately promoted as the impartial champion of reason against the dogmatic and restrictive principles of religion.

2. The conflict between science and religion

Any discussion regarding the relationship of religion and science is now thoroughly tainted with the "conflict metaphor." This is a term which had its genesis in the period just prior to the First World War, from the writings of two authors, A.D. White and J.W. Draper. In 1896 in New York, White published his work, *A History of the Warfare of Science with Theology*. In summary, White's thesis is that religion is wedded to dogma and obedience and therefore it is wholly incompatible with the empirical skepticism that science demands.[100] In 1910 John William Draper, a recently retired professor of physiology at the University of New York, published his work, *A History of the Conflict between Science and Religion*. Draper asserted that religion and science were diametrically opposed, and that religion had suffocated science.[101]

For White and Draper it was impossible for science and religion to coexist, therefore religion should give way to science. They spoke in terms of the conflict of different armies and entrenched camps, with massed legions of followers. This "conflict metaphor" attracted many supporters who continued and developed this thesis into the twentieth century. For example, Arthur Smethurst, in his work, *Modern Science and Christian Belief*, maintains that most Christian theologians adopted an attitude of hostility towards the ideas of Darwinism. This is patently untrue and unhistorical, as the transactions of the Victoria Institute show. Smethurst went further and argued that church and laboratory have been separated throughout history.[102] This is an absurd claim, yet it demonstrates how the "conflict metaphor" has taken root in the history of science and religion.

There were others, however, who were convinced that science and religion could coexist and were complementary disciplines. This is demonstrated by some of the papers presented to the Victoria Institute from the middle of the nineteenth century onwards, and by contemporary scientists right through to the late twentieth century. For example, J.R. Moore published *The Post-Darwinian Controversies* in 1971; the entire first chapter is given over to demonstrating how the "conflict metaphor" has been greatly overblown. It was Moore himself who coined the term "conflict metaphor."[103] Further,

D.N. Livingstone, in 1984, in his book *Darwin's Forgotten Defenders*, says that the assertions of the conflict school are based on "half-baked history."[104]

There are many scholars who view science and religion as complementary and who do not support the conflict scenario, but rather work towards a more balanced and accurate presentation of the issues involved. Unfortunately, it is the conflict metaphor that holds the ring, where religion is seen as being in opposition to science, hindering progress and putting forward dogma instead of reason.

3. The growth of premillennialism

Firstly, we need to explain the term "premillennialism." It is a theological way of looking at Scripture, based on a particular interpretation of the book of Revelation, the last book of the Bible. The book of Revelation is concerned with "last things," or what will happen at the end of this age. It is to do with eschatology, or the study of the end times, where there is a period described of 1,000 years, known as the millennium. It is the nature of this millennium and its relationship to the return of Christ that has given rise to various interpretations. There are basically four ways of interpreting the book of Revelation:

Preterist: All the events of Revelation were fulfilled during the days of either Nero or Domitian, during the Roman Empire. This view was developed by the Jesuits and is still held by many in the Roman Catholic Church and by some Protestant denominations. The book is thus reduced to a curiosity, with no message for later generations.

Historical (postmillennialism): Jesus will return at the end of the millennium. The book of Revelation thus becomes a panorama of church history, from the beginning of the apostolic era to the consummation of the age. This position was espoused by Martin Luther, John Wycliffe and most of the Reformers, except the Anabaptists. The multiple interpretations of the metaphors and symbols employed in the book become very subjective in this view.

Idealist or polemic (amillennialism): There will be no literal millennial reign of Christ on earth. The book of Revelation is not to be taken literally as a description of actual events, whether past or future. This text is only a symbol or metaphor of the great struggle between good and evil, written to encourage believers who were experiencing great persecution at the time. This idea came from the Alexandrian school of philosophy and theology founded by Origen. It is held by very many liberal and some conservative theologians.

Futuristic (premillennialism): Christ will return at the beginning of the millennium and will reign over the earth throughout it. Beginning with chapter 4, the events described in the book of Revelation belong to the future and constitute a prophecy of God's program for the consummation of the age. This view grew in popularity throughout the nineteenth century, and is now held by many evangelicals around the world. The futuristic approach is held to be much more in harmony and consistent with the message of the entire Bible. Far fewer problems are encountered with the metaphors and symbols employed. This no doubt explains its growing number of adherents. The premillennialist view requires a more literal interpretation of the entire Bible, from Genesis to Revelation.

As the nineteenth century progressed, the popularity of premillennialism grew. When Darwin's theory was first published, the prevailing view among Protestant evangelicals was either amillennialism or postmillennialism, depending upon which denomination was in view. These positions are less literal and more liberal in their approach to Scripture. So the initial reaction of evangelicals was at first fairly accommodating. Most of the objections were scientific ones leveled at a brand-new theory, which would naturally attract such criticism from leading intellectuals within the scientific community. Theological criticisms, although always a factor, grew with the increasing popularity of dispensationalism among evangelicals. This method of interpreting Scripture held to an essentially premillennial view. This meant a less symbolic and more literal understanding, especially of Genesis and Revelation. So many evangelicals became more literal in their view of Scripture, thus sharpening the debate with Darwinism and playing into the hands of those who wished to emphasize the "conflict metaphor."

It must not be assumed that all evangelicals opposed Darwinism; as the nineteenth century progressed, the rationalist approach gained ascendancy. It was very difficult to refute scientists of reputation by using scriptural arguments, when the very reliability of Scripture had been damaged by higher criticism and neology. Consequently, those evangelicals who were of a more liberal theological denomination, and who continued to engage with rationalism and Darwinism, more readily compromised over the nature of Scripture. One of the ideas put forward was "theistic evolution," where God was supposed to have used evolution as his method of creation, and the six "days" of creation were seen as the geological ages required by uniformitarianism and evolution. The gap theory; the day-age theory; the revelatory day theory; the framework hypothesis – all these are an attempt to harmonize Scripture with naturalistic science. Their intention was honorable, but the consequences were fatal for scriptural authority.

Science and Scripture

As the debate about Darwinism moved into the realm of revelation, rather than remain in natural theology, the evangelical position on scriptural authority was gradually moved into compromise. This was a gradual process, with ground slowly given up over the years. Not everyone agreed with this change and many maintained the inerrancy of Scripture, especially those who embraced premillennialism. They were slowly marginalized and eventually regarded as irrelevant. The resulting consequence has been the gradual giving up of natural theology as part of the practice of orthodox faith. Thus the intellectual effort of the use of reason, hand in hand with both Divine Scripture and the person of Christ, fell into disuse.

More accurately it has fallen into misuse, where Scripture is harmonized with the natural, the natural having become authoritative. Many people who would call themselves both Christian and evangelical, no longer have a trusting faith in the authority of Scripture; their faith is full of doubts about the reliability of Scripture, because "it conflicts with science." Evangelicals were once in the forefront of scientific endeavor of every kind, yet they seem to have disengaged with science and have confined themselves to a mere "spiritual" interpretation of the Christian faith, where the historical and factual content of Scripture is given up to naturalistic challenges, not only in the biological sciences, but also in the areas of archaeology, geology, and so on. Science has seemingly eaten up Scripture, and nature has eaten up the grace of God.

Many theistic evolutionists, most especially academic clergy, trying to maintain their credibility in both camps, attempted to discount the atheism of Darwinism as an extreme form – but it turned out to be impossible to contain. Atheism is now almost universally espoused by the leaders of evolutionary science.

Higher Criticism

As well as attempting to come to terms with the march of scientific naturalism and evolution, the Church at large, evangelicals included, was simultaneously assaulted by a new theological assault, in the form of Wellhausen's higher criticism. Bishop Colenso and others made their contribution, and the earliest books of the Bible were rendered unreliable. If Moses didn't write the Pentateuch, then it was not history as written down by contemporary eyewitnesses; it loses both its status as a historical document and its claim to be the directly inspired Word of God.

Modern evangelical belief is thus reduced to a faith that the Bible contains "spiritual truth" rather than being factually and historically accurate. Many modern evangelical authorities insist that faith is accepting a personal revelation and experience of the Messiah, not insisting on the rigor of Scripture. Yet the Messiah Himself is defined by Scripture, not only spiritually, but factually and historically. A personal revelation without the context of Scripture can only be subjective and relative. There is thus no factual objectivity to be had from this approach. We will come back to this point in Part III, where we will look at the effects of liberal theology.

Conclusion

By allowing the scientific debate about the natural order of things into the realm of Scripture, Scripture has been virtually destroyed as the trustworthy basis for faith. People have always been full of genuine doubt, but today's Christians are without an authoritative basis to examine their faith in the face of that doubt – Scripture is no longer trusted. So, from the middle of the twentieth century onwards, the next step in the process has been taking place: the gradual destruction of the person and work of Christ. Without Scripture, Christ has no meaning. Throw away Scripture and we automatically throw away Christ. It just takes time for the realization to sink in.

By giving up the ground of natural theology, evangelicalism as a movement has ironically and unwittingly brought about the loss of the authority of Scripture. Many people today view Scripture as untrue, unreliable and ultimately mythical. Certainly they would reject the inspired and error-free attributes of Scripture. Many leaders of church denominations today accept the existence of so-called "errors" and merely attempt to support the "spiritual truths" of the faith. Yet church attendance is diminishing catastrophically and society is moving further and further away from God.

This means that fewer and fewer people have the opportunity for salvation.

The Sword of Truth has been blunted.

PART III

LIBERAL THEOLOGY

Beware lest anyone cheat you through philosophy and empty deceit,
according to the tradition of men, according to the basic principles of the world, and
not according to Christ. For in Him dwells all the fullness of the Godhead bodily;
and you are complete in Him, who is the head of all principality and power.
(Colossians 2:8–10)

CHAPTER 11

THE AUTONOMOUS INTELLECT

When men cease to believe in God, they do not believe in nothing; they believe in anything.

G.K. Chesterton

Pilate therefore said to Him, "Are You a king then?" Jesus answered, "You say rightly that I am a king. For this cause I was born, and for this cause I have come into the world, that I should bear witness to the truth. Everyone who is of the truth hears My voice. Pilate said to Him, "What is truth?"

(John 18:37–38)

In the modern worldview, theism, as a way of defining God, is dead. The higher critics of the Bible have done their work well and have effectively undermined the authority of Scriptures to the point that the existence of God Himself is doubted. As a consequence, almost (but not quite!) all contemporary theological discussion can be considered as meaningless. Many theologians and denominations have come to the point where their traditional understanding of God and His attributes has been diminished to the point of uselessness. Obviously, taken to its logical fulfillment, this would mean the Church has been diminished to the point of uselessness. We see the ever-decreasing attendance at church and the growing unbelief of the mass of the people as the fruit of this process. Consequently, everyone needs a new paradigm, a new point of departure. By this logic a new way to speak of God must be found, before the Church vanishes entirely. There is a great deal of activity in this area, with hundreds of councils and conferences, thousands of books and pamphlets, all desperately seeking to redefine Christ and truth and faith. The Emerging Church is a clear expression of this. There is a major problem, however. How can we find a new way to speak of the God who defines Himself as the same – yesterday, today and forever? The roots of this problem have been laid very deep over a very long period of time.

In search of an answer we must begin with the development of philosophy and theology since the time of Aquinas (1225–74). Aquinas had a view of the fall which put forward the idea, widely accepted, that the intellect remained in an unfallen state. It is this view of the intellect that causes all the subsequent problems. Aquinas had created a part of life that was independent of God, not fallen, and so not bound by Holy Scripture. The intellect was now free to pursue natural theology, or theology outside of the boundaries of the fall. Aquinas hoped for a complementary and related field of human thought. He believed that there was common ground between Holy Scriptures and natural philosophy. History has proven him wrong, but the important point is that Aquinas established an area of autonomy free of God's Holy Writ – the autonomous intellect.

Natural philosophy and the general trend of human thought have always attempted to achieve unity of knowledge. This unity can be expressed as one great interlocking scheme of thought or set of principles, which would explain the whole operation of nature. Every action, every consequence, everything that existed could be described by this great unity of knowledge, if only human beings could work it out. Prior to Aquinas, the search for unity was based upon God and Scripture. God was the point of unity from which all else flowed. Everything owed its existence to God, the Supreme Cause and the Origin of all knowledge. After Aquinas, natural philosophy was free to pursue other avenues. This was the beginning of humanism, where a unity of knowledge was sought based on man rather than God. The assumption that the intellect was independent of Scripture soon placed the autonomous intellect above Scripture and the things of God.

This new freedom expressed itself in art and literature and gradually developed into a man-centered view of the universe and creation, culminating in the Renaissance. This great flowering of philosophy, art, music and science was a great departure from what had gone before; hence we have the term *Renaissance* or "new birth." This was the dawn of a new kind of knowledge, where everyone thought that it would be possible to achieve the unity of knowledge based on the humanist principles of objectivity and progress. This gave birth to the rationalism and empiricism of modern science.

Unfortunately for the autonomous intellect, everyone who has tried to find a universal meaning as an alternative to God has failed. If we look at the progression of art and literature from the Grand Masters of the Renaissance to the present day, we will find an increasing desperation and lack of rationality. We will see an increasing descent into irrationality, meaninglessness and despair. Whereas a work of art was once intended to convey some objective truth to the observer, modern art demands that the observer inject his own meaning into what he sees. It becomes an interactive, experiential exchange of ideas between the artist and the observer; each observer forms his own subjective opinions. It is no longer the transfer of objective, contentful meaning from one person to others. The autonomous intellect has moved mankind further and further away from God as the generations have passed, until there is little objective meaning available to the artist.

The autonomous intellect also affected the progress of philosophy, or how we look at the world around us. Following the Renaissance, Immanuel Kant (1724–1804) and Jean-Jacques Rousseau (1712–78) took philosophy much further than before. Until this time the great debate had been about the relationship between heavenly things and earthly things, that is, between God and man, or grace and nature. The old understanding was that the grace of God redeemed mankind from his fallen nature. Thus the debate centered on the relationship between grace and nature. In a humanist world there is no heaven and no grace. Confined to the natural world the debate inevitably focused on the relationship between nature and man's freedom of action; so Kant and Rousseau replaced the grace of heaven with the concept of "freedom."

This came about because nature had become increasingly deterministic. Newton's mechanics determined the operation of the universe. Where was free will? Kant was trying to find a relationship between an increasingly deterministic natural world and the longing for human freedom. His system could not do it. If divine grace is denied, freedom is also denied. Rousseau attempted to take it further, he and his followers discarding the conventional rules of civilized behavior in an attempt to realize absolute freedom. They were the original dropouts. Latter-day dropouts also see the desperately barren existence of modern life and react in the same way. What the modern dropout lacks is an understanding of why life has become so meaningless. Since we no longer educate our young in the ways of God, they have no standard against which to measure modern thought and society. Unlike Rousseau, their rejection of the modern worldview is instinctive rather than reasoned. Unfortunately, absolute freedom is an impossible and irrational objective. The poet John Donne captured this perfectly when he wrote, "No man is an island, entire of itself . . ."

The effects of natural science were being felt, and although people did not yet fully understand that they were about to be reduced to the level of biological machines, they knew their freedom was being eroded. This erosion of freedom was not caused by science itself, but by the effects of Aquinas's autonomous intellect, working from a mistaken idea about the role of science. The early scientists truly believed in the uniformity of natural laws, based on their belief in a Creator who was consistent and reasonable. What they did not believe in was the uniformity of natural laws *in a closed system*. These four words make all the difference. Francis Schaeffer puts it very well:

> That little phrase makes all the difference in the world. It makes the difference between natural science and a science that is rooted in naturalistic philosophy. It makes all the difference between what I would call modern science and what I would call modern modern science. It is important to notice that this is not a failing of science as science, but rather that the uniformity of natural causes in a closed system has become the dominant philosophy among scientists.[105]

In a closed system there can be no outside interference, no miracles, no God. All you have is cause and effect in a closed mechanical system, which makes machines of human beings and removes all moral force from the universe. By placing science in a man-centered or humanist philosophy, the universe becomes a closed system. God, if He exists, cannot interfere. Mankind is therefore bound by the mechanical laws of the universe, without the ability to affect things, since he is no longer considered to be made in the image of God. Belief in a godless universe creates the need to replace the grace of God with something that would substitute for the lost attributes of divine grace. When real freedom has been lost, a substitute is needed.

Rousseau and others advocated an absolute freedom, a freedom without restraints, an autonomous freedom. This kind of freedom cannot exist in a rational world. It is only a desperate attempt to retain the hope that an individual might find freedom in a universe that has been broken down into a series of mechanical causes and effects. The hope of unity of knowledge has been given up. The autonomous intellect has left no real basis for unity of knowledge. If we look forward to today, we see modern scientists still attempting to achieve the classical ideal of unity of knowledge, even though the basis for such unity has been destroyed. They persist in this useless endeavor because they have no alternative except despair.

Under the philosophy of the closed system, the materialist approach cannot remain within astronomy or physics; it overtakes everything, even life processes and the origin of life itself. Modern scientists do not merely attempt to unify the natural universe of astronomy and physics, but insist on developing a supposed unity of all disciplines: astronomy, biology, mathematics, physics, chemistry, psychology, sociology, anthropology, linguistics and so on . . . Modern science cannot permit any divisions; every discipline must come under the uniformity of natural laws in a closed system, but to do this, freedom, or free will, must be ruled out. The uniformity of natural laws in a closed system thus became (and remains) the dominant philosophy of most scientists within most disciplines. Science as science is not responsible for this. It is the consequence of the belief system which scientists bring to their science, already formed. The final result of the progression of the autonomous intellect is that freedom and free will cannot now exist. We are, at last, in a completely deterministic universe, where grace is dead and freedom is impossible.

What has happened is that the human intellect, unleashed by Thomas Aquinas, has enabled the earthly things of man and nature to destroy the heavenly things of God and grace. Nothing now exists except earthly things; therefore it is meaningless to talk about God in heaven. Jesus is irrelevant. God is dead.

If we return to the philosophers for a moment, we shall get a better idea of how this process has shaped the modern world. After Kant and Rousseau came Georg Wilhelm Friedrich Hegel (1770–1831), who totally transformed the basis upon which we think. Before Aquinas, Western (i.e. Christian) philosophy was based on a God-centered, Biblical view of the world. The Bible is a book full of propositions. It has real content on the ground that in God we have unity of knowledge. The Bible is based on what the philosophers refer to as thesis and antithesis. It follows classical logic in which something cannot be itself and something else at the same time and in the same relationship. For example, I am father to my son in one relationship; I am also the son of my father in another relationship. I cannot be both father and son in the same relationship; this would break the law of non-contradiction. Neither can I be something between father and son – I am either one or the other; I can be both a father and a son at the same time, but in different relationships.

From the Bible we understand that telling the truth is good and telling lies is bad. Refraining from murder is good; committing murder is bad. In all this we see the statement followed by its opposite, or thesis and antithesis, from which we can draw moral conclusions about how to behave. Thesis and antithesis are always in tension and opposed to each other. All philosophies, from time immemorial, not just the Bible, have used thesis–antithesis as their basic method. It can be shown that this is the only way in which it is possible to think. It is how we are able to know and understand anything at all.

By the time of Hegel, all the efforts of natural philosophy to find the unity of knowledge based on the autonomous intellect had failed. It appeared impossible to find an all-encompassing philosophy on a man-centered or humanist basis while still retaining the principles of rationality and the hope for unity of knowledge. So Hegel came up with a world-shaking concept. Since the old way of thinking could not deliver what the natural philosophers wanted, that is, a valid explanation of the universe without God, he proposed that we should think about what we know and how we can know it, in a completely different way than had ever been done before. This was a complete break with traditional philosophical methods, but Hegel saw no other alternative.

Hegel said that we should think in a different way about thesis–antithesis, where the truth is somewhere between the two opposites, with the result being synthesis. The resulting synthesis becomes the next thesis, which in turn has its antithesis, and so we arrive at the second synthesis. By the same method we achieve the third synthesis, then the fourth, and so on. When you think about it, this is a frightening proposal. No longer can any statement and its opposite be considered objectively, that is, as independent axioms. Following the wide acceptance of Hegel's new approach, known as "Hegelian synthesis," the one relates to the other as a father to a mother in giving birth to a child. But consider, what is the synthesis between truth and falsehood: half-truths or half-lies? Are these synthetic constructs new truths? Are they fixed or do they vary with circumstances? Another example is the synthesis between stealing and not stealing – is it partial stealing, or stealing at some times and not others; or is it that stealing is not stealing under certain circumstances? Take the synthesis between murdering and not murdering; when is murder not murder but synthesized into something else? I do not mean here the difference between lawful killing and unlawful killing; nor do I mean, "When does lawful killing become unlawful?" I mean: what is the resulting synthesis when a clear case of murder is contrasted to its opposite – the absence of murder? This goes back to the root of the problem that something cannot be itself and its opposite at the same time and in the same relationship. What is the synthesis in this case – euthanasia, eugenics, abortion? These are obscure labels for the taking of human life, which serve to cover the moral bankruptcy of our age. Gray is the new black and white; and the shade of gray is in the eye of the beholder, according to his inclinations.

Hegel changed everything. His ideas have done a great deal of damage to the way we think. Hegelian synthesis has made it impossible for modern man to think in absolute terms, in black and white, or good and evil. Everything from now on is synthesized into a relative frame with regard to what went before. Nothing is fixed. The process never ends, because every synthesis becomes the next thesis. Every thought is now very slippery when it comes to defining what we really mean. Sadly, to define meaning has become an almost impossible task.

Ludwig Joseph Johann Wittgenstein (1889–1951) spent a rather unhappy life, plagued by depression. He lived for long periods as a recluse. His main work was to do with words and language and "word games." According to Wittgenstein a word did not have a meaning; rather it had a use. An illustration that he gives is an analogy between words and pieces in a chess game. The meaning of a chess piece is not determined by its physical appearance; rather, it is determined by the rules of chess. Similarly the meaning of a word is given by the way it is used, governed by certain rules. No two people have the same rules; therefore no two people, or groups of people, place the same meaning into any given word or use it in the same way. Hegel had removed the relationship between a word and its object. Wittgenstein was struggling with Hegel's legacy: there is now no external, objective meaning in language: everything is now relative and subjective.

Today, a large part of modern work in philosophy is no longer concerned with the big questions of meaning and existence; it consists mostly of trying to define what words really mean. We can no longer be certain that we know anything at all. The very ground upon which we stood has been cut away. The autonomous intellect has destroyed itself. Reason is dead.

After Hegel came Søren Aabye Kierkegaard (1813–55), from whom we get modern existentialism. Kierkegaard's existentialism was Christian in nature. Kierkegaard proposed that Christian doctrine embodies absurd, unnatural paradoxes which are offensive to reason. The crucial paradox is the assertion that the eternal, infinite, transcendent God became incarnated as a temporal, finite human being. Jesus was both God and man simultaneously. Kierkegaard concluded that there are two mutually exclusive attitudes we can take to this paradox: we can have faith, or we can take offense. What we cannot do is reason our way to faith. If we choose faith we must suspend our reason in order to believe in something higher than reason. In fact we must believe by virtue of the absurd. It was, he said, a "leap *to* faith." Kierkegaard never used the phrase "leap *of* faith." He wanted to emphasize that human beings are absolutely reliant on God's grace for salvation and not themselves. Modernist twentieth-century existentialists talk about a "leap of faith" in the context of rationalism and humanism, which is a completely different thing.

Kierkegaard was a Lutheran and in conflict with the liberal theological Church of the time. He eventually came to the position that faith itself is a gift from God; when someone realizes this and that anything he himself might contribute is useless, he is able to take the leap to faith, and into the arms of a loving God. In a Lutheran context, the leap to faith is a clear concept. Some theologians, for example C.S. Lewis, argue that Christianity does not require a "leap of faith" in the modern sense. Lewis maintained that Christianity can be logically deduced based on an argument regarding the source of human reason. However, others would say that religion requires some kind of a "leap of faith."

Martin Heidegger (1889–1971) was greatly influenced by the writings of Kierkegaard, although he never explicitly acknowledged this. Heidegger based his philosophy upon the "hermeneutics of existence," that is, the science of existence.

Kierkegaard accepted that the concept of "being" could define itself. Heidegger did not. Heidegger insisted that a concept must be defined without using itself as reference. Martin Heidegger was very prolific, producing seventy volumes of dense, closely reasoned argument. The disorganized nature of Heidegger's thought, and his obscure writing, makes it difficult to understand why he became so influential. Philosophers, as a class, have divided opinions. His devotees regard him as an inspiring, original thinker. Most find his work difficult to understand and ambiguous. One of his students was Jean-Paul Sartre (1905–80) who, with Albert Camus (1913–60) was one of the most influential twentieth-century existentialists. Through these philosophers, Kierkegaard's Christian concept of the absurd was developed into a humanist notion of the absurd, based on the idea that there is no meaning to be found in the world beyond the meaning we assign to it. This meaninglessness also includes the random unfairness of the world. What happens simply happens, equally to a "good" person or to a "bad" person. It is truly absurd.

The "Theater of the Absurd" is a name for particular plays written between the 1940s and 1960s, mainly in Europe, as well as for the style of existential theater which has evolved from them. The "Theater of the Absurd" demonstrates the logical conclusion that in a godless universe, human existence has no meaning or purpose. This is a huge change from Kierkegaard.

Through the development of the ideas of these existential philosophers, operating in a post-Darwinian worldview, the argument now becomes that we have only the rational and the mechanical (causes and effects) which offer any meaning in a deterministic universe. Yet we cannot trust our own powers of reason or the propositional content of the Bible – Hegelian synthesis has done away with all that. Therefore Biblical truth becomes irrational and cannot hold any meaning. Since there can be absolutely no connection or link between the rational and the irrational, there can now be no rational grounds for faith, or content, or meaning. However, it is impossible to live without content and meaning, so we must validate our existence by making a leap of faith. Existentialism now becomes validating our moment-by-moment existence by assuming a meaning to what we do. This is the basis for the modern existential leap. The assumption of meaning, or the leap of faith, has no rational basis but it is the only way to escape a mechanical explanation and the absurdity of earthly life. It is also a leap of great despair, without hope, or justification. The dismaying side to this leap of faith is that it requires the suspension of all critical thinking. It requires a different kind of faith than that needed in former times to believe in the Bible. It is an absolutely blind faith.

All hope, therefore, becomes non-rational, which can only demand an irrational, or existential, leap of faith. This leap is unique and internal to every individual. This is another terribly important consequence of the autonomous intellect: every individual is now isolated. On this basis proper human relationships become very difficult. All rational contact with the external, objective, ordered universe has been lost. All is now internal, subjective and irrational – we might even say "illusory." By the processes of humanist philosophy, Western thought has accomplished a similar result to the ancient Eastern mystery religions. The autonomous intellect has taken away our grasp of reality, where all is illusion.

We come now to Friedrich Nietzsche (1844–1900) who is recognized as one of the greatest existentialist philosophers. His work is very difficult to read, where almost every sentence is followed by an apparent contradiction. Like Heidegger, Nietzsche has had a mixed reception. He was born in Leipzig, the son of a Lutheran clergyman, and studied at the universities of Bonn and Leipzig. He was appointed to the chair of classical philology at Basle in 1868, at the age of twenty-four. He retired due to ill health in 1879. Between 1880 and 1889 he lived as a virtual recluse. All his work was published between 1872 and 1889, at which point he became insane, and was in a condition of mental and physical paralysis until he died in 1900. Nietzsche was the ultimate subjectivist, denying all external reality, where there are no facts, only interpretations of facts. He was the end product of the autonomous intellect – a nihilist. In his book ominously entitled *Beyond Good and Evil: Prelude to a Philosophy of the Future*, we read: "There are no moral phenomena at all, only a moral interpretation of phenomena."[106]

Theologians were swept along by this same process. The development of liberal theology placed the concept of God into the realm of the non-rational, with no meaningful content to the word "God." According to Schaeffer, this is the only possible conclusion of a theology within a closed system. This denied the very idea of a personal God, but allowed the use of the word "God." At the same time, the theories of the higher critics undermined the authority of the Bible (they proposed that the Bible had errors in the areas of history and reported facts), but the existential leap *of* faith (not Kierkegaard's leap *to* faith) allowed them to believe in it anyway.

Rudolf Bultmann (1886–1976), was an eminent German existentialist, influenced extensively by the works of the philosopher Martin Heidegger. Bultmann adapted existentialism to apply to the New Testament. He is known for what he and his advocates referred to as the "demythologizing" of the New Testament, where the methods of higher criticism placed rationalism over revealed truth in Scripture. Bultmann and his followers reinterpreted the Gospels as metaphor, wherever rationalism could not accept the supernatural. He and his followers, in effect, stripped the Gospels of miracles as historical, supernatural actions of God, interpreting them instead as metaphors applicable to modern existence.

Bultmann offered the German Church an existential Christianity, devoid of those hard-to-believe miracles, and divorced from historical reality, which offered a person the ability to stay churched without believing in the historical Jesus and His miraculous ministry. The effect on the German Church was devastating and it was soon having the same effect outside Germany. Spiritual truth was separated from historical truth in the Scriptures. There could be no way of reasoning about it and no point of contact, because all spiritual truth was now in the realm of the non-rational. Whatever the starting point, any faith becomes a non-verifiable leap, without justification of any kind.

Since the word "God" no longer has any content or meaning, the incarnation becomes meaningless. What we have therefore is another way of looking at God and Jesus that denies the objective reality of their existence and their ability to affect things here on earth. We have the closed system in operation again. How can God come into the universe in any form, since it is a closed system? The miracle of the incarnation is denied. Any miracle is denied. How then can we discuss it if the miracle is denied? We cannot. For all practical purposes God is dead.

The autonomous intellect has reduced mankind to the absurdity of not being able to talk about God and the incarnation in meaningful terms. It has produced an unbridgeable gulf between the eternal transcendent God and finite created humanity. Modern liberal theologians cannot even begin to discuss this problem. They have disqualified themselves by undermining and effectively throwing away the Bible, the original starting point of all their efforts. This has destroyed the intellectual credibility of Christianity.

Religious existentialism thus copied the secular model by requiring an existential, non-rational leap of faith in order to continue believing in the Bible. We can now see how modern theologians can blithely accept the alleged errors and contradictions in the Bible and at the same time insist that it makes no difference. The "God-is-dead" school of theology still uses the word "Jesus," but, of course, it is meaningless. It is just another irrational word, without definable content. It can mean whatever the user wants it to mean. The person and work of Christ have been deconstructed into meaninglessness. The objective, propositional content of the Bible has been removed from the word "Jesus" and the blind existential leap substituted. Not only is it blind, but it is also uniquely personal and individual – a non-transferable personal universe. It is a non-refundable one-way ticket to nowhere. All intellectual capital has been absorbed, leaving nothing behind. Thus we arrive at empty secularism.

The question now arises, since the spiritual truth of the Bible has been separated from rationality and since we cannot discuss the Bible's content where it relates to real history, real people and the universe, why should we accept the non-rational spiritual message, with its meaningless words and irrational terms? The answer is, on this basis, we shouldn't. The autonomous intellect has destroyed it. Faith is dead.

I have heard many modern evangelical people making statements such as: "A meeting with Jesus is what counts, not arguing about the truth of the Bible." When something like this is heard, let the hearer beware. The speakers have substituted irrational existentialism for Biblical faith and are no longer Christian, whether they know it or not. They continue to use "Jesus" words and Christian terminology, and honestly believe they are closer to the "true" spirituality of Jesus than the traditional form of Christianity. What they do not understand is that a unique, subjective, experiential encounter with Christ is meaningless without the objective, external context provided by God's revelation in Holy Scriptures. Actually, it is worse than meaningless: it is downright dangerous. Without the framework of the unchanging Word of God, self-deception is almost inevitable, before spiritual deception is even considered. Francis Schaeffer wrote:

> I have come to the point where, when I hear the word *Jesus* –
> which means so much to me because of the Person of the historic
> Jesus and His work – I listen carefully because I have with sorrow
> become more afraid of the word *Jesus* than almost any other word
> in the modern world. The word is used as a contentless banner,
> and our generation is invited to follow it. But there is no rational,
> Scriptural content by which to test it, and thus the word is being
> used to teach the very opposite things from those which Jesus
> taught . . .

We have come then to this fearsome place where the word *Jesus* has become the enemy of the Person Jesus, and the enemy of what Jesus taught. We must fear this contentless banner of the word *Jesus* not because we do not love Jesus, but because we do love Him. We must fight this contentless banner, with its deep motivations, rooted in the memories of the race, which is being used for the purpose of sociological form and control. We must teach our spiritual children to do the same.[107]

We do not need a new way to speak of God; we need simply to understand the modern condition and how we have arrived at it. We must understand both the problem and the modern solution of the existential leap, and respond with the full gospel of Christianity from the inerrant, inspired Word of God. Otherwise we will be imprisoned in the world of Nietzsche, physically and mentally paralyzed.

CHAPTER 12

MIRACLES

Jesus answered and said to them, "Go and tell John the things which you hear and see: The blind see and the lame walk; the lepers are cleansed and the deaf hear; the dead are raised up and the poor have the gospel preached to them. And blessed is he who is not offended because of Me."

(Matthew 11:4–6)

I n a closed universe with a materialist worldview we have now come to the point where the miracle stories of the New Testament can no longer be interpreted as supernatural events performed by an incarnate Deity. As we have concluded from the previous chapter, modern liberal theology cannot resist this conclusion. All it can do is bow to the inevitable and try to find naturalistic explanations of the miracles recorded in Scripture. For example, I have heard Anglican sermons which stated that the miracle of the feeding of the 5,000[108] was only possible because everyone had brought their packed lunches with them; another sermon was that the miracle of Jesus walking on water[109] can be explained by the fact that He was walking in the shallows and it only appeared that He was walking on water. In both cases a careful reading of the relevant scriptures shows that such naturalistic interpretations are not possible: the apostles had already pointed out to Jesus that the region in which the people were gathering had no food or water and the people were already suffering; the boat is described as in the middle of the Sea of Galilee, which is very deep. These events are either miraculous or complete fabrications.

We should remember that Newton himself had no trouble with the miraculous, since he was not a Darwinian evolutionist and did not believe in the uniformity of natural laws in a closed system. Determinism came later.

We should also remember that we live in a world which has outstripped Newton, and perhaps it would be good at this point to remind ourselves of the quantum theory. It brings the idea of indeterminacy to the scientific view of the natural world, where miracles are possible without "breaking the rules." The natural is not everything: supernatural events are possible from outside the universe as long as we are not shackled by the determinist mindset of modern science. There seems to be an emotional bias against miracles, rather than a reasoned conclusion.

Let us look at four of the miracles that cause the most trouble – the virgin birth, the resurrection, the ascension, and the miracle of prayer. Yes, prayer is a miracle!

The Virgin Birth
The virgin birth, understood as purely natural biology, makes Christ's divinity, as traditionally understood, impossible. It also assumes that the people involved were rather simple-minded with no understanding of their own biological processes.

Joseph, Mary's husband, being an agrarian peasant from a small village, knew full well the biology of making babies. He knew that women do not get pregnant unless they have had sexual intercourse with a man. Also, in his society and as a Jew, it was the greatest of social stigmas to marry a girl already pregnant by another man. So he decided to put her away and have nothing more to do with her. This is the Biblical account. It has all the hallmarks of truth. People still separate today for the same reason; everyone understands the situation.

The modern account, having accepted the authority of the scientific community about the uniformity of natural causes within a closed system, would say that God could not intervene from outside the system, nor could a female become pregnant without sexual intercourse. This view holds Mary as wanton, or (at best) headstrong, or perhaps taken advantage of, or raped. Whatever the actual means, the Messiah becomes the illegitimate child of an unknown man, from a woman of doubtful morals or the victim of a rape. The outworking of the autonomous intellect, using twenty-first-century thought forms, which exclude any possibility of a miracle from outside the system, reduces the incarnation to the level of sleazy sex, where Jesus is the doubtful offspring of a doubtful union. This is one of the driving forces behind many of the recent books and films about Jesus. They reduce the Messiah to just such an individual, with all the problems of a child of a dysfunctional family, just like many of us. The producers of such material, their minds boxed into the worldview of the closed system, cannot accept the concept of Immanuel, or "God-with-us." Thus they reduce the supernatural to the natural, maintaining the closed system at any cost.

Unfortunately for this point of view, the closed and intimate rural society of the time of Joseph and Mary would know all the details of any scandal touching upon any of its members. Yet all the internal evidence of the Gospels is that Mary was a paragon of virtue. Are we to suppose that all the Gospel writers were liars? Are we to suppose that they all concocted the same story, without contradicting each other in even the tiniest detail, and then endured untold persecution, without anyone breaking ranks and telling the awful truth? Are we to suppose that they were all so naive that they did not know the basic facts of biology?

The whole episode is by nature miraculous, which stands outside any naturalistic explanation. Since modern science has only left us with naturalistic explanations, it cannot be explained: angels and divine intervention are not allowed. Thus the modern consensus can only say that it cannot possibly be true. Sadly, much of the Church in general has also accepted this as the truth, despite the testimony of the Biblical authors. Therefore one can only conclude that a large part of the Church has lost faith in Scripture as a source of truth.

However, the traditional view of Christ's divinity is not based upon the well-known biological facts of making babies, but is based on the scriptural account of what next happened to Joseph. An angel appeared and told him that God had made Mary pregnant by the Holy Spirit. How are we to interpret this? Very simply, no life is created on earth without the direct will of God. Normally He operates through earthly fathers, the male seed impregnating the female ovum to produce another human being: a fully human person out of two human parents, given life by the will of God. Just once, however, He chose to dispense with the human father and thus the offspring was both human and divine. Additionally, the child was male, a very significant point in biological terms. If a woman has a child by spontaneous parthenogenesis (not totally unknown, but very rare) the child can only be female. The father determines sex. The fact that Jesus is male is part of the signature of God's intervention. Since God created the human race with the sexual method of reproduction, there is no great leap of faith required to understand that He could directly manipulate the process to fertilize the ovum.

In this case our Heavenly Father sent His Son to earth by means of the Virgin Mary. The term "virgin" is used deliberately. To state the blindingly obvious, it means she had not lain with a man. Her good character is extolled by all the accounts: "Hail! Mary, full of grace . . ." That is why she was chosen of all women in all of history for the privilege of being the mother of the Messiah, fully human, yet fully divine. All other possible women in history were not chosen for this honor. This should teach us something about Mary.

This is the traditional orthodox view of the divinity of Christ: impossible biologically, yet brought about from outside the system by divine intervention.

The Resurrection

The Bible says that the resurrection is an act of God. Jesus was raised into real physical life from real physical death. The modern view states that this cannot be a physical resurrection occurring inside human history. Partly, this is due to the materialism of the modern worldview and partly due to the state of modern theology, where many theologians have come to the view that God is dead, and that most theological "God talk" is meaningless, so there is no one capable of performing a resurrection and no act of God is possible.

In the bleak, modern existential world the philosophers have created for us, the higher critics have removed the real and historical content from the Bible, the scientists have provided the closed system of a deterministic universe, and the liberal theologians have placed all spiritual meaning into the realm of the irrational; therefore no discussion can now take place about the reality of the resurrection. It has become just another contentless symbol, without form and without meaning. This is, in fact, the fruit of the autonomous intellect and the irrational, existential leap. Biblical critics, natural scientists and liberal theologians have left us nothing else.

In opposition to these opinions, stands the testimony of the apostles and the thousands of disciples of Jesus who witnessed the risen Christ. Most of them died horrible and painful deaths without a single one of them recanting their personal testimony of the risen Christ. This was not some ephemeral myth of imagination, but the real, historical life, death and resurrection of their beloved teacher and Messiah. If the resurrection were not true in objective space–time history, why did every single one of these men and women die rather than break under torture? What inspired them to endure unto death? The only answer that fits the facts of history is that the literal, physical resurrection of Jesus Christ is the simple truth.

It cannot be stated too often that Christianity is rooted in space, time and history. As such, it is open to verification and reason. The universe does have objective reality and so does the truth of the Bible. There is judgment and there is redemption by the saving work of Jesus. There are opposites and their consequences are real. They have real effects on real people living real lives in a real universe. These effects can be observed.

In the Bible there is a great emphasis on the real, physical resurrection of the body. Jesus was very careful to show His disciples that His risen body could eat, could be touched, but yet had other special qualities. There is a very important reason for this demonstration of the reality of the body in the life to come. It is to do with personality. In Hindu religious teaching, achieving Nirvana has often been likened to a drop of water falling into and becoming one with the ocean. True, if a drop of water falls into the ocean it does become one with all the other drops, but the price is loss of identity. The drop cannot be distinguished anymore. Its distinctiveness has been lost. This distinctiveness, or personality, is all-important to Biblical doctrine. How can we worship God as a matter of our own free will and choice if we have no distinctiveness, no personality? How can we be distinct and personal without a separate body? Whether we dwell in this life or the next, we shall need a body. Jesus was very careful to demonstrate this reality. He was also at pains to demonstrate the differences between His resurrection and His ascension to heaven. His risen body "ascended to heaven," that is, it left this space–time continuum to dwell outside this universe with the Father and Creator. Jesus will return the same way that He left – bodily personified.

Jesus is the first fruits or the firstborn from the dead. He is the type and symbol of the redemption and resurrection of all of us. If the resurrection of Jesus is not a real, physical event then we are all doomed, for there will be no other life than this one – another consequence of the modern existentialist worldview.

There is a real and objective universe that stands in opposition to Greek philosophy, Hinduism, New Age religions, the tenets of modern science, existential philosophy and liberal theology. More than that, there is a real and objective universe with real bodies supporting real personalities that reflect the personality of the Creator. Admittedly it is all in a fallen state and separated from God, but there is a way back and it is not meaningless. There is cruelty and heartbreak but it all has meaning. In space–time history there is a beginning, a middle and an end. There is true hope.

The Ascension

The story of the ascension has come in for a lot of criticism since the advent of modern astronomy and the space age. Critics attempt to show that the assumption of a three-tiered universe (heaven – earth – hell) is a children's story drawn from the Bible and has no truth in objective reality. We have telescopes that can see to the uttermost ends of the universe and we have sent people into the heavens to see for themselves. The ascension has therefore no credibility in a post-Copernican space age.

Starting from the closed system of scientific naturalism, where the universe is all there is, we can perhaps understand this point of view. However, we do not need to start from this point of view. All of the early scientists had a point of view that included God and the universe as separate entities, related, but quite distinct. For example, Copernicus tried to describe the universe he observed in the language of mathematics. He changed the way we have ever since regarded it. He did this from the point of view of a Christian priest, searching the cosmos according to his faith that God had created something ordered and regular, open to observation and reason. Copernicus never for one moment imagined that the universe was more than one physical level. He knew that, according to Scriptures, God had created the physical universe from nothing.

The universe is not part of God but has a separate, objective existence. It is dependent upon God and sustained by God, but it is not part of Him. It is a complete and finished work. Since the fall it is no longer perfect as God made it, but damaged by the actions of mankind. This damage includes the effect of time upon the universe and the individuals in it. A significant property of this universe is that time always flows in one direction. Everyone is in the flow of time and everyone will die. God is not part of time. He is eternal, that is, outside of time. He pre-existed the universe and will continue to exist after the universe has ceased.

This means that there are at least two modes of existence. One is here on earth, in the physical universe; the other is outside this universe, not part of it but totally separate, with God in His mode of existence in heaven. "Heaven" is a totally inadequate way of describing a place where there is no time and no deterioration, which cannot be bounded by our finite thoughts, which is not describable by any of the terms we use to describe this earth and the universe in which we live.

According to the Bible, the redeemed and chosen ones of God will eventually live outside time with God. This universe will be destroyed and a new universe created, where a New Jerusalem will be the home of God, the angels and redeemed humanity. Those who reject God's salvation will exist in hell. Until that time we have three possibilities.

These possibilities are the result of the immortality of the soul. It is obvious that most people will die before the return of Christ and their bodies will either rot, or be burned, or be destroyed in some other way. The soul, however, does not die but continues. Where then is it to dwell until the return of Christ? We must go back into the Jewish roots of the faith. There is a place called *Sh'ol* in Hebrew, Anglicized to "Sheol." This word is translated "Hades" in Greek. Sheol, or Hades, is not part of the universe, any more than the heaven in which God dwells.

Sheol can simply mean the grave, or, as in this context, the place of torment. On the other hand, paradise, or "Abraham's bosom," is an allegory or symbol of heaven. We can conclude this from the description in Luke 20:19–31, telling us that the rich man and Lazarus both died. The rich man went to Sheol. Lazarus was comforted in paradise. We are told that there is a great divide between them and that it is impossible to cross from one to the other. In passing, we can also conclude from Christ's comments to the thief on the cross that He, too, went to heaven for the three days of His death, before His resurrection:

> *And Jesus said to him, "Truly, I say to you, today you will be*
> *with Me in Paradise."*
>
> (Luke 23:43)

Copernicus did not believe the universe to be a closed system. He knew that God could and did (and does) act into it and perform actions which, to the limited viewpoint of humanity, appear as miracles. The ascension is an act of God from outside the universe, acting into it, to remove the physical body of Christ from the earth and out of the universe, back to His original mode of existence. This does not imply a three-tiered universe. The apostles saw Jesus rise and then vanish behind a cloud. If that is what the removal of a physical body from this plane of existence looks like, so be it. The appearance of it does not even begin to do justice to the reality of the actual process.

The post-Copernican space age does not pretend to remove people from the universe. So far it has only managed to move a tiny handful of human beings from one place to another, over infinitesimal distances, bounded by the laws of this physical universe. These are the same laws that Copernicus helped to formulate from his observations. They are totally irrelevant to the miracle of the ascension.

The great tragedy is that many church leaders, including some conservative evangelicals, are infected with the modern worldview. They are guilty of simplistic teaching. We might teach our children about Baby Jesus, meek and mild, with angels singing. However, we must eventually teach them about the reality of the awesome power and sovereign majesty of our God, who will one day judge the living and the dead. It is the same with simple concepts of heaven and earth. A child might think of three different levels, one above the other, but an adult should have an adult's understanding of the issue.

Prayer

From the beginning, mankind was designed to be in communion with God. In Genesis 1:26 (KJV) God says:

> *Let Us make man in Our image, after Our likeness.*

It is always a good thing to stop what we are doing from time to time, and ask ourselves who we are, and why we are here. What was the purpose for which God created us? Are we living to fulfill that purpose? Our text in Genesis tells us everything we need to know. Mankind's origin and progress are in these few words. His *origin* is in the words, "Let Us make man in Our image . . ." Mankind is the creation of God in the image of God. His nature was made to resemble the divine nature. His *progress* is in the words, ". . . after Our likeness." So mankind is "in" the image and "after" the likeness. "In" is a word which expresses the concept of *being like*. "After" is a word which expresses the concept of *growing like*. The difference between the two is a resemblance that is fixed, and a resemblance that is capable of increasing to an almost unlimited extent. We are therefore taught that man was designed to grow more and more like God. How is he supposed to do this? Quite simply, by study and prayer – by studying God's Word and putting it into practice; and by praying to God for help in the process.

Prayer is a miracle. Since we are part of the created universe, we finite humans cannot reach out of it and into the realm of God. We can travel to the moon, but not out of the physical universe. Nor can we send messages out of it. Prayer is the miraculous two-way means of God hearing and responding to our genuine prayers. He does this by His power and ability to act into this world. Prayer is a supernatural activity, in that it depends upon Him who is outside or above nature. The command to pray in Scripture occurs hundreds of times, in the Old and New Testaments. We are variously commanded to pour out our troubles, and place all our requests before the one true Living God.

If we exist in a closed universe, prayer is pointless. The command of Jesus to pray to "Our Father" is pointless. This is the logical outcome of the closed system and the irrationality of modern existential Christianity. Firstly, prayer cannot be addressed to a God outside of the universe. The closed universe would not allow communications in and out. Secondly, existential Christianity removes content and meaning from all miraculous events. The miraculous is explained away by rationalism. This by definition must include prayer. If the closed system is all there is, then we are truly without God, or hope of anything other than a meaningless life. More than anything else, the denial of the power of prayer is the cruelest feature of the autonomous intellect, cutting mankind off from all hope of contact with his Creator.

In the dark passages of the night, in the hard times of life, in bereavement, in sickness, loneliness and despair, prayer is the one means by which we can pour out our troubles and sins before God. Prayer is the only means to ask for forgiveness, help and comfort. In the end there is only self and God. No spouse, no sibling, no friend can help or comfort. Only Jesus stands for you. Without prayer there is no spiritual life, no contact with the Godhead, no progress "after His likeness." What cruelty! Such cruelty is the long-term result of mankind following its own thoughts rather than seeking after God.

A righteous man regards the life of his animal,
But the tender mercies of the wicked are cruel.

(Proverbs 12:10)

In his book *Miracles*, C.S. Lewis writes:

> One of the things that held me back from Supernaturalism was
> a deep repugnance to the view of Nature which, as I thought,
> Supernaturalism entailed. I passionately desired that Nature
> should exist "on her own." The idea that she had been made,
> and could be altered, by God, seemed to take from her all that
> spontaneity which I found so refreshing . . . the thought that
> she had been manufactured, or "put there," and put there with a
> purpose, was suffocating.[110]

Lewis was explaining that if nature was a contrived thing, interfered with
on a whim by some supernatural entity, then somehow nature became less
real and reduced to mere scenery for a morality play. This took years to
shake off, but the real cure was brought about by writing his book *Miracles*.
Lewis again:

> At every stage in the writing of this book I have found my idea
> of Nature becoming more vivid and more concrete. I set out
> on a work which seemed to involve reducing her status and
> undermining her walls at every turn: the paradoxical result is a
> growing sensation that if I am not very careful she will become
> the heroine of my book. She has never seemed to me more
> great or more real than at this moment . . . To say that God has
> created her is not to say that she is unreal, but precisely that
> she is real.[111]

It is precisely because God has created nature, that nature is dependent
upon Him. Not only that, but it is fallen and corrupted. It is not working
properly. Like any good manufacturer who cares for his products, when
the machinery needs attention God provides it. Creation is currently
malfunctioning but He has a plan to restore it to perfection. This requires
intervention on His part from time to time. We refer to these occasions as

miracles, and prayer is the miraculous means by which God can intervene in individual lives.

What is absolutely essential is that we must understand that all miracles point towards the Creator. These are His signature and reminder that nature, like us, is a creature. The glory for all of it belongs to Him alone. He is the only Sovereign. The miracles are actually the main point! If we deny the miraculous we deny the Creator, and we deprive ourselves of the means of addressing Him through prayer. Ultimately, we are left with nothing, as Nietzsche knew all too well.

"The Greek poet asks, 'If water sticks to your throat, what will you take to wash it down?'"[112] The Bible is the only source of Living Water.

CHAPTER 13

THE MEANING OF THE CROSS

*For Christ did not send me to baptize, but to preach the gospel, not with wisdom
of words, lest the cross of Christ should be made of no effect. For the message of the
cross is foolishness to those who are perishing, but to us who are being saved it is the
power of God. For it is written:*

*"I will destroy the wisdom of the wise,
And bring to nothing the understanding of the prudent."*[113]

*Where is the wise? Where is the scribe? Where is the disputer of this age? Has not
God made foolish the wisdom of this world? For since, in the wisdom of God, the
world through wisdom did not know God, it pleased God through the foolishness of
the message preached to save those who believe. For Jews request a sign, and Greeks
seek after wisdom; but we preach Christ crucified, to the Jews a stumbling block and
to the Greeks foolishness, but to those who are called, both Jews and Greeks, Christ
the power of God and the wisdom of God. Because the foolishness of God is wiser
than men, and the weakness of God is stronger than men.*

(1 Corinthians 1:17–25)

In some "Christian" circles, the cross of Jesus is increasingly portrayed as
barbaric and cruel, and the view of the cross as the sacrifice for the
sins of the world is increasingly viewed as a primitive concept of God
and religion. The progress of liberal theology is blunting the edge of its
true meaning.

In earlier chapters we looked at the progress of theology as it marched
alongside natural philosophy, giving way to existentialism and denial of the
miraculous, and leaving us with a blind faith; we saw how evangelicalism
was unable to stand up against the onslaught of the modern philosophy of
science – how the theory of evolution enticed the evangelical movement
increasingly away from orthodox Biblical truth. These factors have almost

destroyed the credibility of the Church as an institution, and radically diminished the effectiveness of the cross of our salvation.

In opposition to the contentless symbols of modern existential "Christianity" stands the Bible, with its accurate and objective information where it touches the universe and natural things. This information is not fully complete because we, as finite beings, cannot comprehend all there is to know, but what is given in the Bible is sufficient for us to make reasonable and objective observations about the world around us. This is, in fact, the beginning of modern scientific thinking. This is the point of view of Copernicus, Galileo, Kepler and Newton, of Faraday, Maxwell, Einstein and Planck, to name but a few. More than this, the Bible tells us about the personality of God, and about real persons and personalities throughout history. It does this because personality is the touchstone of reality. No materialist, rationalist, determinist philosophy can explain the fact of personality in the universe. Starting from inanimate matter and using only mechanical causes and effects, there is no way of arriving at personality. There is no way personality can evolve from a universal condition of non-personality. There is no blood from the stone.

In Genesis 1:26 (KJV), God says:

Let Us make man in Our image, after Our likeness . . .

This is not a meaningless phrase. We looked at it in the last chapter, from the point of view of prayer. It means that in some way we have a relationship with the Creator. The basis for this relationship can only be the fact that we all have personalities. It distinguishes us from the inanimate and from the animal kingdom. Personality is part of the soul that distinguishes every human being, one from another. Conscious, rational, personal identity is the gift of God to each individual. This is how we are made in the "image" of God.

Do not be misled by the notion that animals can also have a "personality." For example, no two dogs have the same temperament or behavior. This is not the same thing as the gift of human personality, capable of rational thought and moral decision and, most importantly, capable of a direct personal relationship with God.

God has made it plain that His personality will not tolerate even the smallest sin. We are therefore all condemned before the immovable justice of God's law. God has shown us that the only way to return to Him is through an atoning sacrifice. Even at the beginning of the book of Genesis, God made this plain: when Adam and Eve made clothes of fig leaves to cover their nakedness, God took these away and substituted fresh animal skins (Genesis 3:21). Clearly, some animals had to die to provide those skins. God is telling us that there must be blood sacrifice as a covering for sin. This is a foreshadowing of the temple sacrifice of the Jews under the Mosaic Law, and of the final atoning death of the Messiah on the cross.

God is not an evil tyrant, delighting in the countless slaughters of animals in some barbaric ritual. The Bible tells us that life is in the blood (Genesis 9:4). God is telling us as plainly as possible that when we humans sin we are drawing blood. We draw our life and personality from Him. When we sin we are damaging our personalities and drawing upon the lifeblood of God. Sin is the path of separation from God. Sin is the path of death. If we are not redeemed, if there is no restitution, if there is no balancing sacrifice, we will eventually suffer eternal separation from God and suffer the eternal consequences.

God is the God of love. God *is* love. We cannot imagine the pain we inflict upon Him when we sin. He knows, however, that we inevitably sin because of our fallen nature. There is, therefore, no way back to God based on our own efforts or work. The fig leaf is a symbol of all those human works with which we desperately try to cover our own sins and to earn our own salvation. Adam and Eve tried to make their own "garment of salvation" out of fig leaves to cover their sin. This is impossible for finite and sinful mankind. God shows this by removing the fig leaves and substituting the animal skins. The only acceptable "garment of salvation" is provided by the sacrifice of blood. The blood of the sacrificial animal is a symbol, a representation of the restitution needed for salvation. However, we ourselves cannot make a sacrifice that would be wholly acceptable to God. That is why God Himself provided the skins; Adam was not instructed to provide them. In fulfillment of this principle, God sent His only Son to be an atoning sacrifice for our sins, in a once-and-for-all sacrifice on the cross. Jesus, the divine made human, made this personal sacrifice for you, personally, and for every person who ever lived or will live. It is up to you how you respond to this piece of information.

Personality is the gift of God. It is part of the Biblical statement that we are made in the image of God. Within our God-given freedom of choice we have a responsibility to train our personalities in the way God instructs us in His Holy Scriptures. In this way we develop from childhood to maturity and reflect the glory of God in some small way. We become witnesses of the reality of God's love in creating the universe, and of the reality of God's Son in sacrificing Himself for our salvation. These things are intensely personal, and are outside the grasp of the autonomous intellect. They stand for all time as indestructible signposts to the origin and destiny of all things in God.

The cross is the symbol which sums up this very complex process. This simple symbol represents the highest of aspirations, the very antithesis of primitive views of God and the supernatural. It is not a barbarian concept but the exact opposite: it demonstrates and throws into stark relief the love of God against the evil practiced by mankind.

The cross is the only symbol of hope in a fallen world. Do away with it, and we are lost. Without the cross we have only the concept of purposeless mechanical cause and effect to explain our existence. That would indeed be primitive, barbaric and cruel to the real personalities to whom God has given this present life, and the hope of things to come, through the symbol of the cross.

CHAPTER 14

MORALITY, JUDGMENT AND HELL

*And He said to me, "It is done! I am the Alpha and the Omega, the Beginning
and the End. I will give of the fountain of the water of life freely to him who
thirsts. He who overcomes shall inherit all things, and I will be his God and
he shall be My son. But the cowardly, unbelieving, abominable, murderers,
sexually immoral, sorcerers, idolaters, and all liars shall have their part in the
lake which burns with fire and brimstone, which is the second death."*

(Revelation 21:6–8)

At first, sin is like an occasional visitor, then like a guest who stays for a
while, and finally like the master of the house.[114]

Rabbi Yitzhak [Isaac], "Midrash on Genesis 22:6"

In our post-Christian society it is widely put about that there is no
external, objective, ethical standard that will govern our behavior in
all situations. Liberal theologians generally either go along with this or
make no credible rebuttal of it. They cannot. This is another expression of
the autonomous intellect, which, beginning with the uniformity of natural
laws in a closed system, and, proceeding through the process of destroying
God and heavenly things, produces a relativistic moral universe, based
on a situational ethic. This kind of thinking absolves everyone from the
responsibility of hard moral choices – we just move the situational goalposts.

Criminal behavior becomes perfectly acceptable under this kind of
argument. The damage done to other people, or even society at large, is not
the point. Without an external, objective, standard there can be no moral
absolute that says a certain action is a crime in all circumstances and forever.
There are humanist moral arguments which argue that the criminal must
control himself to allow others the rights to life, freedom and property.
However, these humanist arguments implicitly assume an absolute moral

standard, which stands outside both society and the criminal, and demands obedience from both parties. It cannot be a consensual agreement between the parties; society has its own ideas about behavior; the criminal has his; no meaningful consensus is possible.

It is the external, objective law of God to which we must turn for remedy – an impossibility since it has been excluded. This contradiction at the heart of the modern worldview flows into the practice of the legal and judicial system. Victims of criminal behavior and observers of the system can clearly see that something is very wrong, but they have no idea how to set it right, since they also are within the modern worldview.

During His incarnation, Jesus said that He came not to abolish the law of God but to fulfill it, in the sense of filling up or completing something. Jesus was labeling Himself as the pinnacle and the epitome of the law:

> *Do not think that I came to destroy the Law or the Prophets. I did not come to destroy but to fulfill. For assuredly, I say to you, till heaven and earth pass away, one jot or one tittle will by no means pass from the law till all is fulfilled.*
>
> (Matthew 5:17–18)

What did Jesus mean? He meant that justice is an eternal attribute of God. It arises from His holiness. The law that God gave us was meant to point us back to Him, and to make us to consider our own sinful nature and lost situation. The law convicts us all. We need the help of God Himself, to train us by means of His law, until we truly understand our sins and our helplessness. Only then can He teach us repentance and forgiveness. It is a sure and certain thing that no one can escape the absolute justice of God. It is absolute, immovable and unchanging, and by it we are all condemned. We need the Redeemer who did not avoid the absolute judgment of the law, but met it full face. He paid the price for our transgressions that we might be redeemed from ourselves. He fulfilled the law for any of us who genuinely repent of our sins and wish to throw ourselves upon His mercy and compassion.

If we don't wish to do this, however, and continue to satisfy our own ideas, we will be condemned. The Bible tells us that there is true guilt, true moral responsibility for our actions. God has clearly laid out the consequences of certain types of behavior. He has given us our code of conduct for life.

We will all be judged eventually. The Holy Spirit is here as our conscience to convict us of our true sins and true guilt before God. God has given us meaningful choices. Jesus, the fulfillment of the law, said that anyone who harmed a child had better be thrown into the sea with a millstone around his neck than face the Living God. This is recorded in all three Synoptic Gospels (Matthew 18:6; Mark 9:42; Luke 17:2). Jesus gave an absolute judgment on this point. I, for one, believe Him. Do you?

God's law demands real punishment for real sin. There is no sense of rehabilitation or remedial quality about it, or of working off a debt. The punishment is pure retribution, fully deserved for the transgression of the law. In this sense it looks to the past, and a past action that requires punishment as a matter of justice. In the modern world the sense of real sin has been lost. We now talk of "remedial" prison sentences, where the rehabilitation of the criminal is more important than satisfying the demands of justice. In this sense it looks to the future and the utilitarian benefits of reforming the criminal. In earthly terms the demands of justice now come second to the principle of remediation. This is probably why so many victims and their families feel aggrieved.

If God's justice has been undermined, what about hell, the place of retribution? A common and widely held view of hell is as an interim period of rehabilitation after death. This is sometimes known as the "conditional view" of hell and has had various forms throughout church history. Eventually this period of torment ends and the soul ends up in heaven. The Roman Catholics have developed this into their own doctrine of "purgatory," where all eventually pay off their sin-debt and are finally deemed fit for heaven. Protestants would have real trouble with this idea, since it gives to the individual soul some part in "earning their own salvation" whereas salvation is purely the gift of God, "lest anyone should boast" (Ephesians 2:8–9). However, the "conditional view" in various disguises down the centuries has led to the unbiblical doctrine of "universalism," where all are eventually saved. Some are saved at death and go straight to paradise; others come along later, after enduring suitable torment. If all are eventually and actually saved, this makes nonsense of God's justice.

Another, more recent view of hell looks on the idea of never-ending punishment as so harsh that some evangelicals have proposed the concept of "conditional immortality." If this were the case, those judged as wicked would not go to eternal, conscious punishment, but pass out of existence altogether. This view denies the conscious existence of the wicked soul after death and is known as "annihilationism." In this case there can be no punishment at all. This again makes nonsense of God's justice.

Since the sense of true holiness has been lost, the sense of true justice has also been lost and hell is reduced to a concept rather than a reality; and even the concept is under attack, especially the endless nature of the place and the punishment. Many people cannot contemplate the idea of eternal punishment; their feelings forbid it.

It is an interesting question which came first; whether it was the loss of the sense of real sin deserving real punishment, or the loss of the reality of hell. These things are certainly connected. But before anyone accuses God of manipulating people through guilt and fear, remember that it is God Himself who comes to our rescue and provides the payment that requites the punishment on our behalf, through His Son, Jesus Christ. Forgiveness is available to all.

Unless and until people are able to perceive and understand their own faults and sinful natures, there can be no forgiveness. Since forgiveness is at the heart of Christian salvation, redemption can only take place after the true guilt of real sins is made manifest to us. Let us look at this more closely. If a person is a victim of careless theology or deliberate manipulation, and if he is convinced by the prevailing worldview that there are no moral absolutes, and if he understands that "science" declares that his nature has been determined from birth, and no behavior of his can be, therefore, condemned, then he will believe that he is generally good and has nothing to repent. He cannot believe otherwise. How then do we describe to him the loving mercy of God to all sinners if he does not admit to the existence of sin? In his mind there is no need for the cure because the disease doesn't exist.

Hand in hand with the removal of sin has been the deconstruction of hell. There have been many subjective arguments against the existence of hell, such as "How can a loving God torture people forever?" or "I cannot believe that Jesus would send someone to such a place; God is love." Because of such arguments and feelings, many preachers teach that hell is a metaphor, or that there is no conscious existence after death, or that everyone will eventually be saved. There have been many books written on this subject and many people subscribe to these views. But they do so against the clear teaching of the Bible. One such example is the recent book *Love Wins* by megachurch pastor, Rob Bell. Despite his claims to the contrary, he is clearly a universalist who cannot contemplate the justice of a Holy God. He writes on page 109: " . . . at the center of the Christian tradition since the first church has been the insistence that history is not tragic, hell is not forever, and love, in the end, wins." This is very wrong. Until the middle of the nineteenth century, almost all theologians taught the reality of hell and the endless nature of the punishment there. Like other heresies, universalism has been around a long time, but was never mainstream, or at the center of Christian tradition. His book is not well referenced historically and his claims are suspect. He rarely gives complete Bible references when discussing his theology; his exegesis is very strained and distorted to support his position. He condemns traditional orthodoxy as closed-minded; this is a spoiling move, designed to discount criticism before it is made. He also mistranslates part of the parable of the sheep and the goats (Matthew 25:31–46) and claims that the words "everlasting punishment" are a mistranslation of the Greek in Matthew 25:46. He says they should be translated as "a period of pruning" or a "time of trimming"! This goes against most of the serious translations available to us: the King James Version (KJV), New King James Version (NKJV), New American Standard Bible (NASB), New International Version (NIV), New Revised Standard Version (NRSV) and many others. I have not found a version that translates the words in any way other than "everlasting punishment" or the equivalent. His book is aimed at people who have an emotional problem with God's justice and mercy; they want the mercy but don't like the justice. This is false and unbiblical teaching.

If we stick to the Biblical arguments for eternal punishment we have an easy task. Hell is very real because Jesus Himself said so. Jesus cannot lie. He did not make up something to frighten us into behaving as He wants. Jesus would not make up a false threat of a non-existent hell. He was earnestly warning us of our real and present danger. Many Christians do not realize that most of what we know about hell comes from the mouth of Jesus Himself, because only God has the right to exercise judgment and send anyone to hell. If there were no sin and no hell, why then would God tell people about it? Why would Jesus die to rescue us from it? The Bible is clear and conclusive: eternal punishment and hell are real.

However, the emotional argument can only be overruled by the Biblical argument if the authority and inerrancy of the Bible are assumed. One of the main themes of this book is that authority and inerrancy have been removed from the Bible – in which case the Biblical argument is not very convincing. Consequently we need to look at the rational argument for the existence of eternal punishment and the reality of the place where it is carried out. In his book *The Doctrine of Endless Punishment*, W.G.T. Shedd commented:

> So long as the controversy is carried on by an appeal to the Bible, the defender of endless retribution has comparatively an easy task. But when the appeal is made to human reason and sentiment, or to ratiocination, the demonstration requires more effort. And yet the doctrine is not only Biblical but rational. It is defensible on the basis of sound doctrine and pure reason.[115]

There are only three fundamental truths necessary for maintaining the doctrine, namely:

1. There is a just God
2. Man has free will
3. Sin is a voluntary action

If these are denied then there can be no effective defense of the doctrine of endless retribution, or any other doctrine for that matter. The transgression of the law which ought to receive this endless punishment must be an act of free will. Sin, whether inward thought or outward action, must be unforced human agency. Endless punishment is based on the premise of free will, and would be impossible without it. If anyone could prove that his sin is the result of his predetermined nature, without his personal control or decision to sin, then by the same proof he would show that he could not be punished for it; in fact, it would not be sin at all by the above definition. Endless punishment can only be applied to true guilt.

It is no great leap of understanding to realize that the developments of modern medicine and psychiatry, based as they are on the secular existential worldview, are going to remove the basis of the doctrine. They attempt to explain behavior as the result of environmental factors, genetic makeup and other circumstances. Behavior therefore moves out of free agency. Sin therefore becomes (at least partially) an involuntary action. This humanist worldview therefore falsifies the doctrine of endless punishment by invalidating the voluntary nature of sin. It is easy to see why the doctrines of endless punishment and the existence of hell have been gradually undermined in the liberal theology of the modern Church, infected as it is with the secular existential worldview. Today they are frankly rejected by many Christians.

There is a stark difference between the secular existential worldview and the orthodox Christian worldview. The first traps people into a position of victimhood without choices or responsibility. Whatever they are, they are, without responsibility for themselves or their actions. They are trapped in a mindset that it is all someone else's fault, or caused by something outside their conscious control. How can they change what is essentially beyond their control? There is no God and no way out. Modern existentialism traps them in their situation. They have no hope. The orthodox Christian worldview, on the other hand, acknowledges the circumstances and factors that went into someone's present condition, but insists that responsibility rests with the individual about how they respond to their condition. They may not control their birth or childhood circumstances but they can control, at least partially, their response to it. The infinite God of the Bible judges perfectly each and every one of us.

Jesus' command to make disciples of all nations is a reflection of God's great love for us all, and necessitates telling people of His holiness, His justice and His absolute condemnation of sin. It means telling them about their own sinful nature. It means telling them about life after death and the choices they must make regarding their eternal destiny. It means telling them the Bad News about the reality of sin and hell. We cannot preach love and mercy without the foundation of justice – without justice there can be no mercy. After that, they can be given the Good News, but not before. The Bad News must precede the Good News, otherwise there is no Good News; there will be no repentance and they will continue in their sins.

Calamity and Natural Evil

In this chapter I am trying to deal only with human sin and the evil acts of mankind. There is another form of evil known as "natural evil." This kind of evil is without human involvement: natural disasters such as earthquakes, tsunamis, floods, famines and disease. Many people have a problem with "bad" things happening to "good" people. The problem of why God allows such natural evil is outside the scope of this book, but we need to deal with it briefly, to prevent confusion with other evils. Genesis, the first book of the Bible, describes how the fall of man somehow affected nature (Genesis 3:17–19), so that it is not perfect as God originally made it. Bad things now happen, apparently randomly, and indiscriminately (Luke 13:1–5). The sins of mankind have somehow corrupted the world and it is now a very dangerous place. Revelation, the last book of the Bible, tells us it will be restored to perfection in the end (Revelation 21:1–5). In the meantime we all suffer from accidents, diseases and calamities.

There are three possible causes for suffering: natural random causes, such as disasters and accidents; chastisement to improve our nature; and punishment for evildoing. According to Shedd, punishment for evildoing is neither calamity nor chastisement:

> Men suffer calamity, says Christ, not because they or their parents have sinned, "But that the works of God should be made manifest in them" (John 9:3 KJV). Chastisement is inflicted in order to develop a good, but imperfect character already formed. "The Lord loveth whom he chasteneth," and "what son is he whom the earthly father chasteneth not?" (Hebrews 12:6, 7 KJV). Punishment, on the other hand, is retribution, and is not intended to do the work of either calamity or chastisement, but a work of its own. And this work is to vindicate law; to satisfy justice.[116]

Calamities are all around us. We must live in a world where physical death and injury, disease and old age are commonplace. It is a very dangerous place. Bad things happen all the time. Such calamities happen to people not because of their individual failings or sins, or even the actions of their parents or families, but because of the nature of this fallen world. They don't deserve to be caught in an earthquake, or a tsunami, or an influenza epidemic, or to be born with a defect – they just are. What matters is the reaction to such calamities; that is what is important. Jesus' disciples asked this very question in John's Gospel:

> *Now as Jesus passed by, He saw a man who was blind from birth. And His disciples asked Him, saying, "Rabbi, who sinned, this man or his parents, that he was born blind?" Jesus answered, "Neither this man nor his parents sinned, but that the works of God should be revealed in him."*
>
> (John 9:1–3)

Jesus then went on to heal the blind man. What Jesus' words pointed to was the work of God in first creating a perfect world and then providing a path to repairing the damage done by the fall. What Jesus' simple action of individual healing pointed to was the manifestation of God's work in healing the breach between God and man. This is beautifully expressed in the hymn "Amazing Grace:" "I was blind but now I see." All this natural evil will be repaired and put right, not necessarily in this life, but certainly in the next.

In another incident, Jesus' disciples brought this matter of calamity to His attention when Herod slaughtered some worshippers in the temple. They were innocently worshipping God – why should they suffer so? In Luke's Gospel we read:

> There were present at that season some who told Him about the
> Galileans whose blood Pilate had mingled with their sacrifices. And
> Jesus answered and said to them, "Do you suppose that these Galileans
> were worse sinners than all other Galileans, because they suffered such
> things? I tell you, no; but unless you repent you will all likewise perish.
> Or those eighteen on whom the tower in Siloam fell and killed them,
> do you think that they were worse sinners than all other men who
> dwelt in Jerusalem? I tell you, no; but unless you repent you will all
> likewise perish."
>
> (Luke 13:1–5)

Jesus did not answer in the bland tones of meaningless comfort, but taught a hard lesson. Jesus pointed them away from the idea that calamity or natural evil is retribution, and insisted that it could happen to anyone, morally good or morally bad. A person is not morally better because he escapes a random or accidental event. Jesus is saying that we must pay attention to our own moral state, before we die and face judgment for our own lives. We can all die tomorrow, accidentally or otherwise. The next car journey we take may be our last. The focus of our moral concerns should not be natural evil, but our personal evil.

So our response to calamity should be not to think that we are better than those who suffer these things, but to recognize the work of God in creation and redemption, and to pay close attention to our own moral state – which may deserve endless retribution. We could be next! At the existential moment of each person's death, no matter the cause of it, they pass from this life and the natural into the next life and the supernatural. This life is finite; the next is endless. God's perfect justice is applied at the point of transition. In other words we should be focused on the next life and not this one. Nature is not the only reality.

Chastisement and Discipline

When God disciplines and imposes remedial suffering on his children, for the purposes of improving and educating them, the suffering is temporary, as the following two quotations show:

> *He will not always strive with us,*
> *Nor will He keep His anger forever.*

> (Psalm 103:9)

> *For consider Him who endured such hostility from sinners against Himself, lest you become weary and discouraged in your souls. You have not yet resisted to bloodshed, striving against sin. And you have forgotten the exhortation which speaks to you as to sons:*

> *"My son, do not despise the chastening of the LORD,*
> *Nor be discouraged when you are rebuked by Him;*
> *For whom the LORD loves He chastens,*
> *And scourges every son whom He receives."*

> *If you endure chastening, God deals with you as with sons; for what son is there whom a father does not chasten? But if you are without chastening, of which all have become partakers, then you are illegitimate and not sons. Furthermore, we have had human fathers who corrected us, and we paid them respect. Shall we not much more readily be in subjection to the Father of spirits and live? For they indeed for a few days chastened us as seemed best to them, but He for our profit, that we may be partakers of His holiness. Now no chastening seems to be joyful for the present, but painful; nevertheless, afterward it yields the peaceable fruit of righteousness to those who have been trained by it.*

> (Hebrews 12:3–11)

The discipline of God is aimed at getting our attention away from ourselves and this natural world. It is intended to bring people to maturity in their understanding of God and His attributes and intentions. Paul writes in his first letter to Timothy:

> *Therefore I exhort first of all that supplications, prayers, intercessions, and giving of thanks be made for all men, for kings and all who are in authority, that we may lead a quiet and peaceable life in all godliness and reverence. For this is good and acceptable in the sight of God our Savior, who desires all men to be saved and to come to the knowledge of the truth.*
>
> (1 Timothy 2:1–4)

Of course, if prayer is deemed useless and God non-existent, then all we are left with is the fact of suffering. It is pure random calamity without any hint of purpose. There can be no sense of remediation or punishment. We are left only with natural evil and no way to think about it in any moral sense. What a bleak prospect. The real and Living God, however, desires that everyone should be saved and know the truth. God provides purpose to our suffering. If we seek Him out, we must endure His sometimes painful discipline in moral issues and the temporary suffering that this will entail. The fact that most people do not attempt to seek Him out does not invalidate the premise that some suffering is rooted in God's desire to "legitimize" His children as inheritors of the eternal kingdom.

Endless Punishment

Punishment or retribution is entirely retrospective in purpose and is to satisfy the demands of the law which has already been broken. If a man is condemned for murder, he cannot be executed for the purposes of his moral improvement or his personal rehabilitation. There is no future view in mind. It is true that, in any given individual case, there may be social benefit or personal improvement as a consequence of the punishment; but the consequence must not be confused with the purpose. One further consideration is the endless nature of God's retribution. Shedd again:

> Supposing it, now, to be conceded, that future punishment
> is retributive in its essential nature, it follows that it must be

endless, from the nature of the case. For, suffering must continue as long as the reason for it continues.[117]

Shedd is making the point that the suffering is like the law, which lasts as long as the reason for it lasts. When the reason for the law ceases, then the law ceases also, together with the punishment. Suffering that is remedial and corrective may end when its purpose is achieved, because moral weakness is the reason for imposing it in the first place. If the moral weakness is corrected, then the reason for the suffering ceases. Suffering that is penal, based on transgression of the law and true guilt, can never come to an end; guilt is the reason for inflicting it and guilt once assigned is never repealed. Passage of time may convert moral weakness into moral strength, but it does not convert guilt into innocence. Therefore, if the criminal is properly and justly convicted of his crime, no time can ever come that will remove the guilt. The reason for inflicting retribution today is a reason forever.

The real question every Christian must answer is therefore, "Does God punish endlessly?" We know He chastises for remedial purposes; we can easily understand and accept that, but does He ever punish? Does He inflict eternal retribution on the truly guilty? Does He ever inflict suffering that has no element of rehabilitation, but is purely intended to vindicate His law and satisfy His justice? The teaching of Holy Scripture is that He does. In Matthew's Gospel, Jesus teaches:

> *If your hand or foot causes you to sin, cut it off and cast it from you. It is better for you to enter into life lame or maimed, rather than having two hands or two feet, to be cast into the everlasting fire. And if your eye causes you to sin, pluck it out and cast it from you. It is better for you to enter into life with one eye, rather than having two eyes, to be cast into hell fire.*
>
> (Matthew 18:8–9)

In Mark's Gospel (Mark 9:48), Jesus teaches the same thing and adds a quotation from Isaiah 66:24:

> *. . . where "Their worm does not die and the fire is not quenched."*

Some people object that such punishment is cruel, and unworthy of a benevolent God. Paul answers this in his letter to the Romans:

> *But if our unrighteousness demonstrates the righteousness of God,*
> *what shall we say? Is God unjust who inflicts wrath? . . . Certainly*
> *not! For then how will God judge the world?*
>
> (Romans 3:5–6)

So when does God inflict such punishment? The Bible says everyone is born to live once and then comes judgment (Hebrews 9:27). God will continue with His remedial chastisement, training and discipline until we die; then we will be brought before His tribunal for His judgment. We are all in the same situation. No one can escape God's justice. God is claiming our attention and we should take notice.

> *God shall judge the righteous and the wicked,*
> *For there is a time there for every purpose and for every work.*
>
> (Ecclesiastes 3:17)

The reality of sin and hell are established morally, rationally and Biblically. We have free will and our choices are our own. We have true moral responsibility for them. We can choose our path in this life. If we choose not to focus our personalities upon His nature, if we choose not to attempt to walk with Him in this life, if we choose not to dwell in eternal peace in heaven, we will surely dwell in eternal torment in hell, for such is the justice of God (Revelation 14:6–11).

With great humility and dread we would all do well to remember these words, spoken by Jesus Himself, to His own disciples:

> *And do not fear those who kill the body but cannot kill the soul. But*
> *rather fear Him who is able to destroy both soul and body in hell.*
>
> (Matthew 10:28)

CHAPTER 15

SEX AND BIBLICAL MORALITY

*Now the body is not for sexual immorality but for the Lord, and the Lord for
the body. And God both raised up the Lord and will also raise us up by His power.
Do you not know that your bodies are members of Christ? Shall I then take the
members of Christ and make them members of a harlot? Certainly not! Or do you
not know that he who is joined to a harlot is one body with her? For "the two,"
He says, "shall become one flesh." But he who is joined to the Lord is one spirit with
Him. Flee sexual immorality. Every sin that a man does is outside the body, but he
who commits sexual immorality sins against his own body. Or do you not know that
your body is the temple of the Holy Spirit who is in you, whom you have from
God, and you are not your own? For you were bought at a price; therefore glorify
God in your body and in your spirit, which are God's.*

(1 Corinthians 6:13–20)

We examined morality in general in the last chapter. There is a need to
include a short chapter on sexual sin. We often hear that any sexual
activity is fine, as long as no one else is hurt. The reason is that people
don't see the damage. It's not like stealing or physical assault. Unfortunately,
sexual morality has consequences for the individual, society and community,
and has eternal consequences in the next life.

Our civilization is today flooded with sexual references in every context.
Sex is used to sell every conceivable product. Sexual images are everywhere,
cast in words, photographs, movies, advertisements, stories, and the news.
They are unavoidable. Even if we stayed home in an attempt to avoid them,
they are dumped into the home through TV and radio, newspapers and
magazines, not forgetting that pornography is freely available through the
internet. The sexual instinct is one of the most powerful in the human
organism. The new morality has brought about sexual license; modern
marketing techniques make use of this most powerful instinct, and sexual
appetite is being inflamed beyond its normal boundaries. So we need to

look specifically at sexual sin, even though we could say we have already dealt with it in the last chapter.

Any discussion about sex and morality in today's world is bound to attract severe criticism if it contradicts the widely held view that any kind of consensual activity is OK, because the new morality says it's only a personal choice. The Christian view does contradict the "anything goes" society in which we now live. It's not so much the physical act itself, but the loss of the spiritual side of it. God created sex and it's very pleasurable; it's His way of ensuring that it takes both a man and a woman to propagate human life. This means some kind of relationship that endures in time and extends beyond the physical act into the intellectual, emotional and spiritual realms. This implies there must be some kind of boundary or morality around sexual activity which regulates faithfulness, endurance, sharing, serving one another and especially bringing up children, the fruit of sexual union. God has enabled us to create life. He created all life from nothing; we work with His gift to us. Creation of life is a serious business and God has set out His way of doing it. This involves the spiritual origin of relationships, knowledge and reasoning, and the moral and legal aspects of our relationship to Him and to each other.

The postmodern existential worldview, based on rationalism and evolution, excludes the spiritual and restricts us to the natural only. The intellectual, moral and legal aspects are therefore also confined to the natural, and so the only way we can think about sex is reduced to physical considerations. The moral aspect being confined to the natural world means sexual morality can only be based on the natural instincts and the particular situation. We are back to situational ethics and "what is your truth is not my truth."

Paradoxically, how we feel emotionally about sex becomes irrelevant, since it can only be a physical relationship driven by instinct. Some might argue that the emotions are natural things and cannot be dismissed like that. But how we feel about something is based on what we think it "ought" to be. There is a tension between what "is" and what "ought" to be. As we pointed out in Chapter 2, the philosopher David Hume showed that we cannot get an "ought" from an "is" when confined to the natural world of the senses. If our worldview has eliminated the supernatural as a possibility then there can be no spiritual considerations and no "ought." Therefore our finer feelings are reduced to the natural, to mere biochemical interactions and can have no contentful meaning. So sex becomes an instinct that must be gratified. This may explain why our civilization is gradually descending into lust, almost to the exclusion of all other aspects of sexual relations. Loving someone has almost become synonymous with having sex with them. No wonder the divorce rate is so high; that is, among those who still get married. It is worth restating that people behave according to what they think and have been taught to believe.

However, many people live above the basic considerations of lust, even those who don't get married. Even without explicitly obeying God, or even admitting His existence, most people tend to do what is right in most areas of life. It is the conscience which provides the "ought" in their behavior. The "ought" of the conscience comes from the spirit, from outside the natural. As many philosophers and theologians have pointed out, it is the continuous existence of human conscience which points to the spiritual source of morality.

Jesus, Peter and Paul all used the first two chapters of the book of Genesis when teaching about male and female relationships.[118] God's original pattern is the guide for redeemed behavior for a disciple of Jesus Christ. As all Christians would accept, there are two aspects to creation: one is the vertical relationship between God and man, and the other is the horizontal relationship between men and women. Sexuality and gender are integral to both relationships. There is a clear analogy between them, which is basic to an understanding of the whole Bible. In this analogy, most Biblical scholars agree that the man represents the divine and the woman the human side of the relationship. This is why the roles of men and women are never reversed in Scripture. By analogy this would reverse the relationship of God and humans, an unthinkable situation.[119] It is also why homosexuality is so strongly condemned by God, since it is such a severe corruption of the intended pattern of relationships between men and women, and God and human beings. The practice of homosexuality thus strikes at the very root of God's redemptive plan for mankind. It is a salvation issue and it must not be relegated to the level of a mere "lifestyle choice."

The first chapter of Genesis states that both men and women were made in the image of God, and are therefore equal in value and destiny. This is the first statement about gender in Scripture and must be the basis for all subsequent debate. All human beings do bear the image of God, but all are fallen and are imperfect in many ways. One of the ways in which we fall short is the temptation of sexual sin. The Bible contains clear instructions about this, intended to build and maintain the relationship between God and mankind for the purposes of salvation. It is also the best recipe for domestic harmony on earth, not to mention physical and mental health.

Even a cursory reading of the Holy Scriptures will reveal that we Christians are not to tolerate certain sexual practices, such as adultery, promiscuity, and homosexuality. However, the modern worldview has accepted the consensus of the higher critics that the Bible has errors of historical fact. Starting from this (false) premise, it is further assumed that the Bible is also mistaken where it comes to moral pronouncements about personal behavior, therefore no sexual practice can be considered wrong in a moral sense; it is only a matter of lifestyle choice.

The modern politically correct ideas of tolerance of sexual practices and sexual orientation, contained within the secular and liberal worldviews, are, in effect, very damaging to family life and human community in general. They are ostensibly designed to prevent discrimination, but are actually very divisive and are used to prevent any alternative views being heard.

The main thesis of this book is that God does exist and that Holy Scripture is a valid and inerrant source of authority on these matters. According to Scripture, all sexual relations outside a monogamous marriage are sinful. There is a clear description of sexual sins, in both the Old and New Testaments. The modern worldview rejects this as bigotry and discrimination. There is a great deal of pressure to come into line with modern thinking on someone who wishes to follow a scriptural life. This is a very real concern.

It is important that we should understand that discrimination in itself is not necessarily evil. The Bible tells us to discriminate constantly against sinful ways and repent. It also tells us not to associate with those who persist in sinful ways. We therefore have two completely opposing kinds of discrimination: one is good and is to be practiced constantly; the other is bad and to be avoided at all times. The bad kind is where discrimination is based on one's own (prejudiced) viewpoint or agenda, and is essentially selfish. The good kind is based upon God's eternal ethic and unchanging justice, and is essentially selfless. It is better in the long term to be honest with sinful people and their practices, even if it leads to short-term conflict of ideas.

How did we get to the point where theologically informed church leaders have now brought the worldwide Anglican movement to its knees and to the point of schism by "ordaining" actively and openly homosexual clergy? On 10 May 2004, I was listening to the BBC's Radio 4 while driving to work. There was an interview with a Reverend Timothy Rich about the pending appointment of openly homosexual Canon Gene Robinson as a bishop in the New Hampshire Diocese of the Episcopalian Church of the United States of America. Reverend Rich was and is a close supporter of Canon Robinson. I was shocked to the core when he said that "The Holy Spirit guided them in their decision."

This is flatly contradictory to what the Holy Spirit consistently inspired in the Bible. What the Reverend Rich was actually saying (whether or not he understood it) is that the Holy Spirit is fallible and gives contradictory messages — one message in the Bible and another when communicating direct. Also, in coming to terms with the fact that the Holy Spirit has apparently changed His mind, we must trust the New Hampshire Diocese for the truth and not the Bible! There is the whiff of hypocrisy about an attitude which condones what is explicitly condemned in Scripture and then blames everyone else for the ill-feeling and divisiveness that follow.

There is the famous passage on sexual sin in Leviticus 18, which includes adultery, promiscuity, incest, homosexuality, bestiality, and child sacrifice. In this passage God calls these things an "abomination" to Him. What does He mean? According to *Strong's Dictionary of Bible Words*, there are seven Hebrew words and three Greek words variously translated "abominable," "abominably," "abomination" or "abominations." These Hebrew and Greek words have literal meanings that can be summed up as:

Unclean	Illegal	Idolatrous object
Fetid	To loathe	Disgusting idol
To be a moral stench	To abhor	Detestable
To pollute	To be enraged	

All this is to do with the worship of God. If something is "abominable," or an "abomination," it is to do with idolatry. The wholesome fragrance of the prayers of the righteous turns into something polluted, a fetid stench, if prayers are offered to idols. It also is to do with the breaking of God's law, which God hates and abhors and which produces divine wrath. It must be emphasized: sexual sin is a salvation issue. Consider the scriptures below:

> *For this is the will of God, your sanctification: that you should abstain from sexual immorality; that each of you should know how to possess his own vessel in sanctification and honor, not in passion of lust, like the Gentiles who do not know God; that no one should take advantage of and defraud his brother in this matter, because the Lord is the avenger of all such, as we also forewarned you and testified. For God did not call us to uncleanness, but in holiness. Therefore he who rejects this does not reject man, but God, who has also given us His Holy Spirit.*
>
> (1 Thessalonians 4:3–8)

> *Do you not know that the unrighteous will not inherit the kingdom of God? Do not be deceived. Neither fornicators, nor idolaters, nor adulterers, nor homosexuals, nor sodomites, nor thieves, nor covetous, nor drunkards, nor revilers, nor extortioners will inherit the kingdom of God.*
>
> (1 Corinthians 6:9–10)

> *But we know that the law is good if one uses it lawfully, knowing this: that the law is not made for a righteous person, but for the lawless and insubordinate, for the ungodly and for sinners, for the unholy and profane, for murderers of fathers and murderers of mothers, for manslayers, for fornicators, for sodomites, for kidnappers, for liars, for perjurers, and if there is any other thing that is contrary to sound doctrine, according to the glorious gospel of the blessed God which was committed to my trust.*
>
> (1 Timothy 1:8–11)

> *But there shall by no means enter it [heaven] anything that defiles, or causes an abomination or a lie, but only those who are written in the Lamb's Book of Life.*
>
> (Revelation 21:27)

So the Bible is clear; we are to keep ourselves clean from these "abominable" things or suffer the consequences. But of course we need to live in the world, where most people do not share the Christian conviction about these things. How can we do this? Paul writes about this aspect of life in 1 Corinthians:

> *I wrote to you in my epistle not to keep company with sexually immoral people. Yet I certainly did not mean with the sexually immoral people of this world, or with the covetous, or extortioners, or idolaters, since then you would need to go out of the world. But now I have written to you not to keep company with anyone named a brother, who is sexually immoral, or covetous, or an idolater, or a reviler, or a drunkard, or an extortioner – not even to eat with such a person. For what have I to do with judging those also who are outside? Do you not judge those who are inside? But those who are outside God judges. Therefore "put away from yourselves the evil person."*[120]

(1 Corinthians 5:9–13)

Like Paul, I am not writing about those who are not Christians; they have their own lives and will behave as they choose. Those who are outside we leave to the judgment of God, according to Scripture. Like everyone else, I live and work alongside non-Christians and people of every persuasion every day. There should be no problem with this, and we should treat everyone fairly, according to the law of the land. Like Paul, I am merely pointing out that people who claim to be practicing Christians (brothers) should be obedient to the Word of God. Additionally, the Church should exercise discipline and act according to the instructions found in Scripture.

A more honest approach for "Bishop" Robinson would be to resign his office and get on with being a homosexual, or whatever, than to try to rewrite Scripture and keep on drawing the salary, and eventually pension, as a member of the Christian clergy. Either obey the rules or join a different club, one more to your personal liking. As the scriptures quoted above show, this applies to all besetting sins, not just the sexual ones. Such lack of personal integrity on many issues, combined with the unwillingness of the Church hierarchy to expel such people long before the matter reaches such a stage, is one of the main internal causes of the decline of the Church and its loss of credibility. The ability to act Biblically has been fatally undermined by the reduction of Scripture to a "lifestyle option," rather than a truthful revelation from God. What, ask many ordinary people, does the Church actually stand for? Why bother with it?

The institutionalized Church as a whole (and not just the Anglican/ Episcopalian denominations) exhibits the same paralysis. It is the victim of a clever campaign to distort the issues around the practice of all kinds of sexual sin with much politically correct language about "tolerance," "discrimination" and "prejudice." The word "discrimination" has come to mean prejudice, and "tolerance" has come to mean approval. This is the world turned upside down. If we do not approve of something, we can choose to tolerate it for the wider good. If we approve of something then tolerance is not necessary.

There are medical consequences to any human activity. If you play football, you are at risk of breaking a leg. From a medical point of view there are great risks from infectious diseases associated with sexual promiscuity, both heterosexual and homosexual, as many competent studies have shown. There is a very low chance of avoiding all of these diseases or problems unless the sexual behavior pattern is changed. One of the most striking studies notes that, for homosexuals, there is a much higher than usual occurrence of suicide than among the normal population, and there is an average twenty-five to thirty-year decrease in life span.[121] If you find this statement hard to believe, in April 1993 a paper was presented to the Eastern Psychological Association (USA) in which the researchers analyzed the age of death for nearly 7,000 homosexuals and heterosexuals by obituary notices in a large number of gay and non-gay newspapers. They found that the gay male life span, *even apart from AIDS* and *with a long-term partner*, is significantly shorter than that of married men in general by *more than three decades*. AIDS further shortens the life span by more than 7%.[122]

Homosexuality is not a harmless, acceptable lifestyle. It should not be taught to our children as acceptable. We should always point out the medical dangers to young people. It is curious that these well-attested therapeutic studies, which have been replicated by many competent medical organizations around the world, are never brought forward by any responsible organization or the media. An appeal to science, it would seem, is only allowed where it contradicts the Bible and the accepted normal practice of sexuality. Anything which supports the debate for the restraint of sexual behavior is quietly buried. Nevertheless, the medical findings are valid.

In the United Kingdom, the rise of sexually transmitted infections (STIs) has been astronomical. The number of women who cannot have children because of chlamydia infection through casual sex (whether their own or their partner's) is reaching worrying proportions. Chlamydia is an STI caused by the bacterium *Chlamydia trachomatis*. In the UK, the number of new diagnoses has been steadily increasing each year since the mid-1990s, and it has now become the most commonly diagnosed STI. Chlamydia is called the "silent" disease because most people who get it do not experience any noticeable symptoms and many cases of chlamydia remain undiagnosed. Undiagnosed chlamydia can lead to more serious long-term health problems and infertility.

Apart from any moral or theological considerations and even if we ignore the social consequences, there are serious medical issues with unrestricted sexual behavior.

Finally, I should like to discuss the spiritual aspects of sexual sin, with particular reference to Christian beliefs and the teaching of the Holy Bible. Firstly, the Christian standard of sexual morality is very high. It covers all aspects of sexual conduct: promiscuity, adultery, homosexuality and so on. It states clearly that the only acceptable form of sexual activity is within the institution of marriage, between a man and a woman. As we have seen, the Bible is completely consistent on this theme, throughout the whole of the Old and New Testaments. Since all sexual activities outside of the Biblical standard are clearly labeled as sinful, the practice of them is sinful. If we knowingly practice any form of sin, it leads to a weakening of our relationship with God and a gradual slide into the way of eternal death, forfeiting our opportunity of salvation. I repeat once again: it is a salvation issue. Those clergy who teach differently are betraying their sworn office and have no ground, in logic or in reason, to support efforts to weaken the authority of the Holy Scriptures. In Matthew 13 Jesus speaks about the end of the age. In His own words:

> *The Son of Man will send out his angels, and they will weed out of his kingdom everything that causes sin and all who do evil. They will throw them into the fiery furnace, where there will be weeping and gnashing of teeth. Then the righteous will shine like the sun in the kingdom of their Father. He who has ears, let him hear.*
>
> (Matthew 13:41–42 NIV)

It is not just those who sin and do evil that will be sent to hell; the causes of sin will also go there. In this context it means those who create stumbling blocks and cause others to sin. This includes those who teach in contradiction to Holy Scripture. It is not a minor issue when the Bible states that those who teach will be judged more harshly than the rest (James 3:1). False doctrines, leading to a false plan of salvation and consequent sin, get more people into hell than most other means. Teachers beware!

In the New Testament, Jesus said that He came not to replace the law but to complete it, that not one "jot or tittle" of it would pass away until the end of the world. We cannot claim that God's law in the Old Testament is not for us. If we are true followers of Christ then we would be so conformed to His will that we would no longer have the desire to do the things forbidden by God and condemned by Him as sinful. Sin would no longer have a hold on us. If we are true Christians, obedient to the commands of Jesus, any sin would no longer hold us in chains.

It cannot be stated too often that people behave according to what they believe. If they have been wrongly taught, their belief system will be wrong and their behavior will reflect this. Paul wrote to the church at Corinth:

> Do not be deceived: "Evil company corrupts good habits." Awake to righteousness, and do not sin; for some do not have the knowledge of God. I speak this to your shame.
>
> (1 Corinthians 15:33–34)

Again, here Paul is not writing to non-Christians, those who do not have the knowledge of God. He is writing to the shame of Christians – stating that, even though they knew better, they were acquiring sinful habits and practices by keeping bad company. It is not possible to claim to be a Christian if only those parts of Holy Scripture are accepted which happen to fit in with our own particular opinion, prejudice, or habit. If anyone wishes to support the practice of adultery, or indulge the tendency to promiscuity or homosexuality, then he or she must resign and get on with it, and stop trying to condemn those who try to follow a higher standard. Admittedly, Christian standards are very high, but then Christians believe they will receive help through the Holy Spirit when they attempt to obey the requirements of their faith. The law condemns us all, but the grace of our Lord Jesus Christ gives us new life, new birth, where the old ways of sin and death are killed off, and every sinner transformed into a new creation. Dennis Prager writes:

Man's nature, undisciplined by values, will allow sex to dominate his life and the life of society . . . It is not overstated to say that the Torah's prohibition of non-marital sex made the creation of Western civilization possible. Societies that did not place boundaries around sexuality were stymied in their development. The subsequent dominance of the Western world can, to a significant extent, be attributed to the sexual revolution, initiated by Judaism and later carried forward by Christianity.[123]

Dr Jeffrey Satinover comments: "In sum, it is a simple and sobering fact that no society that has sanctioned unconstrained sexuality has long survived."[124]

The secular facts are clear. Report after report documents the deterioration of our society, which is only behaving according to what it has been taught to believe – a godless morality and a menu of lifestyle options. Rationalism, Darwinian evolution, existentialism, liberal theology and the new morality are destroying our civilization.

There are consequences to any choice. The Bible is very clear about it.

PART IV

WHEN FABLES FALL

All Scripture is given by inspiration of God, and is profitable for doctrine, for reproof, for correction, for instruction in righteousness, that the man of God may be complete, thoroughly equipped for every good work. I charge you therefore before God and the Lord Jesus Christ, who will judge the living and the dead at His appearing and His kingdom: Preach the word! Be ready in season and out of season. Convince, rebuke, exhort, with all longsuffering and teaching. For the time will come when they will not endure sound doctrine, but according to their own desires, because they have itching ears, they will heap up for themselves teachers; and they will turn their ears away from the truth, and be turned aside to fables. But you be watchful in all things, endure afflictions, do the work of an evangelist, fulfill your ministry.
(2 Timothy 3:16–4:5)

CHAPTER 16

THE WORLD MOVES ON

The doctrine of Evolution, if consistently accepted, makes it
impossible to believe the Bible.

Thomas Henry Huxley (1825–95)

There are more things in heaven and earth, Horatio,
Than are dreamt of in your philosophy.

William Shakespeare, *Hamlet*, Act 1 Scene 5

The gradual take-up of Darwinian theory by the global scientific community during the late nineteenth century never totally extinguished the flames of scientific criticism. Although the vast majority of scientists eventually took it up, a significant minority remained unconvinced; as we move into the twentieth century, dissenting voices were sustained against the theory. It is worthwhile to document some of the organizations that continue to oppose evolution and whose influence is growing.

The Creation Science Movement (CSM) is the oldest creationist movement in the world. Founded in 1932 as the "Evolution Protest Movement" by leading members of the Victoria Institute who were concerned at the scientific, ethical and theological consequences that belief in evolution brings to society, its aim was to counter the propaganda that was promoting the theory of evolution as if it were scientifically proven. A pamphlet on different subjects giving evidence of creation is published every other month, together with the journal *Creation*, which carries up-to-date news and comment.

The first CSM meeting (or EPM as it was then) was at 21 Essex Gardens, The Strand, London, in 1932. Sir Ambrose Fleming (1849–1945), inventor of the thermionic valve, presided, and what he said then still stands today. His comments were reported in *The Times* on 12 February 1935:

Of late years the Darwinian anthropology had been forced on public attention by numerous books in such a fashion as to create a belief that it was a certainly settled scientific truth. The fact that many eminent naturalists did not agree that Darwin's theory of species production had been sufficiently established as a truth was generally repressed. If there had been no creation, there was no need to assume any Creator; the chief basis for all religion was taken away and morality reduced to mere human expediency. It had seemed to a large number of thoughtful persons that it was of national importance to counteract the effects of reckless and indiscriminate popularisation of the theory of the wholly animal origin of mankind, especially among the young, by the diffusion of a truly scientific cause for all those altruistic, aesthetic, intellectual, spiritual and religious faculties in man, of which not the very slightest trace was seen in the animal species . . . they desired to oppose a one-sided materialistic presentation of human origin which rejected altogether any suggestion of creation. They said that the arguments of the Darwinian anthropologists were defective in logic and did not give the proof they assumed.[125]

This was written over seventy-five years ago. We have already documented some of what the impact has been on individuals, families and society, in the years since then. In the same period of time, more and more scientific evidence opposing evolution and supporting creation has been discovered in various disciplines, notably genetics, biochemistry and information theory. Evolutionists still do not "give the proof they assumed."

In the United States, the Creation Research Society (CRS) was founded in 1963 by a group of ten like-minded scientists, who had corresponded with each other for a number of years. A major impetus for this effort was a problem that each one had experienced. They had been unable to publish in established journals scientific information favorable to the creation viewpoint. Believing that there were probably other scientists with similar experiences, these men saw the need for a journal in which such information could be published. Thus, the CRS was incorporated in the state of Michigan as a non-profit corporation for educational and scientific purposes. The first issue of the *Creation Research Society Quarterly* was published in July 1964.[126]

The Institute for Creation Research (ICR) was first established by Dr Henry M. Morris in 1970 as the research division of Christian Heritage College (now San Diego Christian College), focused on research, communication, and education in those fields of science particularly relevant to the study of origins. ICR became autonomous in 1981. ICR Graduate School degree programs received formal approval from the state of California in 1981 and taught its first courses the summer of the same year. The school offered Master of Science degrees from 1981 to 2010.[127]

Creation Ministries International has its origins in the Australian ministry Creation Science Association (CSA) of Adelaide, South Australia, founded in 1977. In 1978, *Creation* magazine was started, then called *Ex Nihilo*, later *Creation Ex Nihilo*. In 1980, CSA became Creation Science Foundation Ltd (CSF). *Creation* magazine has since developed into a full-color publication with subscribers in over 100 countries worldwide. In 1984, a journal was started, initially called the *Technical Journal*, or *TJ*, now called the *Journal of Creation*, that contains in-depth, peer-reviewed comment, reviews and the latest research findings. The journal covers a wide spectrum of studies, not just science. Academic articles have appeared on topics such as philosophy, theology, history, archaeology, social sciences and many more. This is to complement the popular *Creation* magazine, providing in-depth material from many experts in their field to satisfy the enquiring mind.[128]

In about 1993, the Australian CSF ministry gave assistance to form a ministry independent of ICR in the eastern part of the USA, which eventually became known as Answers in Genesis (AiG). In late 2005, the US AiG separated and still operates under the same name. The parent group was renamed Creation Ministries International and today has offices in Australia, New Zealand, Canada, the United States and the United Kingdom.

There are other organizations, but these four are sufficient to show that opposition to evolution is widespread and significant. This has gradually become known as "creation science" or "creationism," a scientific endeavor to dispel the myths of evolution in favor of an objective, inductive approach to the available scientific evidence. Although creationism is ridiculed by the "established" scientific community, it is conducted by scientists who studied at the same universities and acquired the same degrees as their evolutionary counterparts.

It is the strength of the condemnation and vilification of creationism that is very surprising. We have previously pointed out that creation science is labeled as pseudo-science or dismissed as non-science. It is worth repeating that many scientists, including Nobel laureates, have a strong faith in a Creator God and find no dichotomy between their scientific work and their faith. This should be a matter of open debate. The scientific establishment, permeated as it is by the theory of evolution, constantly tries to prevent other points of view being aired. This is the curious part of the whole affair. As we previously concluded, this single-minded pursuit of evolutionary theory is holding back scientific progress. Back in the eighteenth century, William Paley once said: "There is a principle which is a bar against all information, which is proof against all argument, and which cannot fail to keep man in everlasting ignorance. This principle is contempt prior to examination."

The members of the scientific community claim respect for their views, based on their claim to be dispassionate observers of nature and arbiters of evidenced-based logic, rather than the faith-based and therefore unsubstantiated views of non-scientific alternatives. Why then are they so frightened of alternative views? Why must creationism as one such view be kept out of the classroom? Surely such a collection of unscientific myths would easily be refuted? That would then be that. However, rather than face up to and defeat creationism, they prefer to attempt to erase it. The answer to this conundrum must lie in their fear that creationism would not be refuted; in fact, evolution might suffer that particular fate. There used to be many debates between evolutionists and creationists. These hardly ever now take place. The creationists won almost all of them *on the science* with the information available at the time. Since then, there is much more evidence available that falsifies evolution – at least to the open-minded. No wonder evolutionists refuse to engage in open debate; they are frightened of the outcome. Perhaps this explains much of the name-calling and the attempts to belittle creationism.

As we noted in Part II, Chapter 8, there have been many advances in science since Darwin's day. Genetics and biochemistry have shown more and more complexity in every living cell than was ever imagined. Information theory has shown just how impossible it is to look upon the operations within a cell and dismiss the integrated biological systems and their precise operations as the product of randomness. Although effectively disguised, evolutionists have been retreating from proper science since the middle of the twentieth century, when Sir Julian Huxley pulled together the modern evolutionary synthesis, or neo-Darwinism. This can probably be considered the high-water mark of evolution as a serious scientific theory. Since then, advances in the biological sciences and new evidence from the field are forcing evolution into retreat. As we discussed earlier, some of the evidence claimed for evolution was deliberately fraudulent. These later discoveries are actually fatal to evolution. Evolutionists are in retreat on many fronts.

Geology

One of the classic foundations of evolutionary geology is the concept of uniformitarianism, put forward by Sir Charles Lyell almost 200 years ago. This gives evolution the huge amount of time it needs to work its "magic" and produce life as we know it. As a result of growing evidence from the field, evolutionary geologists have more or less abandoned uniformitarianism and accepted that catastrophism is the mechanism of the formation of the earth's deposits and strata. They have had to accept that the formation of the earth's crust involves extreme events of huge magnitude. David Raup of the University of Chicago stated: "Contemporary geologists and paleontologists now generally accept catastrophe as a 'way of life' although they may avoid the word catastrophe . . . The periods of relative quiet contribute only a small part of the record."[129] They still attempt to protect their position and argue that although many catastrophes went into forming the geologic column, these were only relatively short blips in the long ages of the earth. Unfortunately there is little or no evidence from the field for these long intervals between catastrophes. We just see catastrophe.

Fossils

We dealt with this subject in Chapter 8, but it is worth drawing out that there are four characteristics of the fossil record:

- Abrupt appearances
- Static forms
- Systematic gaps between species
- Lack of identifiable ancestors or descendants

This alone is fatal to gradual evolution. Although these characteristics are recognized by evolutionists, in an attempt to rescue the situation they adopt a similar solution to the geologists. That is, they propose that evolutionary bursts take place in a very short time in a given locality, followed by long periods of stasis – punctuated equilibrium. The point being that if the burst of evolution were very rapid and the population small and localized, fossil evidence for the event would be virtually impossible to find. In other words the evidence has again retreated into a hypothetical scenario where it cannot be observed or measured. Evolutionist Professor Stephen J. Gould stated:

> Paleontologists have paid an enormous price for Darwin's argument. We fancy ourselves to be the only true students of life's history, yet to preserve our favored account of evolution by natural selection we view our data as so bad that we almost never see the very process we profess to study.[130]

Punctuated equilibrium is only the first step in the retreat from evolution.

Biology and Biochemistry

As we pointed out earlier, getting life from non-life cannot be done; Louis Pasteur proved this in 1864 with his "law of biogenesis," where life can only come from pre-existing life. Evolutionists must have a mechanism to get life from inanimate chemicals. Thomas Huxley was one of the first to recognize this and try to come up with an explanation. He coined the term "abiogenesis" to describe the proposition that life can come from non-life. More than a century and a monumental research effort later, the efforts to find the means of a synthesis of life have produced a mountain of evidence against it. The more we have found out about life processes and cell structures, DNA and genetics, the greater is the divide between inert matter and the simplest of single-celled organisms. Evolutionists have had to retreat into proposing that there is some form of "chemical predestination" with unknown laws which somehow self-organize chemicals into complex structures directing themselves towards life.[131] It is worth quoting Sir Fred Hoyle on this aspect of evolution:

> They advocate the belief that tucked away in nature, outside of normal physics, there is a law which performs miracles (provided the miracles are in the aid of biology). This curious situation sits oddly on a profession that for long has been dedicated to coming up with logical [naturalist] explanations of biblical miracles.[132]

It would seem that evolutionists have been forced to invoke some kind of "supernature" to explain nature. Now isn't that interesting!

Mutations

In neo-Darwinian theory, mutations are the biological changes that provide natural selection with its means of providing all the biological diversity we see around us. Unfortunately, recent advances show that mutations are the simple physical result of the mechanical damage that occurs to all machinery, including biological machinery. Cellular error correction and repair mechanisms are also subject to the same damage. Mutations occur at such high rates that their damaging effects can be seen within an individual lifetime. All organisms within a species suffer similar random damage, so natural selection cannot discard them. In his paper "Mutations: Evolution's Engine Becomes Evolution's End!" Alex Williams summarizes the effects of mutations on the living organisms:

> Mutations are not uniquely biological events that provide an engine of natural variation for natural selection to work upon and produce all the variety of life. Mutation is the purely physical result of the all-pervading mechanical damage that accompanies all molecular machinery. As a consequence, *all multicellular life on earth* is undergoing inexorable genome decay because the deleterious [harmful] mutation rates are so high . . . and natural selection is ineffective in removing the damage.
>
> So much damage occurs that it is clearly evident within a single human lifetime. Our reproductive cells are *not* immune, as previously thought, but are just as prone to mechanical damage as our body cells. Somewhere between a few thousand and a few million mutations are enough to drive a human lineage to extinction, and this is likely to occur over a time scale of only tens to hundreds of thousands of years. This is far short of the supposed evolutionary time scales. Like rust eating away the steel in a bridge, mutations are eating away our genomes and there is nothing we can do to stop them.
>
> Evolution's engine, when properly understood, becomes evolution's end.[133]

Mutations eventually damage our genome to the point of extinction. This is the end towards which "evolution" is working. This is the complete opposite of evolutionary claims. Mutations are gradually killing off all cellular life on earth; this will be accomplished in thousands of years, not millions.

There are many more areas of recent discovery that could be quoted here; to be consistent I have stayed with the main areas examined throughout this book. One other thing should be noticed about the increasing evidence for design in the natural world. Design has become so self-evident that evolutionists are forced into the disclaimer that evolution has produced the "appearance" of design, rather than accept the overwhelming evidence for the reality of it. There is no scientific basis for such a statement; it is merely a spoiling move, designed to diminish the appreciation of design (pun intended) and retain the position that evolution is a random statistical process. It is nothing more than a statement of faith.

One of the conclusions that we can draw is that operational science has moved on to such a degree that we can state with great confidence that, on the evidence that has accrued to us in the 150 years since Darwin published *The Origin of Species*, evolution never happened.

Ironically, it is scientists, not church leaders, who are challenging the evolutionary and existential worldview, and it is these evangelical creation scientists who are promoting the cause of scriptural inerrancy. This in turn requires the literalness of the Genesis record, where it touches upon the natural world. So the call back to Christian orthodoxy is being led by scientists and their study of nature. Natural theology is making a strong comeback. In other words, the birth, rise and eventual death of Darwinian evolution will have taken place in the realm of natural theology after all! The Victorian evangelical scientists were forced into retreat, but their modern counterparts have kept the faith and continued to point out the scientific shortcomings of evolution. What irony that the Church should have abandoned the truth of Scripture for a naturalist theory that is slowly falling on its own sword! We are moving back to a position of the mid-nineteenth century, where man's use of intellect in natural theology is a valid form of inquiry as a legitimate part of the Christian faith.

No such movement is apparent from the Church, which seems to be embracing Darwinism still further. For example, in *The Times* newspaper of 11 February 2009, the 200th anniversary of Darwin's birth, we read:

The Vatican has admitted that Charles Darwin was on the right
track when he claimed that Man descended from apes. A leading
official declared yesterday that Darwin's theory of evolution was
compatible with Christian faith, and could even be traced to
St Augustine and St Thomas Aquinas. "In fact, what we mean
by evolution is the world as created by God," said Archbishop
Gianfranco Ravasi, head of the Pontifical Council for Culture.

On 14 September 2008, the Anglican Church posted an apology to
Darwin on its website. The day before, a journalist for the *Daily Mail*, a UK
newspaper, wrote:

The Church of England will tomorrow officially apologise to
Charles Darwin for misunderstanding his theory of evolution.
In a bizarre step, the Church will address its contrition directly
to the Victorian scientist himself, even though he died 126 years
ago. But the move was greeted with derision last night, with
Darwin's great-great-grandson dismissing it as "pointless" and
other critics branding it "ludicrous". Church officials compared
the apology to the late Pope John Paul II's decision to say sorry
for the Vatican's 1633 trial of Galileo, the astronomer who
appalled prelates by declaring that the earth revolved around
the sun. The officials said that senior bishops wanted to atone
for the vilification their predecessors heaped on Darwin in the
1860s, when he put forward his theory that man was descended
from apes. The Church is also anxious to counter the view that
its teaching is incompatible with science. It wants to distance
itself from fundamentalist Christians, who believe in the Biblical
account of the creation of the world in seven [sic] days. An
article to be posted on the Church's website will say: "Charles
Darwin, 200 years from your birth [in 1809], the Church of
England owes you an apology for misunderstanding you and,
by getting our first reaction wrong, encouraging others to
misunderstand you still."[134]

So the Church at large is still embracing evolution and rejecting Scripture;
it is being left behind as both science and theology are beginning to move

on – in fact it seems to be actively going the other way. Although there is no conflict between science and Christianity, we have seen that evolution and creation are mutually exclusive ideas. Well-meaning attempts to fuse the two, or explain away the conflict between them, solve nothing. Such attempts do, however, debase further the authority of Scripture in relation to "science." Actually *apologizing* to Darwin is a sign of terminal decay. The Church is full of its own pride and intellect, but bereft of wisdom, and cannot see that it is "wretched, miserable, poor, blind, and naked" (Revelation 3:17).

Despite the behavior of the Anglican Church, we are beginning to move back to a position similar to that of the early nineteenth century, where man's use of natural theology, reasoning from the world of nature towards an understanding of God, was perfectly in harmony with Scripture and Christ. We have looked at the way that modern science is wriggling on the hook of the latest developments, and cannot much longer hang on to its evolutionary mindset and the philosophy of scientific naturalism. The scientific community is ferociously trying to contain the long slow fall of its monumental folly, because of the complete loss of credibility that goes with it.

There are only two basic origins of life. Either we were created by an omnipotent being or we weren't. There are several variations, but they all boil down to these two. If we weren't created there needs to be some mechanism of bringing forth life and developing the natural world to its present condition. Scientists have called this option evolution, which includes the origin of the universe in the so-called spontaneous big bang, followed by biological evolution. The big bang is another rationalist hypothesis, which is contradicted by much evidence. We have not considered the big bang theory in this book, preferring to focus on biological evolution. In any case, we have seen that biological evolution is impossible.

In conclusion, our choices are that we came into existence by God's hand or without it; we are either created or evolved. If we falsify the one, it proves the other, and vice versa. On the basis of what we have seen, **creation is the only credible, rational option.**

On a personal level, when I thought about this conclusion and the disdain of evolutionists towards those who oppose them, I was reminded of the poem "Ozymandias" by Percy Bysshe Shelley:

OZYMANDIAS

I met a traveler from an antique land
Who said: Two vast and trunkless legs of stone
Stand in the desert. Near them, on the sand,
Half sunk, a shattered visage lies, whose frown,
And wrinkled lip, and sneer of cold command,
Tell that its sculptor well those passions read
Which yet survive, stamped on these lifeless things,
The hand that mocked them, and the heart that fed;
And on the pedestal these words appear:
"My name is Ozymandias, king of kings:
Look upon my works, ye Mighty, and despair!"
Nothing beside remains. Round the decay
Of that colossal wreck, boundless and bare
The lone and level sands stretch far away.

                              Percy Bysshe Shelley (1792–1822)

Shelley eloquently reminds us of a great truth. I was forcibly struck that the poetic fate of Ozymandias will inevitably be the actual fate of evolution, eroded by the sands of evidence and blown away by the winds of time.

CHAPTER 17

THE ANVIL THAT HAS WORN OUT MANY HAMMERS

For we did not follow cunningly devised fables when we made known to you the power and coming of our Lord Jesus Christ, but were eyewitnesses of His majesty. For He received from God the Father honor and glory when such a voice came to Him from the Excellent Glory: "This is My beloved Son, in whom I am well pleased." And we heard this voice which came from heaven when we were with Him on the holy mountain. We also have the more sure prophetic word, which you do well to heed as a light that shines in a dark place, until the day dawns and the morning star rises in your hearts; knowing this first, that no prophecy of Scripture is of any private interpretation, for prophecy never came by the will of man, but holy men of God spoke as they were moved by the Holy Spirit.

(2 Peter 1:16–21)

There is one problem that still remains to be looked at, and that is the credibility of God's revelation to man in Holy Scripture:

For if the trumpet makes an uncertain sound, who will prepare for battle?

(1 Corinthians 14:8)

If the polls are to be trusted, about 70% of people read their horoscope daily. Few read the Bible anymore. The reason is not far to find; its credibility has been reduced to zero: higher criticism, theistic evolution, progressive evolution, the gap theory, the day-age theory, the revelatory day theory, the framework hypothesis – all these are an attempt to harmonize Scripture with naturalistic science. On top of that we have existential Christianity and liberal theology. Most people in today's modern culture would laugh if they were asked to trust the Bible over other possible sources of authority. They would be scathing in their condemnation of the book as a collection of myths and folklore, long ago debunked by science and modern research. Most people have never read the Bible. They live in a period of history that has given up the things of God and the teachings of Holy Scripture. It is no wonder that Scripture is ignored.

It is a strong drive in most people to look for some authority to give them comfort in their current situation and hope for their future prosperity. In his book *When Jesus Returns*, Rev. David Pawson writes that there are basically three groups of source material for such a search.[135] These are: the superstitious, the scientific, and the scriptural. The first is the least trustworthy, consisting of astrology, horoscope reading, fortune-telling, tarot cards, I Ching, Ouija boards and that kind of thing. These predictions are rarely correct. That is, they are wrong 99% of the time, with simple statistics accounting for the occasional success. The second group of source material is the scientific research community, where trends and conditions are critically studied and mathematically calculated, to give some form of prediction about the likely future of some particular item, say environmental trends. These forms of research may achieve modest success in their forecasts. The third source is religious writings, with their prophecies and predictions of the future. In all cases except one there is a very poor record of accuracy. For example, many people swear by the prophecies of the monk Nostradamus, but there are no exact cases of fulfillment of any of the rather vague and ambiguous verses (or quatrains) of poetry he wrote.

Biblical Prophecy

The exception to the rule is the Bible, which, according to *The Encyclopedia of Biblical Prophecy* contains 737 separate prophecies[136] in clear language about future events. We can identify the dates of the authorship of the sixty-six books of the Bible with reasonable accuracy, using well-proven secular methods, thus showing that the predictions were written down many years before the actual events. So far 594 of these prophecies have come true, 80.6% of the total. However, the unfulfilled prophecies deal with events still in the future, at the end of the world, so the Bible actually has 100% accuracy of fulfillment. However, instead of studying this remarkable book, people subject it to ridicule and dismiss it as a collection of myths. It is very peculiar that a culture that prides itself on rationalism dismisses a rational approach to clear evidence.

To re-establish the credibility of the Bible we need to undo the work of the documentary hypothesis, the higher critics and the archaeologists. We also need to disentangle ourselves from the bleak existentialist worldview of liberal theology. We need to establish the accuracy of the Bible where it touches on the natural world and history, and reaffirm the existence of the supernatural and the miracles in a way that is convincing, and do it from the Bible itself. How does the Bible speak about itself in this regard? We have Isaiah, the greatest of all Biblical prophets, to consult:

> *To whom will you liken Me, and make Me equal*
> *And compare Me, that we should be alike?*
> *They lavish gold out of the bag,*
> *And weigh silver on the scales;*
> *They hire a goldsmith, and he makes it a god;*
> *They prostrate themselves, yes, they worship.*
> *They bear it on the shoulder, they carry it*
> *And set it in its place, and it stands;*
> *From its place it shall not move.*
> *Though one cries out to it, yet it cannot answer*
> *Nor save him out of his trouble.*
>
> *Remember this, and show yourselves men;*
> *Recall to mind, O you transgressors.*
> *Remember the former things of old,*
> *For I am God, and there is no other;*
> *I am God, and there is none like Me,*
> *Declaring the end from the beginning,*
> *And from ancient times things that are not yet done,*
> *Saying, "My counsel shall stand,*
> *And I will do all My pleasure."*

(Isaiah 46:5–10)

Here God points out that no other god speaks or helps in any way, except Him. From this passage we see that God is telling us to remember the prophecies that He caused to be written in the Bible and that they came true. Prophetic fulfillment is what distinguishes the one true Living God and His written Word, from all others, which are mere man-made constructs.

In the Scripture citation from Peter's second letter at the head of this chapter, we read that we have "the more sure prophetic word." More sure than what? We must remember that Peter was a witness to the earthly ministry of Christ Himself. Peter saw many miracles, including people raised from the dead, the resurrected Lord, His transfiguration on the Mount of Olives; he heard the voice of God, and much more besides. Despite all these existential events, which were widely known to his audience, Peter wrote that we have "the more sure prophetic word." This, he says, will keep you going to the end because prophecy, by its very nature, cannot come from the natural world or human imagination. It has a supernatural origin in God Himself. This, he says, is more important than personal experiences, because experiences can always be explained away by clever people, especially when memory fades and doubt creeps in.

Peter was emphasizing that the eternal Word of God foretold many events which subsequently came true. These prophecies give a background and context for the ministry of Christ. This is more important than Peter's experiences. There were many false messiahs and holy men around in Jesus' day. Without the supernatural testimony of the Word of God, pointing to Him over many centuries prior to His birth, in over 300 separate and specific prophecies, Jesus would have blended right in. He would have been just another holy man, one among many. His claims to be the supernatural Son of God could easily have been dismissed. We might never have heard of Him.

Following on from this, we can say that the Bible must contain accurate information where it touches upon history. Otherwise the prophecies are meaningless.

Because of the truly terrifying implications of this prophetic accuracy, many attempts have been made to "late-date" certain books of Bible prophecy, especially the book of Daniel. Because of the accuracy of Daniel's predicted world history, many have tried to date Daniel to the second century BC. They want to show that it was written in retrospect. Sadly for this attempt, Daniel and his friends were taken captive in 605 BC when Nebuchadnezzar first invaded Judah, and he wrote his book in exile in Babylon. Some propose that the five books of Moses were compiled by many later editors/authors, in the so-called documentary hypothesis. We looked at the documentary hypothesis in Chapter 10 and found it to be false. The book of Isaiah has come under fire from scholars who propose that there was more than one author; the reason is not far to find: it has more prophecies of the Messiah than any other book except Psalms. These scholars don't want to face the implications. Sadly for the multiple authorship theory, the unity of Isaiah has been effectively demonstrated by the consistent writing style and vocabulary throughout the text. For example, the phrase "the Holy One of Israel" is used twelve times in chapters 1–39 and thirteen times in chapters 40–66, but only six times in the rest of the Old Testament. There are many examples of attempts to deny the prophetic fulfillment of many of the other parts of the Bible. All these challenges have been met with convincing answers.

In addition to many Bible scholars, many secular scholars, using standard secular dating methods, have concluded that the books predate the events they predict. We can conclude that if any book consistently prophesies rightly, in advance and in clear terms understandable to all, it cannot be of a natural origin. By definition it is supernaturally given and independent of the limitations of the mind of man.

Also, following the conquests of Alexander the Great, much of the then known world spoke Greek and followed Greek culture. Many Jews no longer spoke or read Hebrew. To meet this need, the whole of the Old Testament was translated into Greek circa 285–270 BC by a team of seventy-two scholars in Alexandria, in Egypt. The Greek version thus produced is known as the "Septuagint," after the Greek word for "seventy." This means that all the prophecies concerning the Messiah of Israel were in place almost 300 years before His birth. How then can we ignore the fulfilled prophecy of the Bible? It is astounding that many scholars the world over recognize that the Bible is supernaturally unique in this respect, giving us history in advance. Yet we ignore the clear historical fulfillment of these prophecies and treat the Bible as if it were just another book.

An Archaeological Digression

We have already seen how the documentary hypothesis was used to undermine the five books of Moses without proper archaeological support. What support there was came from the absence of archaeological evidence for the Bible itself. We have only briefly mentioned archaeology before this, and we need to take a better look at it at this point. Archaeologists went to the Middle East armed with a Bible and looked for the evidence of the Israelites in Egypt and in the wilderness and found nothing; they looked for the existence of the Hittites and the Canaanites and found nothing. Archaeological evidence for the battle of Jericho was missing, and the same for the existence of David's and Solomon's kingdoms. Almost two centuries of archaeological endeavor failed to produce any tangible evidence in support of the early Bible narratives.

The traditional school of theology always treated the Bible as history, but the archaeology was missing. When literary criticism in the nineteenth century arose, it led to a critical view. The historical reliability of the texts was questioned, but orthodox scholars were hoping to receive help from archaeology – widely regarded as an evidence-based discipline. For a while this seemed to happen, but through the course of the twentieth century a split between archaeologists and Biblical scholars developed. There were two notable issues: the absence of definitive archaeological discoveries has led to some embarrassment for the Biblical scholars; from the archaeological point of view the interpretation of results is now carried out from a much more skeptical stance than the earlier openness of Biblical archaeology. Modern archaeologists initially tend to discount the Biblical record as false, and they require a greater level of proof than for other sources before they will even consider it.

One group, the "minimalists," argues strongly that the Old Testament does not contain any historically reliable information before the sixth century BC (before the Babylonian exile). Based on this, they propose that the Old Testament manuscripts date from after the exile, or after the sixth century BC. They therefore conclude that the amount of historical information contained in them is negligible. Because of the strong connections to the University of Copenhagen, the group is sometimes also called the Copenhagen school.

One of the reasons for the absence of Biblical archaeological evidence is a flawed dating method for ancient history, based on the chronologies of the Egyptian dynasties. David Rohl's book *A Test of Time* is subtitled *The Bible – From Myth to History*.[137] It explains how he believes the accepted dates are wrong. In his research into the Egyptian Third Intermediate Period, Rohl discovered that the timelines for certain pharaohs were artificially extended. This meant that Biblical archaeologists were looking in the right places, but in the wrong times. That is one of the reasons why nothing was found. When the timelines were adjusted, many things seemed to fall into place.

Many discoveries are now being made which are beginning to

demonstrate the historical reality of David and Solomon and the long history of the Hebrews from Abraham onwards. The Amarna letters (baked clay tablets) were discovered in 1887 at El Amarna in Egypt, recording the pleas for help against the *Habiru* (Hebrews); David Rohl compared the detailed political history contained in the Amarna letters with the events and personalities of the Early Monarchy period of Biblical Israel. He believes there is a convincing synthesis to be made that David was a contemporary of Akhenaten and Tutankhamun in Egypt, and the Hittite emperor Suppiluliumas I.[138]

In 1966 Professor Manfred Bietak with his team arrived in Egypt at Tell ad-Daba to try and discover more about the scattered monuments of the twelfth, thirteenth and nineteenth dynasties. His researches led to the discovery of strong evidence that the ancient city of Avaris in Goshen was the place of the Hebrews' sojourn in Egypt.[139]

Digging between the City of David and the southern wall of the Temple Mount during the mid-1980s under the guidance of her grandfather, Dr Eilat Mazar uncovered a large stone gateway complex, 45 by 54 feet, constructed sometime before the Babylonians sacked Jerusalem in the sixth century BC. Attached to the gate was a short section of the city wall of Jerusalem, built by Solomon. Announcing the news at a press conference in 1986, Mazar said the gateway complex was probably one of twelve gates mentioned in the Biblical record.

In 1993, a team digging at Tell Dan in northern Israel found a fragment of a stone tablet, dated to the ninth century BC, with the inscriptions: "House of David" and "King of Israel." It was a definitive find – proof that David existed.

One of the most brilliant language scholars of the twentieth century was Professor Robert "Dick" Wilson, former professor of Semitic philology at Princeton Theological Seminary in the United States. In his student days he set himself a forty-five-year schedule: fifteen years of language study, fifteen years of studying the text of the Old Testament, and fifteen years of publishing his findings. In the course of this tremendous program, which he fulfilled to the letter, he learned twenty-eight languages and dialects, studying under some of the leading professors of his day. In his second slot of fifteen years he collected over 100,000 quotations from these languages and compared them with related statements from the Old Testament itself.

His conclusion was that the Bible was consistently accurate, while all other contemporary records contained inconsistencies or contradictions. For example, he showed that the Bible's details of about forty kings living from 2000 BC to 400 BC were so accurate that: "No stronger evidence for the substantial accuracy of the Old Testament records could possibly be imagined. Mathematically it is one chance in 750 thousand million, million, million that this accuracy is mere circumstance."[140] He eventually summed up his findings like this: "I have now come to the conviction that no man knows enough to assail the truthfulness of the Old Testament."[141]

There are many more examples of archaeological finds from the nations surrounding Israel that corroborate many details of the Old Testament. I recently visited the British Museum and found a very useful booklet entitled *Through the British Museum – with the Bible*[142] which takes the visitor through the exhibits from a Biblical point of view. I recommend a visit.

Sir William Ramsay, founder member of the British Museum and holder of nine honorary doctorates from universities in Britain, Europe and the United States, was one of the most brilliant archaeologists the world has ever known. At one point his studies concentrated on the narrative in the book of Acts, written by Luke. When Ramsay began his work he was convinced that Luke's details were seriously flawed, but the further he went, the more the Bible was vindicated. Eventually the sheer weight of the evidence forced him to change his mind and come to this assessment: "Luke is a historian of the first rank; not merely are his statements of fact trustworthy, he is possessed of the true historic sense . . . in short, this author should be placed along with the very greatest of historians."[143]

Archaeology is a field in which the Bible is open to investigation and the amazing truth is that new discoveries are underlining the Bible's accuracy, not undermining it. Nelson Glück, a renowned Jewish archaeologist, speaks of the "almost incredibly accurate historical memory of the Bible . . . It may be stated categorically that no archaeological discovery has ever controverted a Biblical reference."[144]

The most famous find of all, the Dead Sea Scrolls, confirms the accuracy of the Bible, where they have been compared with our modern texts. The complete Scroll of Isaiah gives us a copy which is 1,000 years earlier than the one we had – the Masoretic text. When this older scroll was compared with the Masoretic text there were only three letter variations in the whole book of Isaiah. This example confirms that the transmission of the Biblical text was phenomenally accurate. Since these scrolls were buried sometime before AD 70, we can conclude that much of the New Testament was in circulation before then. We now have renewed confidence that the text of the modern Bible is accurately handed down to us, and that the New Testament is truly eyewitness testimony, written by people who were there.

As more and more of these discoveries are made, providing examples of history as described in the Biblical record, there has been a rise of open opposition from many archaeologists. They tend to reject the conclusions made from these findings – not because they question the abilities of the archaeologists, but because they have already dismissed the Bible as credible source material. Their academic prejudices are being challenged. Where have we heard that before?

All I wanted to do in this brief diversion was to look at the subject, to show that faith in the historical accuracy of Scripture is increasingly supported by archaeology. There are still many difficulties, but the world is moving on and more and more evidence is coming to light. So we can relax and look at the prophecies with absolute confidence that Scripture is always dependable and accurate in its statements.

The Prophetic Witness of Scripture

We who are not eyewitnesses of the Gospel events, but observers from far off in time, can still know for certain that the Bible is true and that it is the voice of God; Peter was right in his Epistle, that we can be certain because of the fulfilled prophecies. The Bible is the only book in the world that contains prophecies that can be checked out. It is the only holy book that has any credibility as the Word of God.

At various times in history Scripture has been widely studied and consulted for guidance on everything from personal behavior to government policy. In our current age such studies have been neglected even by the Church. This is rather strange, since prophecy makes up a significant proportion of the Bible. About 25%, or one quarter, of the entire Bible consists of prophecy, or predictions about the future. The Bible claims to be the self-revelation of God to man and points us to prophecy as validation of that claim, where prophecies have fulfillment in every detail, fulfillment in exact time, and fulfillment in sequence. Many different types of things are predicted, but nothing is predicted in more detail than the birth, death and resurrection of Jesus Christ. Of the total of 737, no less than 300 separate prophecies are about Him, more than any other person or event in history. He has fulfilled all of them except the ones to do with His second coming. The one thing that stands out above all others is that the probability that Jesus Christ the Messiah could fulfill all these predictions by random accident is very small indeed. Let us tabulate some of the more important ones. Before we do, let us look at how we assess probabilities:

Take any two random events each with a probability of 50% of occurring; the probability that both will occur together is: 0.5 × 0.5 = 0.25 or 25%.

Expressed another way: one chance in four.

Take any two random events each with a probability of 10% of occurring; the probability that both will occur together is: 0.1 × 0.1 = 0.01 or 1%.

Expressed another way: one chance in 100.

So if we have a series of probabilities, all of which must be true, we multiply them all together to get the final answer. We know we have in advance some 300 prophecies for Jesus to become the Messiah. If these were all random events, we would need to assign a probability to each one and then multiply them all together to come up with the final answer. Remember in Chapter 8 where we saw how to write large numbers? We are going to need it! Professor Peter Stoner (1888–1980) calculated the probability of one man fulfilling only a handful of the over 300 Messianic prophecies. In 1944, he published his research results in *Science Speaks: Scientific Proof of the Accuracy of Prophecy and the Bible.* Stoner concluded that the probability of one person fulfilling just eight of the specific prophecies was statistically impossible![145]

I adapted the following from Prof. Stoner's *Science Speaks* by changing the US silver dollar to a UK pound coin. Let us take just eight prophecies as an example and assign probabilities to them:

Prophecies of the Messiah

Micah 5:2	Born in Bethlehem	1:100,000
Zechariah 9:9	King on a donkey	1:100
Zechariah 11:12	30 pieces of silver	1:1,000
Zechariah 11:13	Temple; potter	1:100,000
Zechariah 13:6	Wounds in hands	1:1,000
Isaiah 53:7	Silence; no defense	1:1,000
Isaiah 53:9	Died with the wicked	1:1,000
Psalm 22:16	Crucified	1:10,000

Total Composite Probability 1:10,000,000,000,000,000,000,000,000,000

That's one chance in 10^{28} or one chance in ten thousand trillion trillion! We multiplied all the probabilities together to get the answer. When Stoner assigned the individual probabilities to the prophecies, he had to decide how likely these things were to happen by accident, or randomly. In all eight cases Stoner chose conservative odds. If you wish to argue, to either increase or decrease them, please do so. My personal opinion is that the true probabilities in all cases would be much higher than those chosen by Stoner. However, what does one chance in 10^{28} mean? Firstly, it has been estimated that the total number of individuals who ever lived is about 100 billion, or 10^{11}. It means that the odds of any one individual fulfilling all these eight conditions are $10^{28}/10^{11}$ or 10^{17}. In plain English, this is one chance in ten thousand trillion!

Imagine the United Kingdom (area = 242,900 km^2) covered with 10^{17} pound coins. Each coin has a volume of about 1141 mm^3. They would cover the country about half a meter deep.[146] Mark one of them and stir well. Blindfold yourself and roam over the UK wherever you like. Choose a coin at random. How likely is it you would get the marked coin?   ·

If we take another 8 prophecies and conservatively assume the same composite probability, then for 16 prophecies we get odds of: $10^{28} \times 10^{28} = 10^{56}$. If we again divide by the number of people who ever lived, we get $10^{56} / 10^{11} = 10^{45}$. So what does 10^{45} mean? The UK covered with pound coins half a meter deep is woefully inadequate. We need a ball of pound coins with a radius of 93 times the distance of the earth to the sun![147] Mark one of them and stir well. Put on a spacesuit and roam wherever you like. Choose a coin at random. How likely is it you would get the marked coin?

If we multiply our 16 prophecies by 3 and conservatively assume the same composite probability, for 48 prophecies we get: $10^{56} \times 10^{56} \times 10^{56} = 10^{168}$. If we again divide by the total population of the earth, we get: $10^{168}/10^{11} = 10^{157}$. What does 10^{157} mean?

The solar model with pound coins doesn't cut it. We need to use something much smaller: the atom, the smallest discrete object in the universe, excluding subatomic structures. The size of the atom is difficult to state exactly, since the atomic radius increases with increasing atomic number, ranging from about 0.1 to 0.5×10^{-9} meters. If we take the smallest size, it gives a tiny volume of about 4.2×10^{-30} cubic meters.[148] That's 4.2 million trillion trillionths of a cubic meter! Now, scientists conservatively estimate there are between 10^{78} and 10^{82} atoms in the universe. For the purposes of this argument we shall assume there are 10^{80}. So if we make a ball of every atom in the universe, this would have a volume of about $4.2 \times 10^{-30} \times 10^{80} = 4.2 \times 10^{50}$ cubic meters. But we can't stop at our own universe's worth of 10^{80} atoms; we need to consider another $10^{157}/10^{80} = 10^{77}$ universes worth of atoms! This would give us a total volume of $4.2 \times 10^{50} \times 10^{77}$, or 4.2×10^{127} cubic meters. If we scale up to kilometers, we get a sphere of 4.2×10^{118} cubic kilometers, full of tiny atoms! Mark one of them and stir well. By the way, a volume of 4.2×10^{118} cubic kilometers in the shape of a sphere would have a diameter of 4.3×10^{39} kilometers.[149] Just to try and give you an idea of the size of this ball, when converted to light years it is 242,942,006,574,221,951,817,206,209 light years across![150] So now, in your new atomic spacesuit, how long would it take you to wander through all those light years? Just how likely is it you would choose the marked atom? That's what one chance in 10^{157} means. And we've only dealt with 48 out of 300 prophecies! It's mind-boggling!

Why do we bother with mathematics like this? Quite simply, to show the absolute absurdity of thinking that the fulfillment of all 300 prophecies was random. It is just not possible. Remember Emile Borel, who said that one chance in 1050 was no chance at all? We are way past that. The only explanation that makes sense is that there was no randomness about it. The prophecies correctly predicted Jesus who, according to God's plan, came to earth and carried out His ministry of redemption. The American Scientific Affiliation commented on Stoner's work:

> The manuscript for *Science Speaks* has been carefully reviewed by a committee of the American Scientific Affiliation members and by the Executive Council of the same group and has been found, in general, to be dependable and accurate in regard to the scientific material presented. The mathematical analysis included is based upon principles of probability which are thoroughly sound and Professor Stoner has applied these principles in a proper and convincing way.[151]

I am more certain that Jesus Christ is exactly who He said He is than I am of any other fact in the universe.

Conclusion

The Bible claims to be the supernatural Word of God and points us to the fulfillment of prophecy as proof. We have shown that there is much historical evidence that Biblical prophecy has been fulfilled hundreds of times throughout history. Secular dating methods and archaeology support this conclusion. It is impossible for anyone to fulfill all the prophecies in a random way. It was supernaturally planned and carried out.

The Anvil has indeed worn out many hammers. We can say that all attempts to reduce the Bible to a man-made collection of myths have failed. The Bible stands outside and above everything that science, philosophy and theology can bring to bear.

Existentialism is blown away, higher criticism is blown away, and scientific naturalism cannot contain the Bible.

CHAPTER 18

A CALL TO ACTION

Go now, write it on a tablet for them, inscribe it on a scroll, that for the days to come it may be an everlasting witness. These are rebellious people, deceitful children, children unwilling to listen to the Lord's instruction. They say to the seers, "See no more visions!" and to the prophets, "Give us no more visions of what is right! Tell us pleasant things, prophesy illusions. Leave this way, get off this path, and stop confronting us with the Holy One of Israel!"

(Isaiah 30:8–11 NIV)

Nevertheless, when the Son of Man comes, will He really find faith on the earth?

(Luke 18:8)

And to the angel of the church of the Laodiceans write, "These things says the Amen, the Faithful and True Witness, the Beginning of the creation of God: 'I know your works, that you are neither cold nor hot. I could wish you were cold or hot. So then, because you are lukewarm, and neither cold nor hot, I will vomit you out of My mouth. Because you say, "I am rich, have become wealthy, and have need of nothing" – and do not know that you are wretched, miserable, poor, blind, and naked – I counsel you to buy from Me gold refined in the fire, that you may be rich; and white garments, that you may be clothed, that the shame of your nakedness may not be revealed; and anoint your eyes with eye salve, that you may see. As many as I love, I rebuke and chasten. Therefore be zealous and repent. Behold, I stand at the door and knock. If anyone hears My voice and opens the door, I will come in to him and dine with him, and he with Me. To him who overcomes I will grant to sit with Me on My throne, as I also overcame and sat down with My Father on His throne. He who has an ear, let him hear what the Spirit says to the churches.'"

(Revelation 3:14–22)

So where are we at the beginning of the twenty-first century? Various strands of history, the development of philosophy, and the growth of modern science have come together to radically change the way we view the world and our role in it. What must be the response of a Christian to the crisis of spiritual faith in our society? It must surely be to place his or her faith in the Word of God. As we have seen, this is not only rational, but realistic.

Postmodern science with its evolutionary worldview now stands in direct and total opposition to the Bible. These two worldviews – one might say these two faiths – cannot coexist. I agree that the world has come once more to a point where great issues are at stake. I believe that the current moral paralysis of the West and its slide into anarchy, with a rising tide of violence, moral degeneration, paganism and superstition, is a consequence of the undermining of its traditional Christian worldview. We need a restatement of the basic Christian fundamentals. We need to embrace the Bible as our worldview *against* the culture and consensus of the West. God said a great delusion would happen and it has:

> *Beloved, I now write to you this second epistle (in both of which I stir up your pure minds by way of reminder), that you may be mindful of the words which were spoken before by the holy prophets, and of the commandment of us, the apostles of the Lord and Savior, knowing this first: that scoffers will come in the last days, walking according to their own lusts, and saying, "Where is the promise of His coming? For since the fathers fell asleep, all things continue as they were from the beginning of creation." For this they willfully forget: that by the word of God the heavens were of old, and the earth standing out of water and in the water, by which the world that then existed perished, being flooded with water. But the heavens and the earth which are now preserved by the same word, are reserved for fire until the day of judgment and perdition of ungodly men.*
>
> (2 Peter 3:1–7)

Does this not foresee evolution? God really does know what is going on; He has a plan and has everything under control. We simply must ensure that our response is Biblical, so that we are not counted among the ungodly, but are "overcomers:"

He who overcomes shall inherit all things, and I will be his God and
he shall be My son.

(Revelation 21:7)

Therefore, beloved, looking forward to these things, be diligent to be
found by Him in peace, without spot and blameless; and consider that
the longsuffering of our Lord is salvation – as also our beloved brother
Paul, according to the wisdom given to him, has written to you, as also
in all his epistles, speaking in them of these things, in which are some
things hard to understand, which untaught and unstable people twist
to their own destruction, as they do also the rest of the Scriptures. You
therefore, beloved, since you know this beforehand, beware lest you also
fall from your own steadfastness, being led away with the error of the
wicked; but grow in the grace and knowledge of our Lord and Savior
Jesus Christ.

(2 Peter 3:14–18)

We have been warned not to twist the Biblical message, because that will
lead to our destruction – as indeed it is doing, even in this life. We must
not water down the gospel message in an attempt to retain church members
or accommodate the world. What happened when Jesus taught hard and
difficult things?

From that time many of His disciples went back and walked with Him
no more. Then Jesus said to the twelve, "Do you also want to go away?"

(John 6:66–67)

Did Jesus tone down His arguments or His teaching to remain popular?
Did He say to Peter, "Quick! Go after them and tell them we'll have a
different style of service tomorrow. They'll be sure to enjoy it and have a
good time. Go on! We must not lose them." He said nothing of the kind.
He even turned to His twelve nearest and closest disciples and asked if they
wanted to leave as well. He was quite prepared to start over. The gospel
message was the important thing, not how the people felt about it. You can
search the New Testament from beginning to end and the idea of pleasing
the people or accommodating the world is conspicuous by its absence. Jesus
loved sinners and wept over them, but He didn't water down His message

to spare their feelings. Not only did many leave Him but many actively persecuted Him, culminating in the crucifixion. He warned His disciples that this would be their lot in life also:

> *Behold, I send you out as sheep in the midst of wolves . . . Now brother*
> *will deliver up brother to death, and a father his child; and children*
> *will rise up against parents and cause them to be put to death. And*
> *you will be hated by all for My name's sake. But he who endures to the*
> *end will be saved.*
>
> (Matthew 10:16, 21–22)

The disciples took this to heart, and we read later, in Acts chapter 4, about Peter and John, who were arrested for preaching the gospel, charged before the Jewish authorities, beaten, imprisoned and threatened with death. The church had a prayer meeting and decided to go on preaching with boldness. In fact, they did not stop daily preaching that Jesus is the Christ, in the temple and in various homes. They didn't cave in under threats, or water down the message to please the authorities. They were eventually scattered by persecutions and went everywhere, preaching the gospel. By Acts chapter 17 we read how they turned the world upside down!

We should also endure the pressures of our modern world and, like the original disciples, embrace the Word of God:

> *And do this, understanding the present time. The hour has come for you*
> *to wake up from your slumber, because our salvation is nearer now than*
> *when we first believed. The night is nearly over; the day is almost here.*
> *So let us put aside the deeds of darkness and put on the armor of light.*
> *Let us behave decently, as in the daytime, not in orgies and drunkenness,*
> *not in sexual immorality and debauchery, not in dissension and jealousy.*
> *Rather, clothe yourselves with the Lord Jesus Christ, and do not think*
> *about how to gratify the desires of the sinful nature.*
>
> (Romans 13:11–14 NIV)

All those who testify to the power of the gospel testify to its separating power, of conviction of sin, of repentance, and the salvation that follows. The early church preached Jesus Christ crucified, risen and ascended. We know it was effective. The cross is a symbol of redemption and cleansing, restitution and healing, perfection and holiness. It stands against all the ideas and practices of this fallen world. It is only meaningful within a very highly developed view of God. It is only meaningful once it is understood that we can have a relationship with Him. It is only meaningful once we understand that we are special creatures, destined to live with Him. It is the way back to Him. Without the cross we are all lost. It is only found within the pages of Holy Scripture, nowhere else. If the Bible is rejected, so is salvation. Salvation comes through the hearing of the Word:

> *In Him you also trusted, after you heard the word of truth, the gospel of your salvation.*
>
> (Ephesians 1:13)

The crucifixion, resurrection and ascension of Jesus Christ are integral to the Christian faith. To imagine that God could not accomplish these events is to limit Him to the level of our own understanding and completely destroy the basis of the faith. Paul, in his first letter to the Corinthians, addresses this very problem:

> *Moreover, brethren, I declare to you the gospel which I preached to you, which also you received and in which you stand, by which also you are saved, if you hold fast that word which I preached to you – unless you believed in vain. For I delivered to you first of all that which I also received: that Christ died for our sins according to the Scriptures, and that He was buried, and that He rose again the third day according to the Scriptures, and that He was seen by Cephas [Peter], then by the twelve. After that He was seen by over five hundred brethren at once, of whom the greater part remain to the present, but some have fallen asleep. After that He was seen by James, then by all the apostles. Then last of all He was seen by me also, as by one born out of due time . . .*
>
> *Now if Christ is preached that He has been raised from the dead, how do some among you say that there is no resurrection of the dead? But if there is no resurrection of the dead, then Christ is not risen. And if Christ is not risen, then our preaching is empty and your faith is also empty. Yes, and we are found false witnesses of God, because we have*

testified of God that He raised up Christ, whom He did not raise up –
if in fact the dead do not rise. For if the dead do not rise, then Christ
is not risen. And if Christ is not risen, your faith is futile; you are still
in your sins! Then also those who have fallen asleep in Christ have
perished. If in this life only we have hope in Christ, we are of all men
the most pitiable.

But now Christ is risen from the dead, and has become the
firstfruits of those who have fallen asleep. For since by man came
death, by Man also came the resurrection of the dead. For as in Adam
all die, even so in Christ all shall be made alive.

(1 Corinthians 15:1–8, 12–22)

Doubting the physical reality of the resurrection is not new, but one of the earliest manifestations of lack of faith. As Paul records, either the eyewitness testimony of those present at the time is correct, or we are the most pitiable of human beings. The eyewitness testimony is that Jesus did die physically, rose again three days later, and ascended to heaven forty days after that. When the people of the first century read and heard what the disciples were preaching, no one objected or said, "That's not true!" There were still hundreds of eyewitnesses to the events who could say, "I was there! I heard! I saw!"

The modern world of Christendom from top to bottom seems to have forgotten the basics of the faith. The foundations are very weak:

For though by this time you ought to be teachers, you need someone to
teach you again the first principles of the oracles of God; and you have
come to need milk and not solid food. For everyone who partakes only
of milk is unskilled in the word of righteousness, for he is a babe. But
solid food belongs to those who are of full age, that is, those who by
reason of use have their senses exercised to discern both good and evil.

(Hebrews 5:12–14)

We should remind ourselves that Scripture validates itself as the Word of God by means of historical accuracy, supernatural prophecies and their fulfillment. There is no need for a new way to speak of God. We must rediscover the meaning of the Scriptures.

That which was from the beginning, which we have heard, which we
have seen with our eyes, which we have looked upon, and our hands
have handled, concerning the Word of life – the life was manifested,
and we have seen, and bear witness, and declare to you that eternal
life which was with the Father and was manifested to us – that which
we have seen and heard we declare to you, that you also may have
fellowship with us; and truly our fellowship is with the Father and
with His Son Jesus Christ.

(1 John 1:1–3)

The Battle for Faith

The Bible is an ultimatum. It is not an interesting piece of spiritual
theory or a collection of myths. It is a challenge to be met in our daily
lives. Christianity is a response to a message that is clearly spelled out in
the Bible.

For the word of God is living and powerful, and sharper than any
two-edged sword, piercing even to the division of soul and spirit,
and of joints and marrow, and is a discerner of the thoughts and
intents of the heart. And there is no creature hidden from His sight,
but all things are naked and open to the eyes of Him to whom we
must give account.

(Hebrews 4:12–13)

In the early part of this book I wrote about the need for a Reformation
on the same principles as Martin Luther's Reformation, that is, let us
return to the Bible as the source of our guidance and not the cruel and
empty promises of worldly authorities. I also asked how this should be
done, and what form it should take. Martin Luther posted his theses
on the church door as a challenge for debate. Today we have different
issues to deal with. I have placed some simple theses for debate in the
Appendix, based on the main themes of this book. There are many things
to debate along the road of faith. Some are more important that others
in different centuries and different eras. In our day many Christians
have ceased going to church, yet perhaps still hold to the orthodoxy
of the Bible. Others are still churched, but have growing fears about
the future viability of their faith in such a compromising environment.

A great number have lost their faith entirely, just like the Dutch Protestant Church described in the Preface.

The "Call to Action" at the end of this book is a call back to a trusting faith in the authority of Scripture. This applies to everyone, whether churched or unchurched, whether lapsed in faith or currently ignorant of it. There is no party line, no denominational view. There are a great number of Christians who have been disenfranchised, but who, like the evangelical movement, belong to no single organization or denomination. They do form a movement, but they constitute a cloud of people difficult to pin down or reach. They are like that new concept in information technology – the "Cloud." So into that cloud I contribute this book, in the hope that the information within it will reach the souls who need to know that faith in the Bible is not misplaced.

> *Finally, my brethren, be strong in the Lord and in the power of His might. Put on the whole armor of God, that you may be able to stand against the wiles of the devil. For we do not wrestle against flesh and blood, but against principalities, against powers, against the rulers of the darkness of this age, against spiritual hosts of wickedness in the heavenly places. Therefore take up the whole armor of God, that you may be able to withstand in the evil day, and having done all, to stand.*
>
> (Ephesians 6:10–13)

That is all we have to do – stand. The Church must not be timid but proclaim its faith in God the Creator and Redeemer. Compromise with evolution and other philosophies simply will not do; these man-made fables will certainly fall. The only questions are "when?" and "how far?" We have seen that full confidence and faith can be placed in the Bible; it is worthy of our faith. We have the evidence to support our case. Let us stop dithering and do it.

> *Now faith is the substance of things hoped for, the evidence of things not seen.*
>
> (Hebrews 11:1–2)

So let us call for a renewal of faith and get back to basics. Let us reform the practice of Christianity into what it once was – a living faith. Let us:

> *... contend earnestly for the faith which was once for all delivered to the saints.*

(Jude 3)

THESES FOR DEBATE

I ended the book with a "Call to Action." I was not originally going to put forward any theses for debate. During the years and the course of writing I did put down some headings to help me think clearly. I added separate thoughts, and, as time went on, they coalesced into the individual statements you see below. Each thesis can be debated individually or within a grouping. Many of them overlap and many relate to the same thing, even when in different categories. They were very useful to me and I hope that they may be useful for others.

Some may think I am being overbearing and dogmatic – perhaps fundamentalist! Many of the statements below are basic theology. Well, proper debate about the basics is what is needed. The foundations of the faith are very weak. Whatever agreement or disagreement there may be over the statements below, it is the debate and the search for the truth that is important. Let us pray to Almighty God for wisdom.

God
1. God is an uncreated eternal Being
2. God exists in a Trinity of three Persons: Father, Son, and Holy Spirit
3. God is holy and good
4. God is just and wise

5. God is sovereign
6. God is omnipotent and omniscient
7. God is the Judge of all the earth and always does right
8. God's nature is unchanging

Holy Scripture – The Bible
9. The Bible is what it claims to be – the supernaturally revealed Word of God
10. The Bible was inerrantly inspired by the Holy Spirit through human agency
11. Fulfilled prophecy testifies to the authority and inerrancy of the Bible
12. The Bible is self-contained and self-interpreting
13. The Bible is designed for the salvation of mankind
14. The Bible contains an accurate account of the origins of the universe and life
15. The Bible is the true source of morality and provides a template for godly living

Jesus Christ
16. The incarnation of the Second Person of the Godhead is an historical fact
17. Jesus is both God and man – Immanuel, or "God-with-us"
18. The virgin birth is an historical fact
19. The crucifixion under Pontius Pilate is an historical fact
20. The resurrection after three days is an historical fact
21. The ascension from the Mount of Olives is an historical fact
22. All prophecies of the Messiah in the Old Testament are fulfilled in Jesus
23. The earthly ministry of Jesus was a miraculous fulfillment of prophecy
24. Jesus came into the world to bear witness to the truth
25. Jesus lived a sinless life under the law
26. The atoning sacrifice of the sinless Son of God paid for our sins if we accept it
27. The only path to salvation is through repentance and the atonement of Christ

Man

28. Man is a dependent creation made in the image of a Holy God
29. Man was originally created perfect
30. Man is an immortal being from the point of conception
31. God has placed us in families with defined relationships and roles
32. Adam's choice has separated us from God – the fall of man
33. Man has a free choice in this life which will determine his destiny in the next
34. Man is born to live once, then comes judgment
35. The destiny of man is either in heaven or in hell; there is no third option
36. Man must show humility before the transcendent, omnipotent, omniscient God

Science and Philosophy

37. The theory of evolution (Darwinism) has no definitive evidence to support it
38. Evolution is not science properly so-called – it is outside the scientific method
39. Evolution is a faith – a way of looking at the world
40. The fossil record supports the creation of life by "kind"
41. The geological record supports catastrophism and the flood
42. Most physical evidence points to a young earth
43. Life does not come from non-life
44. Genetics and cell biochemistry point to a complexity unexplainable by science
45. The appearance of design means the existence of design – Occam's Razor
46. Humanist philosophies deny God and remove the hope of salvation from man
47. Both religious and secular leaps of faith are equally irrational and meaningless
48. All that modern philosophy offers is bleak, motiveless existence
49. The autonomous intellect has destroyed the things of God and His grace
50. The sense of sin and accountability to the Living God has been lost

51. Secular humanism and modern evolutionary science are enemies of humanity
52. The consequence of Darwinism is endless war between nations and individuals

Creation

53. The universe had a beginning and will have an end
54. The universe was a perfect creation of the uncreated eternal and perfect God
55. The universe is separate, finite, but dependent on God
56. Without the uncreated eternal God there could be no such universe
57. The universe and the earth are fine-tuned to support human life
58. All life comes from God and has a purpose
59. The fall of man has damaged the created universe – bad things now happen

Miracles

60. Miracles in the Bible are historically real both by evidence and authority
61. Miracles taken as a whole are a sign of God's reality and activity
62. Miracles authenticate Jesus Christ and His claim to being God
63. Miracles authenticate the reality of redemption and salvation
64. Miracles individually point to different aspects of God's plan of salvation
65. Miracles give God all glory and honor and praise
66. The virgin birth produced the miracle of the incarnate Deity
67. The crucifixion, resurrection and ascension are supernatural miracles of God
68. The historical miracles are recorded and testified by hundreds of eyewitnesses
69. Prayer is a miracle of communication between the natural and the supernatural

Sin and Morality

70. God loved us all before the beginning of time and creation
71. Everyone is fallen and sins continuously – we are not naturally good
72. All conscious choices in thought, word and deed will be judged by God
73. We cannot escape God's judgment by our own efforts
74. We need the help of Jesus Christ to be acquitted of our sins
75. The Bible gives the standard of morality pleasing to God
76. Biblical morality is designed for mankind and gives the best results

Heaven and Hell

77. Heaven is a place of endless joy and release from all pain, suffering and death
78. Heaven is a place of reward for faithful service for the child of God
79. Heaven is a place of endless fulfillment in the presence of God
80. No sinful person will enter heaven
81. Most of what we know about hell comes from the mouth of Jesus Himself
82. Hell is a place of endless, conscious torment required by the justice of God
83. Hell is necessary if there is even one unrepented sin
84. If there is no hell there is no heaven and no hope

The Church

85. The Biblical church is the ministering brotherhood of all believers
86. The church exists to teach the salvation of Christ to all who will listen
87. The church has a duty to preach the reality of heaven and hell
88. The institutional Church is infected with secular humanism and existentialism
89. The institutional Church supports evolution, contradicting Scripture and Christ
90. The institutional Church no longer teaches the salvation of Christ with conviction
91. The institutional Church has lost the faith once given to the saints

Salvation

91. God desires that everyone should come to salvation
92. Salvation cannot be earned from a Sovereign God – it can only be His gift
93. Salvation comes through the hearing of the Word of God
94. Personal conviction of sin and acceptance of responsibility for sin is the starting point
95. Repentance of past sins by the grace of God is the essential beginning
96. Acceptance of the atonement of Jesus Christ is the only way of salvation

BIBLIOGRAPHY AND SUGGESTED FURTHER READING

Ankerberg, John and John Weldon. *Darwin's Leap of Faith: Exposing the False Religion of Evolution* (Harvest House, 1998).

Ashton, John F. (ed.). *In Six Days: Why 50 Scientists Choose to Believe in Creation* (New Holland Books, 1999).

Augustine. *City of God* (Penguin Classics, 1984). First published 1467.

Ayer, A.J. *Language, Truth and Logic* (Penguin, 1986).

Behe, Michael J. *Darwin's Black Box* (Simon & Schuster, 1996).

Berkhof, Louis. *Systematic Theology* (Banner of Truth, 1958).

Bohm, David. *Quantum Theory* (Dover Publications, 1989).

Bouwmeester, Dirk, Artur Ekert and Anton Zeilinger (eds). *The Physics of Quantum Information* (Springer-Verlag, 2000).

Chesterton, G.K. *Orthodoxy* (Hodder & Stoughton, 1999).

Clark, R.E.D. *Creation* (Tyndale Press, 1953).

Coder, S. Maxwell and George F. Howe. *The Bible, Science and Creation* (Moody Bible Institute, 1966).

Darwin, Charles. *The Descent of Man and Selection in Relation to Sex* (2nd edn, John Murray, 1882).

Darwin, Charles. *The Origin of Species by Means of Natural Selection, Or The Preservation of Favoured Races in the Struggle for Life* (6th edn, John Murray, 1882).

Dennett, Daniel C. *Darwin's Dangerous Idea: Evolution and the Meaning of Life* (Simon & Schuster, 1995).

Geisler, Norman L. *Christian Ethics: Options and Issues* (Baker Books, 1989).

Greene, Brian. *The Elegant Universe* (Vintage, 2000).

Guinness, Os. *The Dust of Death* (Crossway Books, 1994).

Guinness, Os. *God in the Dark: The Assurance of Faith beyond a Shadow of Doubt* (Crossway Books, 1996).

Hawking, Stephen W. *A Brief History of Time: From the Big Bang to Black Holes* (Bantam Press, 1988).

Hayward, Alan. *Creation and Evolution: The Facts and the Fallacies* (Triangle Books, 1985).

Heisenberg, Werner. *The Physical Principles of the Quantum Theory* (Dover Publications, 1949).

Hobbes, Thomas. *Leviathan* (Penguin, 1982). First published 1651.

The Holy Bible

Hume, David. *A Treatise of Human Nature: Book One*, ed. D.G.C. Macnabb (Fontana, 1982). First published 1739.

Hume, David. *A Treatise of Human Nature: Books Two and Three*, ed. Páll S. Árdal (Fontana, 1982). Book 2 first published 1739; Book 3 first published 1740.

Koop, C. Everett and Francis A. Schaeffer. *Whatever Happened to the Human Race?* (Crossway Books, 1983).

Lewis, C.S. *The Abolition of Man* (Fount, 1978).

Lewis, C.S. *God in the Dock* (Fount, 1990).

Lewis, C.S. *Miracles* (Fount, 1990).

Lewis, C.S. *Present Concerns: Ethical Essays* (Fount, 1991).

Lyell, Charles. *The Student's Elements of Geology* (2nd edn, John Murray, 1874).

Mackay, D.M. (ed.). *Christianity in a Mechanistic Universe and Other Essays: A Symposium* (Inter-Varsity Fellowship, 1965).

Margenau, Henry and Roy Abraham Varghese (eds). *Cosmos, Bios, Theos: Scientists Reflect on Science, God and the Origin of the Universe, Life and Homo Sapiens* (Open Court Publishing, 1992).

Morison, Frank. *Who Moved the Stone?* (Faber and Faber, 1930).

Morris, Henry M. *Evolution and the Modern Christian* (Presbyterian Reformed Publishing, 1967).

Morris, Henry M. *The Genesis Record: A Scientific and Devotional Commentary on the Book of Beginnings* (Baker Books, 1976).

Nietzsche, Friedrich. *Beyond Good and Evil*, trans. R.J. Hollingdale (Penguin, 2003).

Paley, William. *Evidences of Christianity* (Longman and Co., 1843).

Pascal, Blaise. *Pensées* (Penguin, 1987).

Pawson, David. *When Jesus Returns* (Hodder & Stoughton, 1995).

Payne, J. Barton. *Encyclopedia of Biblical Prophecy: The Complete Guide to Scriptural Predictions and Their Fulfillment* (Baker Books, 1980).

Peacock, Roy E. *A Brief History of Eternity: A Considered Response to Stephen Hawking's* A Brief History of Time (Monarch, 1989).

Popkin, Richard H. and Avrum Stroll. *Philosophy* (3rd edn, Butterworth-Heinemann, 1993).

Prigogine, Ilya. *The End of Certainty: Time, Chaos, and the New Laws of Nature* (The Free Press, 1997).

Radice, Betty (ed.). Clifton Wolters (trans.) *The Cloud of Unknowing and Other Works* (Penguin Classics, 1961).

Rendle Short, A. *The Bible and Modern Research* (2nd edn, Marshall, Morgan and Scott, 1938).

Satinover, Jeffrey. *Cracking the Bible Code* (William Morrow, 1997).

Satinover, Jeffrey. *Homosexuality and the Politics of Truth* (Hamewith Books, 1998).

Schaeffer, Francis A. *A Christian Manifesto* (rev. edn, Crossway Books, 1982).

Schaeffer, Francis A. *The Church before the Watching World* (Inter-Varsity Press, 1972).

Schaeffer, Francis A. *A Francis A. Schaeffer Trilogy: The God Who Is There; Escape from Reason; He Is There and He Is Not Silent* (Crossway Books, 1990).

Schaeffer, Francis A. *Genesis in Space and Time* (Inter-Varsity Press, 1972).

Shedd, W.G.T. *The Doctrine of Endless Punishment* (Banner of Truth, 1986). First published 1885.

Sheler, Jeffrey L. *Is the Bible True?* (HarperCollins, 1999).

Simmons, Geoffrey. *What Darwin Didn't Know* (Harvest House, 2004).

Sire, James W. *The Universe Next Door* (3rd edn, Inter-Varsity Press, 1997).

Sproul, R.C. *Not a Chance: The Myth of Chance in Modern Science and Cosmology* (Baker Books, 1994).

Tillich, Paul. *Systematic Theology* (3 vols; University of Chicago Press, 1951, 1957, 1963).

Walvoord, John F. *Every Prophecy of the Bible* (David C. Cook, 1999).

Watson, David C.C. *The Great Brain Robbery: Creation or Evolution?* (Henry E. Walter, 1975).

Whitcomb, John C. *The Early Earth* (Baker Books, 1998).

Whitcomb, John C. and Henry M. Morris. *The Genesis Flood: The Biblical Record and Its Scientific Implications* (Presbyterian Reformed Publishing, 1961).

White, Joe and Nicholas Comninellis. *Darwin's Demise* (Master Books, 2001).

Wilson, A.N. *God's Funeral* (Abacus, 2000).

Notes

Preface

1 C.S. Lewis, *Mere Christianity* (HarperCollins, 2002), p. 41.
2 John Ankerberg and John Wheldon, *Darwin's Leap of Faith: Exposing the False Religion of Evolution* (Harvest House, 1998), p. 12.
3 Robert Pigott, BBC religious affairs correspondent, "Dutch Rethink Christianity for a Doubtful World." http://www.bbc.co.uk/news/world-europe-14417362 (5 August 2011).

Chapter 1: Faith Under Assault

4 James W. Sire, *The Universe Next Door* (3rd edn, Inter-Varsity Press, 1997), inside front cover.
5 Hermann Diels and Walther Kranz (eds), *Fragments of the Pre-Socratics* (1967).
6 Francis Bacon, *The New Organon, or True Directions Concerning the Interpretation of Nature* (1620), trans. James Spedding, Robert Leslie Ellis and Douglas Denon Heath, *The Works*, vol. 8 (Taggard and Thompson, 1863).

7   http://www.usatoday.com/tech/science/discoveries/2007-05-21-coelacanth-indonesia_N.htm.

8   W. Roush, "'Living Fossil' Is Dethroned," *Science*, vol. 277, no. 1436 (5 September 1997).

9   L. Sunderland, *Darwin's Enigma* (Master Books, 1998), pp. 101–102.

10   John F. Ashton PhD, *In Six Days: Why 50 Scientists Choose to Believe in Creation* (New Holland, 1999).

11   *The Spectator* (1860), in David L. Hull, *Darwin and His Critics: The Reception of Darwin's Theory of Evolution by the Scientific Community* (Harvard University Press, 1973), pp. 155–170.

12   Os Guinness, *God in the Dark: The Assurance of Faith beyond a Shadow of Doubt* (Crossway, 1996), p. 14.

Chapter 2: Faith, Knowledge and Wisdom

13   David Hume, *A Treatise of Human Nature*, ed. Páll S. Árdal (Fontana/Collins, 1982), Book 3, Section 1.1, p. 203.

Chapter 3: A Fight to the Death

14   A.C. Dixon, R.A. Torrey (eds), *The Fundamentals: A Testimony to the Truth* (12 vols; Bible Institute of Los Angeles, 1910–15).

15   Pam Sheppard, "A Call Back to Truth," Answers in Genesis–US (11 September 2007).

16   *ibid*.

Chapter 4 : Unchanging Truth

17   Daniel C. Dennett, *Darwin's Dangerous Idea: Evolution and the Meaning of Life* (Simon & Schuster, 1995).

18   D. Dennett, "Darwin's Dangerous Idea," *The Sciences* (May–June 1995), pp. 34–40. Cited in *Creation*, vol. 19, no. 2 (4 March 1997).

Chapter 5: The Reformation of 1517

19   Herbert Spencer, *The Data of Ethics* (London, 1879), p. 32.

20   Sir Julian Huxley, "The New Divinity," in *Essays of a Humanist* (Penguin, 1969).

Chapter 6: Astronomy, Mathematics and the Bible

21   David Bohm, *Wholeness and the Implicate Order* (Routledge Classics, 2002), p. 36.

22   Quoted in Professor Roy E. Peacock, *A Brief History of Eternity: A Considered Response to Stephen Hawking's* A Brief History of Time (Monarch, 1989), p. 33.

23   *ibid*, p. 38.

24   *ibid*, p. 38.

25   *ibid*, p. 143.

26   In 1616 the system of Copernicus was denounced as dangerous to faith, and Galileo was called to Rome and warned not to teach it. In 1632 he published a work written for the non-specialist and in Italian, readable by any literate person: "Dialogo sopra i due massimi sistemi del' mondo" (Dialogue on the Two Chief Systems of the World). This work supported the Copernican system and opposed the Ptolemaic system; it provided great challenges to scientific and philosophical thought. Galileo was subsequently tried in 1633 by the Inquisition and brought to the point of denying all ideas and proposals that argued the sun to be the central body, with the earth and all the planets moving around it. After the trial Galileo was sentenced to house arrest in Siena, and later in Arcetri near Florence. In spite of ill health and eventual blindness, Galileo continued his scientific studies until his death.

27   Peacock, *A Brief History of Eternity*, p. 143.

28   *ibid*, p. 144.

29   *ibid*, p. 46.

30   Quoted in Francis A. Schaeffer, *Escape from Reason* (Crossway, 1990), p. 226.

Chapter 7: From Determinism to Uncertainty

31 Ilya Prigogine, *The End of Certainty: Time, Chaos and the Laws of Nature* (The Free Press, 1997), Acknowledgments, p. viii.

32 Jeffrey Satinover MD, *Cracking the Bible Code* (William Morrow, 1997), p. 244.

33 J.J. O'Connor and E.F. Robertson, "Louis Victor Pierre Raymond duc de Broglie," found at http://uk.geocities.com/magoos_universe/broglie.htm (June 2004).

Chapter 8: Evolution and Biblical Creation

34 Francis Crick, *Life Itself: Its Origins and Nature* (Simon & Schuster, 1981), p. 88.

35 H.J. Muller, "Is Biological Evolution a Principle of Nature That Has Been Well Established by Science?" Privately duplicated and distributed by the author (May 1966).

36 Cited in John Blanchard, *Evolution: Fact or Fiction?* (Evangelical Press, 2002), p. 9.

37 John Ankerberg and John Wheldon, *Darwin's Leap of Faith: Exposing the False Religion of Evolution* (Harvest House, 1998), Preface, p. 14.

38 Howard Byington Holroyd, "Darwinism Is Physical and Mathematical Nonsense," *Creation Research Society Quarterly* (June 1972), pp. 6, 9.

39 Michael Russell, Andrew Pomiankowski, George Turner, Paul Rainey and Robin Dunbar, "Evolution: Five Big Questions," *New Scientist*, no. 2399 (14 June 2003). Quoted in the *Journal of the Creation Science Movement*, vol. 13, no. 10 (September 2003). Creation Science Movement, PO Box 888, Portsmouth PO6 2YD, United Kingdom. www.creationsciencemovement.com.

40 Jacques Monod, *Chance and Necessity* (Vintage, 1972), pp. 112–113.

41 Prof. John C. Whitcomb and Prof. Henry M. Morris, "Modern Geology and the Deluge," in *The Genesis Flood* (P&R Publishing, 1961), ch. 5, p. 135 et seq.

42 Whitcomb and Morris, *The Genesis Flood*, pp. 180–211.

43 *ibid*, pp. 171, 206–207.

44 O.D. von Engeln and Kenneth E Caster, *Geology* (McGraw-Hill, 1952), pp. 417–418. Quoted in Whitcomb and Morris, *The Genesis Flood*, p. 206.

45 *Voices for Evolution* ([US] National Center for Science Education, 1989), p. 141.

46 Thomas Huxley, *Three Lectures on Evolution* (1882).

47 Charles Darwin MA, LLD, FRS, *The Origin of Species* (6th edn, John Murray, 1882), p. 134.

48 Stephen Jay Gould, "The Return of Hopeful Monsters," *Natural History* (June–July 1977), pp. 22, 24. (*Natural History* was a magazine formerly published by the American Museum of Natural History in New York.)

49 David Raup, "Conflicts between Darwin and Paleontology," *Field Museum of Natural History Bulletin* (January 1979).

50 *Philosophical Transactions of the Royal Society of London*, vol. 29 (1715), pp. 296–300. Quoted in *Creation*, vol. 21, no. 1 (1998), p. 16.

51 *Scientific Transactions of the Royal Dublin Society*, new series, vol. 7, no. 3 (1899). Quoted in *Creation*, vol. 21, no. 1 (1998), p. 16.

52 S.A. Austin and D.R. Humphreys, "The Sea's Missing Salt: A Dilemma for Evolutionists," *Proceedings of the Second International Conference on Creationism*, vol. 2 (1990), pp. 17–33. Quoted in *Creation*, vol. 21, no. 1 (1998), p. 16.

53 K.L. McDonald and R.H. Gunst, "An Analysis of the Earth's Magnetic Field from 1835 to 1965," *ESSA Technical Report*, IER 46-IES1 (US Govt Printing Office, 1967). Quoted in *Creation*, vol. 20, no. 2 (1998), pp. 15–17.

54 R.T. Merrill and M.W. McElhinney, *The Earth's Magnetic Field* (Academic Press, 1983), pp. 101–106. Quoted in *Creation*, vol. 20, no. 2 (1998), pp. 15–17.

55 D.R. Humphreys, "Reversals of the Earth's Magnetic Field during the Genesis Flood," *Proceedings of the First International Conference on Creationism*, vol. 2 (Creation Science Fellowship, 1986), pp. 113–126. Quoted in *Creation*, vol. 20, no. 2 (1998).

56 R.S. Coe and M. Prévot, "Evidence Suggesting Extremely Rapid Field Variation during a Geomagnetic Reversal," *Earth and Planetary Science*, vol. 92, nos 3/4 (April 1989), pp. 292–298.

Quoted in *Creation*, vol. 20, no. 2 (1998), pp. 15–17.

57   James Hutton, "Theory of the Earth with Proof and Illustrations," discussed by F. Press and R. Siever in *Earth* (4th edn, W.H. Freeman, 1986), pp. 33, 37, 40. Quoted in *Creation*, vol. 22, no. 2 (2000).

58   Ariel Roth, *Origins: Linking Science and Scripture* (Review and Herald Publishing, 1998), p. 264. Quoted in *Creation*, vol. 22, no. 2 (2000). A number of references about the growth and preservation of continental crust are cited.

59   *ibid*, p. 266.

60   Don Batten, "Where Are All the People?" *Creation*, vol. 23, no. 3 (2001), pp. 52–55. For the nth square, the number of rice grains = $2^{(n-1)} = 2^{63}$ for the last square, or about 10^{19} grains (ten million trillion).

61   *Encyclopaedia Britannica*, "Trends in World Population" CD (2000).

62   Don Batten, "Where Are All the People?" *Creation*, vol. 23, no. 3 (2001), p. 54. If r = % rate of growth per annum, and the number of years of growth = n, then after n years, the population produced from a starting population of y people is given by: $y(1 + r/100)^n$.

63   *ibid.*

64   David J. Rodabaugh, "The Queen of Science Examines the King of Fools," *CRS Quarterly* (June 1975), p. 14.

65   David J. Rodabaugh, "Mathematicians Do It Again," *CRS Quarterly* (December 1975), pp. 173–175.

66   Cited in *Nature* (12 November 1981), p. 105.

67   William Broad and Nicholas Wade, *Betrayers of the Truth: Fraud and Deceit in the Halls of Science* (Century, 1983). Cited in Ankerberg and Wheldon, *Darwin's Leap of Faith* (Harvest House, 1988), p. 94.

68   Wendell R. Bird, *The Origin of Species Revisited*, vol. 2, pp. 135–136. Cited in Ankerberg and Wheldon, *Darwin's Leap of Faith*, pp. 94–95.

69   H. Kettlewell, "Darwin's Missing Evidence" (1959), in *Evolution and the Fossil Record: Readings from* Scientific American (W.H. Freeman, 1978), p. 23. Quoted in *Creation*, vol. 21, no. 3 (1999), p. 56.

70   *The Washington Times* (17 January 1999), p. D8.

71 J.A. Coyne, "Not Black and White," *Nature*, vol. 396, no. 6706 (5 November 1998), pp. 35–36.

72 *Technical Journal*, vol. 18, no. 1 (2004), pp. 71–75.

73 R. Youngson, *Scientific Blunders: A Brief History of How Wrong Scientists Can Sometimes Be* (Carroll and Graf, 1998); Russell Grigg, "Ernst Haeckel: Evangelist for Evolution and Apostle of Deceit," *Creation*, vol. 18, no. 2 (1996), pp. 33–36.

74 Russell Grigg, "Fraud Rediscovered," *Creation*, vol. 20, no. 2 (1998), pp. 49–51.

75 Michael Richardson et al., *Anatomy and Embryology*, vol. 192, no. 2 (1997), pp. 91–106.

76 Nigel Hawkes, *The Times*, London (11 August 1997), p. 14.

77 Francis Hitching, *The Neck of the Giraffe: Where Darwin Went Wrong* (Ticknor and Fields, 1982), p. 204.

78 Michael J. Behe, *Darwin's Black Box* (1st Touchstone edn, Simon & Schuster, 1998), p. 185.

79 Søren Løvetrup, *Darwinism: The Refutation of a Myth* (Croom Helm, 1987), p. 352. Cited in Ankerberg and Wheldon, *Darwin's Leap of Faith*, p. 95.

80 http://www.newscientist.com/article/dn14094-bacteria-make-major-evolutionary-shift-in-the-lab.html.

81 Journal reference: *Proceedings of the National Academy of Sciences* (DOI: 10.1073/pnas.0803151105).

82 Quoted in http://www.newscientist.com/article/dn14094-bacteria-make-major-evolutionary-shift-in-the-lab.html.

Chapter 9: Science, Faith and Consequences

83 Wendell R. Bird, *The Origin of Species Revisited: The Theories of Evolution and Abrupt Appearance*, vol. 1 (Philosophical Library, 1989), p. 1.

84 Robert B. Downs, *Books That Changed the World* (rev. edn, New American Library/Mentor, 1983), pp. 286–287. Cited in Ankerberg and Wheldon, *Darwin's Leap of Faith* (Harvest House, 1988), p. 95.

85 Adolf Hitler, *Mein Kampf* (1924), p. 286.

86   Adolf Hitler, quoted in Joachim Fest, *Hitler* (Harcourt, 1974), pp. 679–680.

87   Sir Arthur Keith, *Evolution and Ethics* (1947), p. 14.

88   *ibid*, p. 230.

89   *ibid*, p. 149.

90   Eric Fromm, "Alienation under Capitalism," in Ed Josephson, *Man Alone* (Dell, 1964), p. 54.

Chapter 10: The Response of Evangelicalism

91   D.W. Bebbington, *Evangelicalism in Modern Britain: A History from the 1730s to 1980s* (Unwin Hyman, 1989), p. 131.

92   *ibid*.

93   Allan Peter Green, "Darwin and God: Evangelical Response to Darwinism 1860–1960." Unpublished dissertation, University of Stirling, 2010.

94   George P. Landow, *The Aesthetic and Critical Theories of John Ruskin* (Princeton University Press, 1971).

95   Right Rev. John William Colenso DD, Bishop of Natal, *The Pentateuch and Book of Joshua Critically Examined* (Longman, Green, Longman, Roberts & Green, 1865), introductory remarks, p. 26.

96   Allan Peter Green, "Darwin and God: Evangelical Response to Darwinism 1860–1960." Unpublished dissertation, University of Stirling, 2010.

97   *ibid*.

98   J. Reddie, *Transactions of the Victoria Institute*, vol. 1 (1866), p. iv.

99   The phrase "Nature, red in tooth and claw" comes from the poem "In Memoriam A.H.H." by Alfred, Lord Tennyson, completed in 1849; it is from Canto 56, referring to humanity: "Who trusted God was love indeed / And love Creation's final law / Tho' Nature, red in tooth and claw / With ravine, shriek'd against his creed." "Tooth and claw" was already in use by Tennyson's day as a phrase representing brute nature. This poem was his elegy to the untimely death of a dear friend, and contrasted the Christian idea of a loving God with the impersonal savagery of nature.

This extensive philosophical poem didn't try to give answers, but it is very profound and became part of the debate in the Victorian period about the major scientific and theological issues of the day. It was completed ten years before the publication of Darwin's *Origin of Species*.

100 A.D. White, *A History of the Warfare of Science with Religion* (New York, 1896), pp. 1–5.

101 J.W. Draper, *A History of the Conflict between Religion and Science* (New York, 1910), p. 2.

102 Arthur Smethurst, *Modern Science and Christian Beliefs* (London, 1953).

103 J.R. Moore, *The Post-Darwinian Controversies* (Oxford, 1971), p. 42.

104 D.N. Livingstone, *Darwin's Forgotten Defenders* (Oxford, 1984), p. 3.

Chapter 11: The Autonomous Intellect

105 Francis A. Schaeffer, *Trilogy: Escape from Reason* (Inter-Varsity Press, 1990), p. 229.

106 Friedrich Nietzsche, *Beyond Good and Evil* (Penguin), p. 96, #108.

107 Francis A. Schaeffer, *Trilogy: Escape from Reason* (Inter-Varsity Press, 1990), p. 259.

Chapter 12: Miracles

108 Matthew 14:13–21; Mark 6:30–44; Luke 9:10–17; John 6:1–14.

109 Mathew 14:22–33; Mark 6:45–52; John 6:15–21.

110 C.S. Lewis, *Miracles* (Fontana, 1960), p. 67.

111 *ibid*, p. 68.

112 *ibid*, p. 68.

Chapter 13: The Meaning of the Cross

113   Isaiah 29:14.

Chapter 14: Morality, Judgment and Hell

114   Rabbi Dr H. Freedman and Maurice Simon (trans. and eds),
       "Midrash on Genesis 22:6," in *Midrash Rabbah Genesis I and
       Midrash Rabbah* (10 vols; The Soncino Press, 1939).
115   W.G.T. Shedd, *The Doctrine of Endless Punishment* (Banner of
       Truth, 1986), p. 119. First published 1885.
116   *ibid*, p. 120.
117   *ibid*, p. 127.

Chapter 15: Sex and Biblical Morality

118   David Pawson, *Leadership is Male* (Highland, 1992), p. 13.
119   *ibid*, p. 14.
120   Deuteronomy 17:7; 19:19; 22:21, 24; 24:7.
121   Jeffrey Satinover MD, *Homosexuality and the Politics of Truth*
       (Hamewith Books, 1996), pp. 49–51.
122   *ibid*, p. 69. Cites P. Cameron, W.L. Playfair and S. Wellum,
       "The Homosexual Lifespan," presentation to the Eastern
       Psychological Association USA (April 1993); emphasis added.
123   Dennis Prager, "Judaism, Homosexuality and Civilization,"
       Ultimate Issues, vol. 6, no. 2 (1990), p. 2.
124   Jeffrey Satinover MD, *Homosexuality and the Politics of Truth*
       (Hamewith Books, 1996), Introduction, p. 18.

Chapter 16: The World Moves On

125   http://www.csm.org.uk/whoweare.php (accessed 30 September
       2010).
126   W.H. Rusch, "A Brief Statement of the History and Aims of the

CRS," *CRS Quarterly*, vol. 19, no. 2 (1982), p. 149.

127 http://www.icr.org/discover/index/discover_history/ 30 September 2010.

128 http://creation.com/about-us#who_we_are/ 30 September 2010.

129 D.M. Raup, "Geology and Creationism," *Field Museum of Natural History Bulletin*, vol. 54, no. 3 (16–25 March 1983), p. 21. Cited in Dave Woetzel, "Evolutionists Retreating from Science," *Journal of Creation*, vol. 23, no. 3 (2009), pp. 123–127.

130 Prof. Stephen J. Gould, *The Panda's Thumb* (W.W. Norton, 1980), pp. 181–182.

131 Paul Davies, *The Fifth Miracle* (Simon & Schuster, 1999), p. 259.

132 Fred Hoyle, "The Big Bang in Astronomy," *New Scientist*, vol. 92 (1981), pp. 526–527.

133 Alex Williams, "Mutations: Evolution's Engine Becomes Evolution's End!" *Journal of Creation*, vol. 22, no. 2 (August 2008), pp. 60–66.

134 http://www.dailymail.co.uk/news/article-1055597/Church-makes--8216-ludicrous-8217-apology-Charles-Darwin--126-years-death.html#ixzz111db2fru.

Chapter 17: The Anvil That Has Worn Out Many Hammers

135 David Pawson, *When Jesus Returns* (Hodder & Stoughton, 1995), pp. 1–4.

136 J. Barton Payne, *Encyclopedia of Biblical Prophecy* (Hodder & Stoughton, 1974).

137 David Rohl, *A Test of Time: The Bible – From Myth to History* (Century/Random House, 1995).

138 *ibid*, pp. 221–232.

139 *ibid*, pp. 263–274.

140 Robert Dick Wilson, *A Scientific Investigation of the Old Testament* (Moody Press, p 70).

141 *ibid*.

142 Brian H. Edwards (series ed.), *Through the British Museum – with the Bible* (Day One Publications, 2005), PO Box 66, Leominster HR6 0XB, United Kingdom.

143 William Ramsay, *The Bearing of Recent Discovery on the Trustworthiness of the New Testament* (Hodder & Stoughton), p. 222.

144 Nelson Glück, *Rivers in the Desert: History of Neteg* (Jewish Publications Society of America, 1969), p. 31.

145 Peter Stoner, *Science Speaks: Scientific Proof of the Accuracy of Prophecy and the Bible* (Moody Press, 1944), pp. 109–110.

146 Pound coin has a radius of 11 mm and thickness of 3 mm, giving a volume of 1,141 mm^3. So total volume of coins is 1141×10^{17} mm^3. This equals area of UK x height. Area of UK is 242,900 km^2, giving a height of approximately 0.47 meters.

147 Total volume of coins is 1141×10^{45} mm^3, or 1141×10^{27} km^3. Volume of sphere of coins is given by $4\pi r^3/3$ so $r = \sqrt[3]{((3 \times 1141 \times 10^{27})/4\pi)} = 1.4 \times 10^{10}$ km. Earth orbit mean radius $= 1.5 \times 10^8$ km. Therefore size factor is $1.4/1.5 \times 10^2 = 93.33$.

148 The volume of a sphere is given by $(4\pi/3) \, r^3$, where r is the radius. The volume of an atom of radius 0.1×10^{-9} $(= 10^{-10})$ meters is therefore $(4\pi/3)(10^{-10})^3 = 4.2 \times 10^{-30}$ cubic meters to one decimal place.

149 Diameter of a ball of radius r is given by $D = 2[\sqrt[3]{\oplus(3V/4\pi)}]$ where volume, $V = 4.2 \times 10^{118}$ cubic kilometers. Therefore $D = 4.3 \times 10^{39}$ kilometers to one decimal place.

150 Speed of light is approximately 300,000 kilometers per second. Therefore in one year light travels $300,000 \times 60 \times 60 \times 24 \times 365.25 = 9,467,280,000,000$ kilometers. Therefore 2.3×10^{39} divided by 9,467,280,000,000 gives 242,942,006,574,221,951, 817,206,209 or 2.4×10^{26} light years to one decimal place.

151 H. Harold Hartzler PhD (American Scientific Affiliation), Secretary-Treasurer, Goshen College, Indiana, in Peter Stoner, *Science Speaks: Scientific Proof of the Accuracy of Prophecy and the Bible* (Moody Press, 1944), Foreword.

We hope you enjoyed reading this
Sovereign World book.
For more details of other Sovereign
books and new releases see our website:

www.sovereignworld.com

Find us on Twitter @sovereignworld

Our authors welcome your feedback on their books.
Please send your comments to our offices.
You can request to subscribe to
our email and mailing list online or by writing to:

Sovereign World Ltd, PO Box 784,
Ellel, Lancaster, LA1 9DA, United Kingdom
info@sovereignworld.com

Sovereign World titles are available from
all good Christian bookshops and eBook vendors.

For information about our distributors in the UK,
USA, Canada, South Africa, Australia and Singapore, visit:
www.sovereignworld.com/trade

If you would like to help us send a copy of this book and
many other titles to needy pastors in developing countries,
please write for further information or send your gift to:

Sovereign World Trust, PO Box 777,
Tonbridge, Kent TN11 0ZS
United Kingdom
www.sovereignworldtrust.org.uk

The Sovereign World Trust is a registered charity